100 SMART Board™ LESSONS

TERMS AND CONDITIONS

IMPORTANT - PERMITTED USE AND WARNINGS - READ CAREFULLY BEFORE USING

Minimum specification:
- PC/Mac with a CD-ROM drive and at least 128 MB RAM
- Microsoft Office 2000 or higher
- Adobe® Reader®
- Interactive whiteboard
- Notebook™ software
- Facilities for printing and sound (optional)

PC:
- Pentium II 450 MHz processor
- Microsoft Windows 2000 SP4 or higher

Mac:
- 700 MHz processor (1 GHz or faster recommended)
- Mac OS X.4 or higher

For all technical support queries, please phone Scholastic Customer Services on 0845 6039091.

YEAR 5

Scottish Primary 6

CREDITS

Authors
Giles Clare (science), Anthony David (mathematics),
Rhona Dick (history), Martin Flute (foundation subjects),
Eileen Jones (English), Alan Rodgers and Angella Streluk (geography)

Development Editor
Niamh O'Carroll

Editor
Nicola Morgan

Assistant Editors
Kim Vernon and Margaret Eaton

Illustrators
Andy Keylock (book illustrations), Jim Peacock (Notebook file
illustrations), Theresa Tibbetts (additional book and
Notebook file illustrations)

Series Designer
Joy Monkhouse

Designers
Rebecca Male, Allison Parry,
Andrea Lewis and Melissa Leeke

CD-ROM developed in association with
Q & D Multimedia

ACKNOWLEDGEMENTS

SMART Board™ and Notebook™ are registered trademarks of SMART Technologies Inc.

Microsoft Office, Word and Excel are either registered trademarks or trademarks of
Microsoft Corporation in the United States and/or other countries.

With grateful thanks for advice, help and expertise to Angus McGarry (Trainer) and
Fiona Ford (Education Development Consultant) at Steljes Ltd.

All Flash activities designed and developed by Q & D Multimedia.

Interactive Teaching Programs (developed by the Primary National Strategy)
© Crown copyright. Extracts from the Primary National Strategy's *Primary Framework
for literacy and mathematics* (2006) www.standards.dfes.gov.uk/primaryframework
© Crown copyright. Reproduced under the terms of the Click Use Licence.

Extracts from The National Literacy Strategy and The National Numeracy Strategy
© Crown copyright. Material from the National Curriculum © The Queen's Printer and
Controller of HMSO. Reproduced under the terms of HMSO Guidance Note 8.
Extracts from the QCA Scheme of Work © Qualifications and Curriculum Authority.

Every effort has been made to trace copyright holders for the works reproduced in this
book, and the publishers apologise for any inadvertent omissions.

Designed using Adobe InDesign.

Published by Scholastic Ltd
Villiers House
Clarendon Avenue
Leamington Spa
Warwickshire CV32 5PR

www.scholastic.co.uk

Printed by Bell and Bain Ltd, Glasgow

1 2 3 4 5 6 7 8 9   7 8 9 0 1 2 3 4 5 6

Text © 2007 Giles Clare (science), Anthony
David (mathematics), Rhona Dick (history),
Martin Flute (foundation subjects), Eileen Jones
(English), Alan Rodgers and Angella Streluk
(geography)

© 2007 Scholastic Ltd

**British Library
Cataloguing-in-Publication Data**
A catalogue record for this book is available
from the British Library.

ISBN 978-0439-94541-7

Due to the nature of the web, the publisher cannot
guarantee the content or links of any of the websites
referred to in this book. It is the responsibility of the
reader to assess the suitability of websites. Ensure you
read and abide by the terms and conditions of websites
when you use material from website links.

CONTENTS

100 SMART BOARD™ LESSONS

Interactive whiteboards are fast becoming the must-have resource in today's classroom as they allow teachers to facilitate children's learning in ways that were inconceivable a few years ago. The appropriate use of interactive whiteboards, whether used daily in the classroom or once a week in the ICT suite, will encourage active participation in lessons and should increase learners' determination to succeed. Interactive whiteboards make it easier for teachers to bring subjects across the curriculum to life in new and exciting ways.

'There is a whiteboard revolution in UK schools.'

(Primary National Strategy)

What can an interactive whiteboard offer?

For the **teacher**, an interactive whiteboard offers the same facilities as an ordinary whiteboard, such as drawing, writing and erasing. However, the interactive whiteboard also offers many other possibilities to:

- save any work created during a lesson
- prepare as many pages as necessary
- display any page within the Notebook™ file to review teaching and learning
- add scanned examples of the children's work to a Notebook file
- change colours of shapes and backgrounds instantly
- use simple templates and grids
- link Notebook files to spreadsheets, websites and presentations.

Using an interactive whiteboard in the simple ways outlined above can enrich teaching and learning in a classroom, but that is only the beginning of the whiteboard's potential to educate and inspire. a

For the **learner**, the interactive whiteboard provides the opportunity to share learning experiences, as lessons can be delivered with sound, still and moving images, and websites. Interactive whiteboards can be used to cater for the needs of all learning styles:

- kinaesthetic learners benefit from being able to physically manipulate images
- visual learners benefit from being able to watch videos, look at photographs and see images being manipulated
- auditory learners benefit from being able to access audio resources such as voice recordings and sound effects.

With a little preparation all of these resource types could be integrated in one lesson, a feat that would have been almost impossible before the advent of the interactive whiteboard!

Access to an interactive whiteboard

In schools where learners have limited access to an interactive whiteboard the teacher must carefully plan lessons in which the children will derive most benefit from using it. As teachers become familiar with the whiteboard they will learn when to use it and, importantly, when not to use it!

Where permanent access to an interactive whiteboard is available, it is important that the teacher plans the use of the board effectively. It should be used only in ways that will enhance or extend teaching and learning. Children still need to gain practical first-hand experience of many things. Some experiences cannot be recreated on an interactive whiteboard but others cannot be had without it. *100 SMART Board™ Lessons* offers both teachers and learners the most accessible and creative uses of this most valuable resource.

About the series

100 SMART Board™ Lessons is designed to reflect best practice in using interactive whiteboards. It is also designed to support all teachers in using this valuable tool by providing lessons and other resources that can be used on a whiteboard with little or no preparation. These inspirational lessons cover all National Curriculum subjects. They are perfect for all levels of experience and are an essential for any SMART Board users.

Safety note: Avoid looking directly at the projector beam as it is potentially damaging to eye s, and never leave the children unsupervised when using the interactive whiteboard.

Introduction

About the book

This book is divided into four chapters. Each chapter contains lessons and photocopiable activity sheets covering:

- English
- Mathematics
- Science
- Foundation subjects.

At the beginning of each chapter a **planning grid** identifies the title, the objectives covered and any relevant cross-curricular links in each lesson. Objectives are taken from the relevant Primary National Strategy, National Curriculum Programmes of Study (PoS), or the QCA Schemes of Work. All of the lessons should therefore fit into your existing medium-term plans. The planning grids have been provided in Microsoft Word format on the CD-ROM for this purpose.

Lesson plans

The lessons have a consistent structure with a starter activity, activities for shared and independent work, and a plenary to round up the teaching and learning and identify any assessment opportunities. Crucially, each lesson plan identifies resources required (including photocopiable activity sheets and Notebook files that are provided on the CD-ROM). Also highlighted are the whiteboard tools that could be used in the lesson.

Photocopiable activity sheets at the end of each chapter support the lessons. These sheets provide opportunities for group or individual work to be completed away from the board, but link to the context of the whiteboard lesson. They also provide opportunities for whole-class plenary sessions in which children discuss and present their work.

Two general record sheets are provided on pages 170 and 171. These are intended to support the teacher in recording ways in which the interactive whiteboard is used, and where and how interactive resources can be integrated into a lesson.

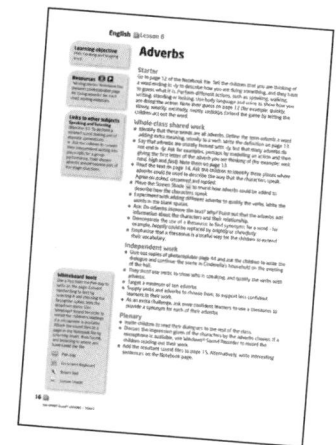

What's on the CD-ROM?

The accompanying CD-ROM provides an extensive bank of Notebook files. These support, and are supported by, the lessons in this book. As well as texts and images, a selection of Notebook files include the following types of files:

- Embedded Microsoft Office files: These include Microsoft Word and Excel documents. The embedded files are launched from the Notebook file and will open in their native Microsoft application.

- Embedded interactive files: These include specially commissioned interactive files as well as Interactive Teaching Programs (ITPs) from the Primary National Strategy.

- Printable PDF versions of the photocopiable activity and record sheets, as well as the answers to the mathematics activities, are also provided on the CD-ROM.

- 'Build your own' file: This contains a blank Notebook page with a bank of selected images and interactive tools from the Gallery, as well as specially commissioned images. It is supported by lesson plans in the book to help you to build your own Notebook files.

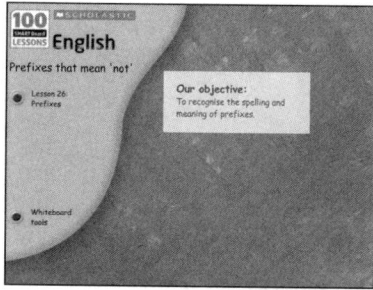

The Notebook files

All of the Notebook files have a consistent structure as follows:

Title and objectives page

Use this page to highlight the focus of the lesson. You might also wish to refer to this page at certain times throughout the lesson or at the end of the lesson to assess whether the learning objective was achieved.

Starter activity

This sets the context to the lesson and usually provides some key questions or learning points that will be addressed through the main activities.

Main activities

These activities offer independent, collaborative group, or whole-class work. The activities draw on the full scope of Notebook software and the associated tools, as well as the SMART Board tools.

What to do boxes are also included in many of the prepared Notebook files. These appear as tabs in the top right-hand corner of the screen. To access these notes, simply pull out the tabs to reveal planning information, additional support and key learning points.

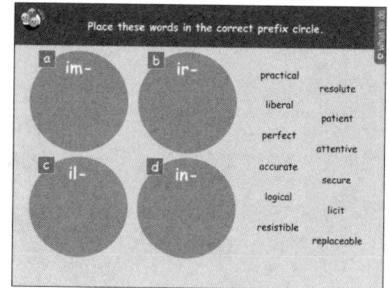

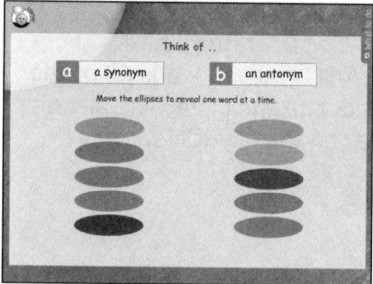

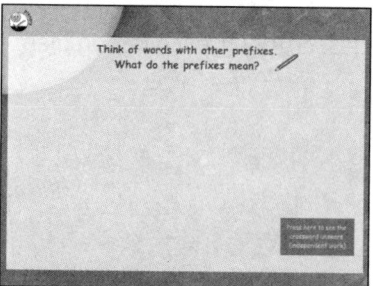

Plenary

A whole-class activity or summary page is designed to review work done both at the board and away from the board. In many lessons, children are encouraged to present their work.

Whiteboard tools page

The whiteboard tools page gives a reminder of the tools used in the lesson and provides instructions on how they are used.

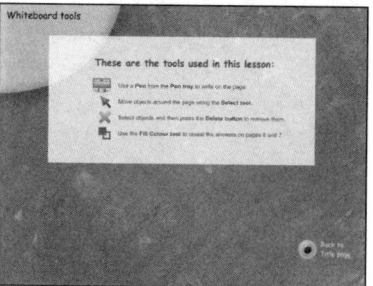

HOW TO USE THE CD-ROM

Setting up your screen for optimal use

It is best to view the Notebook pages at a screen display setting of 1280 × 1024 pixels. To alter the screen display, select Settings, then Control Panel from the Start menu. Next, double-click on the Display icon and then click on the Settings tab. Finally, adjust the Screen area scroll bar to 1280 × 1024 pixels. Click on OK.

If you prefer to use a screen display setting of 800 × 600 pixels, ensure that your Notebook view is set to 'Page Width'. To alter the view, launch Notebook and click on View. Go to Zoom and select the 'Page Width' setting. If you use a screen display setting of 800 x 600 pixels, text in the prepared Notebook files may appear larger when you edit it on screen.

Viewing the printable resources

Adobe® Reader® is required to view the printable resources. All the printable resources are PDF files.

Visit the Adobe® website at **www.adobe.com** to download the latest version of Adobe® Reader®.

Introduction

Getting started

The program should run automatically when you insert the CD-ROM into your CD drive. If it does not, use My Computer to browse to the contents of the CD-ROM and click on the *100 SMART Board™ Lessons* icon.

When the program starts, you are invited to register the product either online or using a PDF registration form. You also have the option to register later. If you select this option, you will be taken, via the Credits screen, to the Main menu.

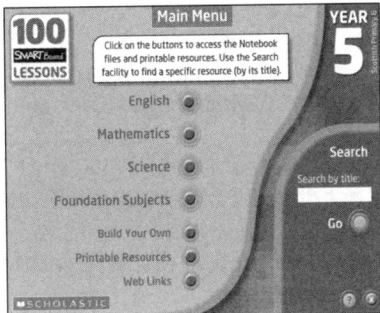

Main menu

The Main menu divides the Notebook files by subject: English, mathematics, science and foundation subjects. Clicking on the appropriate blue button for any of these options will take you to a separate Subject menu (see below for further information). The 'Build your own' file is also accessed through the Main menu (see below). The activity sheets are provided in separate menus. To access these resources, click on Printable resources.

Individual Notebook files or pages can be located using the search facility by keying in words (or part words) from the resource titles in the Search box. Press Go to begin the search. This will bring up a list of the titles that match your search.

The Web Links button takes you to a list of useful web addresses. A help button ? is included on all menu screens. The Help notes on the CD-ROM provide a range of general background information and technical support for all users.

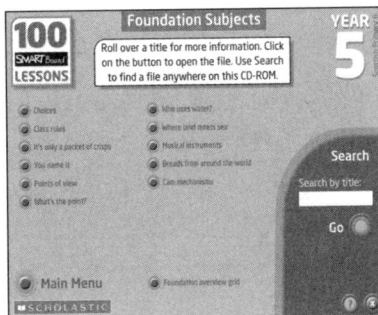

Subject menu

Each Subject menu provides all of the prepared Notebook files for each chapter of the book. Roll over each Notebook file title to reveal a brief description of the contents in a text box at the top of the menu screen; clicking on the blue button will open the Notebook file. Click on Main menu to return to the Main menu screen.

'Build your own' file

Click on this button to open a blank Notebook page and a collection of Gallery objects, which will be saved automatically into the My Content folder in the Gallery. You only need to click on this button the first time you wish to access the 'Build your own' file, as the Gallery objects will remain in the My Content folder on the computer on which the file was opened. To use the facility again, simply open a blank Notebook page and access the images and interactive resources from the same folder under My Content. If you are using the CD-ROM on a different computer you will need to click on the 'Build your own' button again.

Printable resources

The printable PDF activity sheets are also divided by chapter. Click on the subject to find all the activity sheets related to that subject/chapter. The answers to Chapter 2, mathematics, are also provided.

To alternate between the menus on the CD-ROM and other open applications, hold down the Alt key and press the Tab key to switch to the desired application.

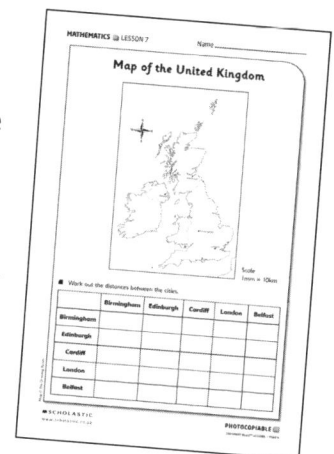

English

This lessons in the English chapter match the objectives in the Primary National Strategy's *Primary Framework for literacy*. These objectives are listed in the curriculum grid below, along with the corresponding objectives from the medium-term planning in the National Literacy Strategy. The curriculum grids in this book are also provided on the accompanying CD-ROM, in editable format, to enable you to integrate the lessons into your planning.

The interactive whiteboard offers pace and visual excitement to the lessons. Words can be made to appear or disappear, text can be manipulated, the children can see sentences being constructed, and they will watch paragraphs and stories emerging.

Be generous with the use of the interactive whiteboard and involve the children as much as possible in operating the board's tools. This will bring special benefits to children with dominant visual and kinaesthetic styles of learning. Above all, use the interactive whiteboard as another resource for the teaching of English. The whiteboard should support the interaction between you, the children and literacy.

Lesson title	PNS objectives	NLS objectives	Expected prior knowledge	Cross-curricular links
Lesson 1: Clarity and correctness	**Sentence structure and punctuation** • Punctuate sentences accurately.	**S3:** To discuss, proof-read and edit their own writing for clarity and correctness. **S6:** To understand the need for punctuation as an aid to the reader.	• Editing can improve their writing.	**PE** PoS (4b) Pupils should be taught to warm up and prepare appropriately for different activities. **PE** PoS (4c) Why physical activity is good for health and well-being.
Lesson 2: Words ending in vowels	**Word structure and spelling** • Group and classify words according to their spelling patterns.	**W4:** To examine the properties of words ending in vowels other than the letter *e*.	• The term *vowel*.	**Science** QCA Unit 5A 'Keeping healthy'
Lesson 3: Adapting and simplifying	**Sentence structure and punctuation** • Adapt sentence construction to different readers.	**S4:** To adapt writing for different readers and purposes by changing vocabulary, tone and sentence structures to suit.	• Text should have a target audience.	**ICT** QCA Unit 5A 'Graphical modelling'
Lesson 4: Mapping texts	**Creating and shaping texts** • Experiment with different narrative forms and styles; write their own stories. **Text structure and organisation**	**T14:** To map out texts showing development and structure.	• Narrative needs a structure.	**History** QCA Unit 11 'What was it like for children living in Victorian Britain?'
Lesson 5: Direct and reported speech	**Creating and shaping texts** • Vary the pace and develop the viewpoint through the use of direct and reported speech. **Sentence structure and punctuation** • Adapt sentence structure to different text-types, purposes and readers. • Punctuate sentences accurately, including use of speech marks.	**S5:** To understand the difference between direct and reported speech. **S7:** From reading, to understand how dialogue is set out.	• The term *direct speech*.	**Speaking and listening** Objective 51: To perform a scripted scene making use of dramatic conventions.
Lesson 6: Adverbs	**Creating and shaping texts**	**W10:** To use adverbs to qualify verbs in writing dialogue.	• The term *adverb*.	**Speaking and listening** Objective 51: To perform a scripted scene making use of dramatic conventions.
Lesson 7: Story openings	**Understanding and interpreting texts** **Creating and shaping texts**	**T1:** To analyse the features of a good opening and compare a number of story openings.	• Familiarity with stories.	**History** QCA Unit 11 'What was it like for children living in Victorian Britain?'
Lesson 8: Verbs	**Sentence structure and punctuation** • Adapt sentence structure to different text-types, purposes and readers.	**S8:** To revise and extend work on verbs.	• Verbs have different forms.	**Science** QCA Unit 5A 'Keeping healthy'

Lesson title	PNS objectives	NLS objectives	Expected prior knowledge	Cross-curricular links
Lesson 9: Reading journals	**Engaging with and responding to texts** • Reflect on reading habits and preferences.	**T13:** To record their ideas, reflections and predictions about a book.	• Experience of commenting on books.	**Speaking and listening** Objective 55: To analyse the use of persuasive language.
Lesson 10: Plurals	**Word structure and spelling** • Group and classify words according to their spelling patterns.	**W5:** To investigate, collect and classify spelling patterns in pluralisation.	• The terms *singular* and *plural.*	**ICT** PoS (3a) Pupils should be taught how to share and exchange information in a variety of forms.
Lesson 11: Instructions	**Understanding and interpreting texts** • Compare information texts and identify how they are structured. **Sentence structure and punctuation** • Adapt sentence structure to different text-types, purposes and readers.	**T22:** To read and evaluate a range of instructional texts. **T25:** To write instructional texts, and test them out.	• The term *instructions.*	**ICT** QCA Unit 5E 'Controlling devices' **Design and technology** QCA Unit 5C 'Moving toys'
Lesson 12: Word class revision	**Sentence structure and punctuation**	**S4:** To revise from Year 4 the different kinds of noun; the function of pronouns; agreement between nouns, pronouns and verbs.	• Words are grouped in word classes.	**Speaking and listening** Objective 57: To use and recognise the impact of theatrical effects in drama.
Lesson 13: Suffixes	**Word structure and spelling** • Know and use less common suffixes such as *-cian.* • Group and classify words according to their spelling patterns and meanings.	**W8:** To recognise and spell the suffix *-cian,* etc.	• The term *suffix.*	**Mathematics**
Lesson 14: Myths	**Understanding and interpreting texts** • Compare different types of texts and identify how they are structured. • Infer writers' perspectives from what is written and from what is implied.	**T1:** To identify and classify the features of myths, legends and fables. **T8:** To distinguish between the author and the narrator, investigating narrative viewpoint and the treatment of different characters.	• Stories are in different genres.	**History** QCA Unit 15 'How do we use ancient Greek ideas today?'
Lesson 15: Spoken and written language	**Speaking** • Tell a story using notes. **Understanding and interpreting texts** • Compare different types of texts and identify how they are structured. • Infer writers' perspectives from what is written and from what is implied.	**S6:** To be aware of the differences between spoken and written language, including conventions to guide the reader. **T1:** To identify and classify the features of myths, legends and fables.	• The difference between telling and reading a story.	**Speaking and listening** Objective 48: To tell a story using notes designed to cue techniques, such as repetition, recap and humour.
Lesson 16: Imagery	**Understanding and interpreting texts** • Infer writers' perspectives from what is written and from what is implied.	**T10:** To understand the differences between literal and figurative language.	• Experience of descriptive language.	**History** QCA Unit 11 'What was it like for children living in Victorian Britain?'
Lesson 17: Homophones	**Word structure and spelling** • Group and classify words according to their spelling patterns and their meanings.	**W6:** To distinguish between homophones.	• Some words sound the same.	**ICT** PoS (2a) To develop and refine ideas by bringing together, organising and re-organising text, tables, images and sounds.
Lesson 18: Explanations	**Understanding and interpreting texts** • Make notes and use evidence from across a text to explain events or ideas. • Compare information texts and identify how they are structured. **Creating and shaping texts** • Adapt non-narrative forms and styles to write factual texts.	**T15:** To read a range of explanatory texts, investigating and noting features. **T21:** To convert personal notes into notes for others to read, paying attention to appropriateness of style, vocabulary and presentation.	• Experience of information texts.	**Geography** QCA Unit 11 'Water'
Lesson 19: Letter strings	**Word structure and spelling** • Group and classify words according to their spelling patterns.	**W5:** To investigate words which have common letter strings but different pronunciations.	• Pronunciation varies.	**History** QCA Unit 6C 'Why have people invaded and settled in Britain in the past? A Viking case study'
Lesson 20: Note-making	**Understanding and interpreting texts** • Make notes on and use evidence from across a text to explain events or ideas.	**T20:** Note-making: to discuss what is meant by *in your own words* and when it is appropriate to copy/quote/adapt. **T21:** To convert personal notes into notes for others to read.	• Information can be given in other words.	**Science** QCA Unit 5A 'Keeping healthy'

Lesson title	PNS objectives	NLS objectives	Expected prior knowledge	Cross-curricular links
Lesson 21: Prepositions	Sentence structure and punctuation	S3: To search for, identify and classify a range of prepositions.	• Words have different names and functions.	PE QCA Unit 29 'Athletic activities' (3) To understand the basic principles of warming up.
Lesson 22: Empathy	Engaging with and responding to texts • Compare the usefulness of techniques such as visualisation and empathy in exploring the meaning of texts.	T2: To identify the point of view from which a story is told and how this affects the reader's response. T3: To change point of view. T7: To write from another character's point of view.	• Stories can be related in different ways.	Speaking and listening Objective 55: To analyse the use of persuasive language.
Lesson 23: Performance poetry	Drama • Use and recognise the impact of theatrical effects in drama.	T4: To read, rehearse and modify performance of poetry. T11: To use performance poems as models to write and to produce poetry in polished forms through revising, redrafting and presentation.	• Language can be spoken as well as written or read.	Speaking and listening Objective 56: To understand different ways to take the lead and support others in groups.
Lesson 24: Spelling rules	Word structure and spelling • Group and classify words according to their spelling patterns.	W5: To investigate and learn spelling rules.	• Some spellings follow rules (experience of reading text closely).	ICT PoS (3b) To be sensitive to the needs of the audience and think carefully about the content and quality when communicating information.
Lesson 25: Longer sentences	Sentence structure and punctuation • Punctuate sentences accurately.	S4: To use punctuation marks accurately in complex sentences. S6: To investigate clauses. S7: To use connectives to link clauses within sentences and to link sentences in longer texts.	• The purpose of the comma.	Geography PoS (1e) To communicate in ways appropriate to the task and audience. History PoS (5c) To communicate their knowledge and understanding of history in a variety of ways.
Lesson 26: Prefixes	Word structure and spelling • Know and use less common prefixes, such as im- and ir-.	W7: To recognise the spelling and meaning of prefixes.	• The term prefix.	Design and technology QCA Unit 5C 'Moving toys'
Lesson 27: Connecting ideas	Listening and responding • Analyse the use of persuasive language. Creating and shaping texts • Adapt non-narrative forms and styles to write factual texts. Sentence structure and punctuation • Adapt sentence structure to different text-types, purposes and readers.	S7: To use connectives to link clauses within sentences and to link sentences in longer texts. T19: To construct an argument in note form or full text to persuade others of a point of view.	• Arguments should follow on from one another.	Geography QCA Unit 20 'Local traffic – an environmental issue'
Lesson 28: Persuasive letters	Listening and responding • Analyse the use of persuasive language. Creating and shaping texts • Adapt non-narrative forms and styles to write factual texts. Sentence structure and punctuation • Adapt sentence structure and punctuation to different text-types, purposes and readers.	T17: To draft and write individual or group letters for real purposes. T19: To construct an argument in note form or full text to persuade others of a point of view.	• How letters are set out.	Geography QCA Unit 20 'Local traffic – an environmental issue'
Lesson 29: Word transformations	Word structure and spelling • Know and use less common prefixes and suffixes.	W6: To transform words.	• The terms suffix and prefix.	History QCA Unit 11 'What was it like for children living in Victorian Britain?'
Lesson 30: Persuasion	Listening and responding • Identify different question types and evaluate their impact on the audience. • Analyse the use of persuasive language. Sentence structure and punctuation • Adapt sentence structure to different texts-types, purposes and readers.	T14: To select and evaluate a range of texts, in print or other media, for persuasiveness, clarity, quality of information. T15: From reading, to collect and investigate use of persuasive devices.	• Text must be aimed at an audience.	PE QCA Unit 30 'Outdoor and adventurous activities'

Clarity and correctness

Starter
On a new Notebook page, type:

Solomon and Max discussed their plans. They decided on the Lake District. There would be places to camp. Some could be crowded. They would find somewhere peaceful. It could take all day.

Ask: *What do you notice about the sentences?* (They are all quite short.) Explain that each one is a 'simple sentence': a sentence consisting of one clause. Look at some of the children's most recent stories, and count how many simple sentences they have used.

Whole-class shared work
● Introduce the term *compound sentence*: a sentence of two or more clauses joined by a conjunction – for example, *and, or, but,* or *so.* For example, *Solomon and Max discussed their plans and they decided on the Lake District.*
● Introduce the term *complex sentence.* Define a complex sentence as one consisting of a main clause and one or more subordinate clauses.
● Write up a complex sentence: *After Solomon and Max discussed their plans, they decided on the Lake District.* Highlight the main clause *(they decided on the Lake District)* and subordinate clause *(Solomon and Max discussed their plans)* in different colours.
● Point out the conjunction at the beginning of the sentence and the comma between the clauses. A comma is needed when a subordinate clause begins a sentence, in order to separate the two clauses.
● Repeat the process to demonstrate another complex sentence, such as: *There would be places to camp although some could be crowded.*
● Highlight the conjunction, comma, the main clause *(There would be places to camp)* and the subordinate clause *(some could be crowded).*
● Ask the children to think of other conjunctions (for example, *because, after, although, unless, whereas, while, until, as, if, since*) and make a note of these.

Independent work
● Give out copies of photocopiable page 41 and ask the children to create complex sentences using the chart provided.
● Emphasise that every sentence must use every column and begin with a subordinate clause.
● Support less confident learners by colouring the different parts of the sentence the same colour in each column, using highlighter pens or underlining in felt-tipped pens.
● As an extra challenge, ask the children to make up another set of complex sentences without the help of a chart.

Plenary
● Ask the children to write up some of their sentences.
● Ask them to identify the two clauses.
● Look at the children's opening story paragraphs from previous work. Ask them to demonstrate how they could create complex sentences.

Words ending in vowels

Learning objective
PNS: Word structure and spelling
● Group and classify words according to their spelling patterns.

Resources 🅿
Photocopiable page 42 'A tour of tastes' for each child; writing materials; pictures of the different foods mentioned on the photocopiable page.

Links to other subjects
Science
QCA Unit 5A 'Keeping healthy'
● Link the independent work poem to science work on eating a varied and balanced diet.

Starter

On a new Notebook page, type: *orange, cake, chocolate, cabbage, grape*. Ask: *What do they have in common?* Point out that all these words end in *e*. Ask the children to write the plural forms on their individual whiteboards. Compare answers and explain that a word ending in *e* normally forms a plural in the usual way: adding *s*.

Whole-class shared work

● Ask the children to think of some examples of words ending in a vowel other than *e* (for example, *piano*).
● On a new Notebook page, use the Shapes tool 🖳 to add a large outlined rectangle to the page. Divide the rectangle into three columns and then use the Lines tool ↘ to divide the second column into two, as follows:

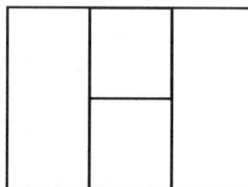

● In the first column, type: *panda, piano, corgi, tornado, tarantula, viola, armadillo, cello, kiwi, radio, paella, sofa, puma, chapatti*. Point out the final letter of each: *a*, *o* or *i*.
● Ask the children to make the plural forms (by adding an *s* to each word).
● In the top half of the second column type: *kangaroo, zoo, domino*. Let the children write and show plurals on individual whiteboards before you demonstrate the correct forms: *kangaroos, zoos, dominoes*.
● Explain that most singular nouns ending in *o* form their plural by adding *s*; a few add *-es*.
● Select *dominoes* and drag it to the bottom half of the second column. Add more *-es* examples, such as *heroes, buffaloes, potatoes*.
● Demonstrate how to check plural spelling in a dictionary: a dictionary shows *-es* forms; if no plural form is shown, the noun follows the regular rule of adding *s*.
● In the third column, type: *bacteria, tagliatelle, ravioli, antennae, phenomena*.
● Ask: *What do you notice?* (They are plural forms already, without an *s*.) These words keep the plural spelling of their original language.
● Write the rules for each set of plural spellings at the top of each column.

Independent work

● Give out copies of photocopiable page 42 and ask the children to write an alliterative food poem using plural forms, drafting lines in rough first.
● Less confident learners could work in pairs. Display pictures of the different foods to aid visualisation.
● As an extra challenge, ask the children to use the same format for an 'alliterative animals' poem.

Plenary

● Let the children read their poems aloud. Encourage active listening by asking the audience to say which phrases and lines they particularly enjoyed.
● Write interesting alliterative phrases on the board using a Pen from the Pen tray. Ask the children to vote on which ones they like the best.

Whiteboard tools
Use the Shapes and Lines tools to create a table.

🖳 Pen tray

🖈 Select tool

✐ Highlighter pen

🖳 Shapes tool

↘ Lines tool

⌨ On-screen Keyboard

Adapting and simplifying

Learning objective
PNS: Sentence structure and punctuation
● Adapt sentence construction to different readers.

Resources ◉
'Storytelling' Notebook file; individual whiteboards and pens; writing materials.

Links to other subjects
ICT
QCA Unit 5A 'Graphical modelling'
● Provide experience of an object-based graphics package, asking the children to find ways to use it to contribute to the pictures in their books.

Starter
Ask: *What do you like reading? Why?* Focus on style, language, sentence construction and tone, rather than subject. Ask: *What advice would you give for writing for your age group?* Compare ideas and agree on the top three rules. Write them on page 2 of the Notebook file, under the heading 'Ages 9-10'. For example:
 1. Use a variety of sentences.
 2. Don't make your sentences too long.
 3. Include complex sentences with interesting connectives.

Whole-class shared work
● Go to page 3 of the Notebook file. Identify places where the writer has followed the golden rules decided by the class.
● Discuss other rules that the writer seems to have followed. Add them to the list on page 2, for example:
 ● Give plenty of detail and description.
 ● Use questions as well as statements.
 ● Use interesting, informative vocabulary *(isolated, furtively, rattled)*.
 ● Involve the reader, making the reader feel you are talking directly to him or her. *(You can guess his plan.)*
● Explain that writers write for different readers by varying their rules. On the right-hand column on page 2, work together to create a list of golden rules for writing for five- to six-year-olds. For example:
 1. Have pictures as well as text.
 2. Keep sentences short.
 3. Only have simple sentences.
 4. Use statements, not questions.
 5. Use easy, straightforward vocabulary.
● Go to page 4 and read the story with the children. Investigate the extract, identifying where the writer has followed the rules.
● Compare the picture story to the narrative on page 3. Discuss and mark up how the narrative has been broken up into six pages for the picture story.
● Go to page 5 and read the text out loud. Ask: *Which of the two age groups is this for?* (Nine- to ten-year-olds.) Highlight the details that show this.
● Print a copy of page 5 for each pair of children. Display the golden rules on page 2.

Independent work
● Ask the children to write the story of Cinderella for a five- to six-year-old reader.
● Suggest retelling the story in six pages.
● The children must write text for each page and make notes on what the pictures will be.
● Suggest sentence openings to support less confident learners, and discuss a suitable overall length for the story.
● As an extra challenge, ask the children to adapt one of their own stories for a younger reader.

Plenary
● Write a sentence plan for one of the children's stories on page 6 of the Notebook file.
● Scan and view more stories on screen, inviting the children to talk about their planned pictures.

Whiteboard tools
Use a Highlighter pen to highlight particular words or parts of text. Upload scanned images by selecting Insert, then Picture File, and browsing to where you have saved the image.

▭ Pen tray

▭ Highlighter pen

▭ Select tool

▭ On-screen Keyboard

Mapping texts

Learning objective
PNS: Creating and shaping texts
● Experiment with different narrative forms and styles to write their own stories.
PNS: Text structure and organisation

Resources ● ▣
'Writing stories' Notebook file; photocopiable page 43 'Mapping texts' for each child; writing materials.

Links to other subjects
History
QCA Unit 11 'What was it like for children living in Victorian Britain?'
● Repeat the task with a story set in Victorian Britain: one narrative about a working Victorian child, the other about Dr Barnardo rescuing homeless children.

Starter
Discuss with the children what methods they use to plan stories - for example, storyboards, box plans, mind maps and notes. Make notes on page 2 of the Notebook file.

Whole-class shared work
● Point out that stories do not always contain one narrative: two narratives (perhaps set in different times or in different places) are often woven into one story. Careful planning is even more important when writing this kind of story.
● Ask: *What would the writer have to consider?* Write suggestions on page 3 of the Notebook file. Ask: *How will the story be divided between the two narratives? In what order will the two narratives be dealt with? How will the two narratives come together?*
● Go to page 4 and display the box plan, in which the writer is planning two narratives. Ask: *Which characters have a narrative?* Point out the two orange boxes on the left. Ask: *In what order will the writer plan to relate the narratives?* (Alternately.) Discuss why it is not a good idea to tell one narrative first and then to tell the other.
● Fill the boxes and talk about the contents of each box, one at a time. Each box briefly summarises what that paragraph or section will be about. Use the Lines tool ◥ to draw arrows to emphasise:
  ● how the story alternates between the narratives, shifting between characters and places (different places in the forest);
  ● the way the two narratives are drawn together at the end.
● Discuss different narratives that can be used in stories. For example: reality versus a dream; the present versus the past. On page 5 of the Notebook file, write examples of stories and the types of narratives that are used.
● Go to page 6. Discuss the ways in which writers move smoothly from one narrative to another (for example, with connective words and new paragraphs) and write down ideas. The writer has to use interesting and varied ways to 'flag' these narrative changes. Warn the children against repetition of overused phrases, such as *Meanwhile at the...*

Independent work
● Give out copies of photocopiable page 43 and ask the children to plan the story of Cinderella (traditional or their own version).
● Their story should have two narratives that meet at the end.
● Provide less confident learners with ideas for some of the boxes.
● As an extra challenge, ask more confident learners to write their opening connective words beside each paragraph box.

Plenary
● Complete the table on page 7 of the Notebook file, to review one child's plan for the story.
● Discuss other story plans. Do the rest of the class understand the plans? Talk about the connectives that could be used to move between the two narratives.

Whiteboard tools
Use the Fill Colour tool to reveal hidden text. Use arrows from the Lines tool to show how a writer alternates between narratives to tell a story.

🖥 Pen tray

⬚ Select tool

▣ Fill Colour tool

◥ Lines tool

Direct and reported speech

Starter
Read through page 8 of the Notebook file. Ask what the children notice about the two texts. They should realise that both tell the same story but are presented differently: (a) uses the actual words spoken; (b) reports the words that were spoken. Pull out the tabs to reveal this.

Whole-class shared work
● Use and define the terms *direct speech* and *reported speech* (or *indirect speech*):
  1. Direct speech uses the speaker's original words.
  2. Reported speech does not quote the original words of the speaker.
● Go to page 9. Use a Highlighter pen 🖉 to highlight the sentence: *"Will you do me a favour, Red Riding Hood?" she asked.* Ask the children to identify the equivalent sentence in (b) and highlight it in the same colour.
● Repeat this for the other direct speech sentences. Use different colours for each pair of sentences.
● Investigate the differences between the direct and reported speech:
  ● verb tense (*Will* becomes *would*)
  ● person (*you* becomes *she*)
  ● subordinating words (*if* is added)
  ● word order (*Will you* changes to *she would*)
  ● punctuation (*?* becomes *.*)
● Demonstrate differences between *"I'd love to," answered Red Riding Hood* and *Red Riding Hood said that she would love to go*:
  ● verb tense (*I'd* becomes *she would*)
  ● person (*I* becomes *she*)
  ● subordinating words (*that* is added).
● Focus on *that*. The connective *that* is often omitted but the meaning of the sentence remains the same. Ask the children which version they would write in a story, and why.

Independent work
● Go to page 10 of the Notebook file. This gives the basic structure of a later scene in the Red Riding Hood story. Discuss where dialogue could be introduced in this scene (for example, between Grandma and the wolf, before and after he enters the cottage).
● Ask the children to write this section of the story, using a mixture of direct and reported speech. Place a limit of three sentences of direct speech.
● Give less confident learners a writing frame of sentence openings, to support their work.
● Ask more confident learners to transform part of a playscript into a story.

Plenary
● Listen to some of the children's scenes. If a microphone is available, record the children reading out their work.
● Add the sound files to page 11 of the Notebook file. Alternatively, write up interesting sentences.
● Discuss how characters are being presented. Point out that using direct speech sparingly gives greater impact to characters' words.

Adverbs

Learning objective
PNS: Creating and shaping texts

Resources 💿 🅿
'Writing stories' Notebook file; thesauri; photocopiable page 44 'Using adverbs' for each child; writing materials.

Links to other subjects
Speaking and listening
Objective 51: To perform a scripted scene making use of dramatic conventions.
● Ask the children to convert their independent writing into playscripts for a group performance. Their chosen adverbs should become part of the stage directions.

Whiteboard tools
Use a Pen from the Pen tray to write on the page. Convert handwriting to text by selecting it and choosing the Recognise option from the dropdown menu. Use Windows® Sound Recorder to record the children's readings if a microphone is available. Attach the sound files to a page in the Notebook file by selecting Insert, then Sound, and browsing to where you have saved the file.

🖥 Pen tray

🖾 On-screen Keyboard

🔖 Select tool

🔲 Screen Shade

Starter
Go to page 12 of the Notebook file. Tell the children that you are thinking of a word ending in *-ly* to describe how you are doing something, and they have to guess what it is. Perform different actions, such as speaking, walking, writing, standing or looking. Use body language and voice to show how you are doing the action. Note their guess on page 12 (for example: *quickly, slowly, wearily, excitedly, neatly, untidily*). Extend the game by letting the children act out the word.

Whole-class shared work
● Identify that these words are all adverbs. Define the term *adverb*: a word adding extra meaning, usually to a verb. Write the definition on page 13.
● Say that adverbs are usually formed with *-ly*, but that many adverbs do not end in *-ly*. Ask for examples, perhaps by modelling an action and then giving the first letter of the adverb you are thinking of (for example: *well, hard, high* and *fast*). Note them on page 13.
● Read the text on page 14. Ask the children to identify three places where adverbs could be used to describe the way that the characters speak. Agree on *asked, answered* and *replied*.
● Move the Screen Shade 🔲 to reveal how adverbs could be added to describe how the characters speak.
● Experiment with adding different adverbs to qualify the verbs. Write the words in the blank spaces.
● Ask: *Do adverbs improve the text? Why?* Point out that the adverbs add information about the characters and their relationship.
● Demonstrate the use of a thesaurus to find synonyms for a word – for example, *happily* could be replaced by *brightly* or *cheerfully*.
● Emphasise that a thesaurus is a useful way for the children to extend their vocabulary.

Independent work
● Give out copies of photocopiable page 44 and ask the children to write the dialogue and continue the scene in Cinderella's household on the evening of the ball.
● They must use verbs to show who is speaking, and qualify the verbs with adverbs.
● Target a minimum of ten adverbs.
● Supply verbs and adverbs to choose from, to support less confident learners in their work.
● As an extra challenge, ask more confident learners to use a thesaurus to provide a synonym for each of their adverbs.

Plenary
● Invite children to read their dialogues to the rest of the class.
● Discuss the impression given of the characters by the adverbs chosen. If a microphone is available, use Windows® Sound Recorder to record the children reading out their work.
● Add the resultant sound files to page 15. Alternatively, write interesting sentences on the Notebook page.

Story openings

Starter
Discuss the importance of a story's opening: it is the writer's chance to 'hook' the reader. Ask the children to suggest some examples of good story openings and discuss these. Write their comments on page 2 of the Notebook file.

Whole-class shared work
● Read the opening of your current class novel. Ask: *Do you want to read on?* Encourage the children to give reasons for their answers.
● Read other story openings and ask the children to evaluate them, giving reasons for their opinions.
● Discuss some reasons why openings may succeed:
    ● funny or unusual descriptions (for example, *Matilda* by Roald Dahl)
    ● details to arouse your interest in the characters (for example, *Charlotte Sometimes* by Penelope Farmer)
    ● characters with wide appeal (*The Hundred and One Dalmatians* by Dodie Smith).
● Go to page 3 of the Notebook file. Agree on a class list of important features for story openings.
● Press the button to reveal a list of 'Important features for story openings'.
● Add any features that the children have not identified by highlighting the text and dragging it onto page 3 in the Page Sorter 🖿.
● Go to page 4 of the Notebook file. Ask for the children's opinions of this story opening.
● Investigate the text closely, identifying examples of the features listed. For example:
    1. Answers important questions:
        a. *who?* - Bennie, Kurt, Dad
        b. *where?* - computer laboratory
        c. *when?* - at night.
    2. Uses expressive language: *almost controls you; lost his nerve; extraordinary; amazing.*
    3. Introduces intrigue/problems/questions: *Whose voice is it? What does this game do?*
● Explain that the children are going to write their own story opening. Suggest possible themes linked to a different curriculum area, such as:
    ● A moving toy, made in Design and technology, shows strange powers.
    ● An archaeological dig unearths a piece of ancient Greek pottery. Myths and legends are linked to the pottery.
    ● A Victorian toy is found in the house. How did it get there?

Independent work
● Encourage the children to write their story opening. Emphasise that they must make the reader want to read more.
● Support less confident learners by helping with planning and setting the scene.
● Challenge more confident learners to provide a second opening, aimed at a different age group.

Plenary
● Let the children read their story openings aloud. Does the audience (the class) want to find out more?
● If a microphone is available, record the children reading their work aloud.
● Add the sound files to page 5. Alternatively, write good opening sentences on the Notebook page.

Verbs

Starter
Type (and save) this text on the whiteboard:
If you try to stay healthy, you were needing a balanced diet. When people took just one food group and they should ignore the other types, they lack essential vitamins and their health will suffer. It has made a poor diet. They would improve with all the food groups. That proved a balanced diet.

Ask the children to read the text. Ask: *Does this sound right? Which words are wrong?* Prompt them to discuss the mixture of verbs tenses. Identify examples of the present and past tense, using different colours.

Whole-class shared work
● Remind the children that verbs have three tenses: past, present and future. The same verb can be used in different tenses but it changes its form.
● Highlight the verb *has made*. Ask: *What tense is it?* (Past.) *Which is the main verb?* (made.) Highlight *were needing*. Repeat the question, identifying *needing* as the main verb.
● Underline the other two verbs: *has* and *were*. Ask: *What is their role?* Identify them as auxiliary verbs: auxiliary verbs help the main verb to form its tense.
● Point out that English has only two inflected tenses: past and present. (*Inflected* means that the tense is made by changing the form of the verb itself, for example, *cooks, cooked.*) All other tense formations need an auxiliary verb. For example, *have cooked, shall cook,* and so on.
● Introduce and define the term *modal verbs*: a type of auxiliary verb used to form the future tense. Highlight *will suffer* and underline *will*, identifying it as a modal verb.
● Other modal verbs express possibility: *could, would, should, might* and *ought.* Identify an example in the text *(would improve).*
● Display the PDF of photocopiable page 45 and explain its context: the school nutrition advisor is watching what children are eating. For speed, she makes a commentary on what she sees (present tense).

Independent work
● Ask the children to pretend that this commentary was made a week ago. They must change the text into a recount in the past tense for the advisor's report.
● Identify the verbs for less confident learners.
● As an extra challenge, ask more confident learners to use modal verbs to write a prediction about next term, when the school will change to healthy eating.

Plenary
● Display the 'Keeping healthy' text on the screen.
● Identify the verbs and agree on appropriate past tense forms.

Reading journals

Learning objective
PNS: Engaging with and responding to texts
● Reflect on reading habits and preferences.

Resources ◎ ▣
'Reading journals' Notebook file; photocopiable page 46 'Reading journal' for each child.

Links to other subjects
Speaking and listening
Objective 55: To analyse the use of persuasive language.
● After the Starter activity, ask the listeners to assess the persuasiveness of the speakers.

Starter
Open page 2 of the Notebook file. Working in pairs, the children should take turns to sell a favourite book to their partner. Afterwards, ask: *What did the speakers need to say?* (Enough to make the book seem worth reading.) *What did the listeners want to hear?* (Not so much that there was no point in reading the book.) Make notes on page 2 and suggest that book reviews need to do this, too. Repeat the 'selling' exercise, taking account of these points.

Whole-class shared work
● Read a book review to the class. Ask: *When is the best time to write a book review?* (When you finish the book.) *Why might this be a problem?* (Forgetting early reactions or predictions.)
● Point out the advantage of keeping a reading journal. Used regularly, it could show how you feel at different stages of the book.
● Discuss information that could be useful in a reading journal entry. Make a list on page 3 of the Notebook file. For example:
  1. title
  2. author
  3. first impressions
  4. cover
  5. story opening
  6. predictions
  7. changes in opinion
  8. memorable incidents or words
  9. thoughts on how the story will finish
  10. recommendations.
● Read the story on page 4. The story is for younger children. It is short, so would probably need only one reading journal entry.
● Read the completed journal entry for this picture story on page 5. Point out important features, such as:
  ● mention of the cover
  ● references to memorable details in the pictures
  ● quoting of words from the text
  ● recommendation about who might enjoy the book.

Independent work
● Display the story opening on page 6 of the Notebook file.
● Give out copies of photocopiable page 46. Ask the children to read the story opening and then write a reading journal entry. Remind them to make a prediction about the rest of the book.
● Less confident learners could work in pairs.
● Encourage more confident learners to write an entry for the latest reading from the class novel.

Plenary
● Insert scanned examples of the children's journal pages onto page 7 of the Notebook file, or discuss and write up their ideas.
● Talk about the children's different reactions to the story and their predictions. Did the story opening entice them to read further?
● Stress the need for a clear layout in a reading journal. Encourage the children to start keeping a journal, using the layout on the photocopiable sheet or designing their own layout.

Whiteboard tools
Use a Pen from the Pen tray to write on the page. Text can be added using the On-screen Keyboard, accessed through the Pen tray or the SMART Board tools menu. Use a Highlighter pen to make a note of important features. Upload scanned images by selecting Insert, the Picture File, and browsing to where you have saved the image.

▭ Pen tray

▱ On-screen Keyboard

▣ Select tool

▨ Highlighter pen

Plurals

Starter
Open page 2 of the Notebook file. Read the four words in the centre of the page. In pairs, ask the children to take turns to use the plural forms of two of the words. Listening partners must write the plural form as they hear it on their individual whiteboards. Compare results and write the correct plural endings for each word.

Ask: *What is the basic rule for making the plural form?* (Add *s*.) Explain that adding -*es* is very common.

Whole-class shared work
● Explain that typical words follow the rule of adding *s* for plurals. Ask: *How can you identify words needing* -*es?* Nouns ending in hissing, buzzing or shushing sounds *(s/x/ch/sh)* add -*es*: a syllable is added, making the plural easier to say. Write some examples on page 2 *(churches, hutches)*.
● Suggest saying words aloud or silently before writing. In pairs, ask one child to write *s* on an individual whiteboard, and the other -*es*. Ask pairs to decide which board to hold up, as you work through each of the nouns on pages 3 to 9. Allow 30 seconds' collaboration before asking the children to show their whiteboards. Then use the Eraser from the Pen tray to reveal the correct answer in the box.
● Go to page 10. Ask the children to vote on where to place the words. The words are split into typical words (add *s*); hissing and buzzing words (add -*es*); consonant + y words (change the *y* to *i* and add -*es*).
● Discuss general rules for changing singular words to plural. Point out the rules for words ending in y: for consonants + y, you change the *y* to *i* and add -*es*, but you just add *s* for vowels + y words.
● Apply the rules for spelling plural words to the text on page 11. Allow time for the children to decide how to spell a plural form before changing the word. Pull the screen over the text to reveal the correct plural spellings.
● Highlight *scissors*, a word that only has a plural form, and *children*, a plural with an ending other than *s*.

Independent work
● Ask the children to design a memorable poster to advertise a spelling rule.
● Allow less confident learners to work in pairs.
● Encourage more confident learners to list words with only one form:
  ● words that have no singular, such as *trousers, scissors, news;*
  ● words that are the same in singular and plural, such as *sheep, deer.*

Plenary
● Use the scanner to view designs on screen or add them to page 12 of the Notebook file.
● Ask children to present their ideas to the class. Write catchy slogans on the Notebook page. An example of a poster is given on page 13.
● Save the Notebook file to use in a subsequent lesson.

Instructions

Learning objectives
PNS: Understanding and interpreting texts
● Compare information texts and identify how they are structured.
PNS: Sentence structure and punctuation
● Adapt sentence structure to different text-types, purposes and readers.

Resources 💿
'Spelling plurals' Notebook file; writing materials. (Microsoft Word is required to view the embedded text document in the Notebook file.)

Links to other subjects
ICT
QCA Unit 5E 'Controlling devices'
Design and technology
QCA Unit 5C 'Moving toys'
● Link the independent work to these objectives. Reinforce the understanding that the user of the device will rely on a clear set of instructions.

Whiteboard tools
Use a Highlighter pen to highlight particular words. Edit text with the On-screen Keyboard, accessed through the Pen tray or the SMART Board tools menu. Upload scanned images by selecting Insert, then Picture File, and browsing to where you have saved the image.

🖵 Pen tray

🔖 Select tool

🖼 On-screen Keyboard

🖊 Highlighter pen

🖼 Page Sorter

Starter
Read the sentences on page 14 of the Notebook file. Allow thinking time before using prompts, such as: *Think about sentence types.* Conclude that they are all command sentences. Ask: *How can you tell?* Guide the children towards noticing the imperative verbs *(keep, watch, look, tell).* Give the children practice in making up command sentences.

Whole-class shared work
● Discuss the context for command sentences. Ask: *When/where do you read command sentences?* (In instructions.) Talk about everyday examples, such as instructions in games or recipes.
● Look around the classroom, checking for sets of instructions. Talk about notices around the school - for example, next to the fire extinguisher, near an alarm button, or in the computer room.
● On page 15 of the Notebook file, make a list of features important to an instructional text.
● Press on the star to show the ready-made list. Add any features that the children have not identified by highlighting the text and dragging it onto page 15 in the Page Sorter 🖼 .
● Look at the text on page 16, a set of instructions to create a spelling poster display. Ask: *Where would you find this text?* (In a school textbook; on a worksheet.)
● Investigate the text more closely to identify command sentences and highlight these.
● Point out: *The children can plan their collages and paintings on the computers.* Ask: *What is wrong with this sentence?* (It is a statement.) Experiment with converting it to a command, for example: *Plan the collages and paintings on the computers.*
● Experiment with including other features, such as bullet points.
● Press on the button to edit the text as a Microsoft Word document. Stress the need for clarity.
● Page 17 demonstrates a possible result.

Independent work
● Return to the list of important features on page 15.
● Ask the children to write a set of instructions to support practical work in ICT or Design and technology. For example, they could write a set of instructions to control a simple device (such as a buzzer, small motor or lights) or to create a moving toy.
● Support less confident learners by allowing them to discuss their instructions with a partner first.
● As an extra challenge, ask more confident learners to write a set of instructions on how to improve a classroom or school.

Plenary
● Use the scanner to view the instructions. Discuss clarity and usefulness. They can be added to page 18 of the Notebook file.
● Provide opportunities for personal or partner evaluation as instructions are tested.

Word class revision

Learning objective
PNS: Sentence structure and punctuation

Resources ⊙ ◘
'Pandora's Box' Notebook file; individual whiteboards and pens; photocopiable page 47 'School life' for each child.

Links to other subjects
Speaking and listening
Objective 57: To use and recognise the impact of theatrical effects in drama.
● Link this objective to the poetry performances in the Plenary.

Starter
Read the text on page 2 of the Notebook file. Test the children's knowledge of word classes by identifying the classes of the highlighted words. Change the colour of words to show the different word classes.

Revise the meanings of the following terms: nouns, pronouns, verbs and adverbs. Pressing on the red box at the bottom of the page brings up word classes and definitions. Point out that the position of adverbs in sentences may vary.

Ask: *Which noun is replaced by 'It'?* (box.) Emphasise verb agreement: *was* agrees with *box*; *were* agrees with *dangers*. Experiment with moving *desperately* to a new sentence position for a changed sentence structure. Ask the children to identify other examples of these word classes.

Whole-class shared work
● Highlight the nouns on page 2. List the different kinds of nouns: singular, plural, collective, proper, noun phrases, noun clauses.
● Go to page 3 to emphasise these types of nouns.
● Read the text on page 4. Talk about the highlighted words. Ask which noun group they belong to. (Noun phrases.)
● Identify the main noun in each noun phrase and discuss how it is modified.
● Drag out the noun phrases and place them in the appropriate columns in the table. Do this by double-pressing on the text, dragging to highlight the word, and dragging it out from the text.
● Read the text on page 5. Explain that adverbs are hidden in the spaces. In pairs, ask the children to write a suggestion for each adverb on their individual whiteboards.
● After they have done this, pull the screen across the text to reveal the hidden words.
● Emphasise that alternatives may present a different picture. Write good examples on the Notebook page.

Independent work
● Give out copies of photocopiable page 47 and ask the children to write a poem about school life. The poem should visit different rooms and places and create images of what is happening there.
● Discuss some places, characters and activities to include.
● Encourage initial rough drafts before writing the poem in neat.
● Encourage use of strong verbs, different kinds of nouns and appropriate adjectives and adverbs. The children should try to follow the pattern set up in the first two lines.
● Less confident learners could work in pairs, speaking lines before writing.
● As an extra challenge, ask more confident learners to investigate a paragraph of a novel and identify different kinds of noun.

Plenary
● Ask children to read their 'School life' poems aloud.
● Small-group work would allow children to use different voices within one poem.
● If a microphone is available, use Windows® Sound Recorder to add the children's recitals to page 6 of the Notebook file.

Whiteboard tools
If a microphone is available, use Windows® Sound Recorder (accessed through Start> Programs>Accessories> Entertainment) to add the children's recitals to the Notebook page.

🖥 Pen tray

🖈 Select tool

A Text tool

🖉 Highlighter pen

Suffixes

Learning objectives
PNS: Word structure and spelling
● Know and use less common suffixes such as -cian.
● Group and classify words according to their spelling patterns and meanings.

Resources ● P
'Using 'shun' endings' Notebook file; photocopiable page 48 'Same sound – different suffixes' for each child; writing materials.

Links to other subjects
Mathematics
● Ask the children to list mathematical words that have a shun ending (for example: equation, operation, decision, fraction, calculation, proportion).

Starter
Read the words on page 2 of the Notebook file and discuss what they have in common. If necessary, encourage the children to say them to a partner. The children should realise that the words are all nouns ending in a *shun* sound. Ask: *How could we group them?* Demonstrate with some examples: physi**cian** and opti**cian**; posse**ssion** and profe**ssion**. Highlight the different types of *shun* endings.

Challenge the children to think of any other *shun* words (regardless of ending). Write them in a different place on the whiteboard. Ask if one ending seems to be more common than others. Point out that -*tion* is the most common spelling for *shun* words.

Whole-class shared work
● The *shun* sound is made by a number of different suffixes. There are no fixed spelling rules to help recognise which suffix to use, but there are some patterns.
● Ask the children to work in threes. On individual whiteboards, they should write either *cian, ssion* or *sion*. Call out base words on page 3, and ask each group to hold up the correct suffix. Then reveal the correct answer. Alternatively, ask everyone to make and show a *shun* fan.
● Identify and highlight spelling patterns:
  ● -*cian:* where base words end in *c*
  ● -*sion:* where the base word ends in -*de* or -*se*
  ● -*ssion:* – where a clear soft *sh* sound is made.
● Emphasise that there are many more patterns to discover.
● Go to page 4 and do the *shun* words quiz. The children have to choose one out of four suffixes for each base word, to make its *shun* form.
● Repeat the game in subsequent lessons, to see if the children's spelling improves.
● The answers are all repeated on page 5 of the Notebook file. This can be printed out for a homework spelling list.

Independent work
● Give out copies of photocopiable page 48 and ask the children to match two word roots to each suffix.
● When they have finished the first question, they can go on to find *shun* endings for the second list of base words.
● Encourage the children to check spelling with dictionaries.
● Less confident learners could just do one word for each suffix.
● Challenge more confident learners to list and give examples for all the spelling patterns they have identified.

Plenary
● Add the base words and new words with suffixes on page 6 of the Notebook file.
● Demonstrate how the base words and endings link to form the new words.

Whiteboard tools
Change the words on page 3 with the On-screen Keyboard, accessed through the Pen tray or the SMART Board tools menu, to make them simpler or more difficult.

▭ Pen tray

▣ Select tool

▣ Fill Colour tool

▨ On-screen Keyboard

Myths

Starter
Read the story on pages 2, 4, 5 and 7 of the Notebook file. Go to page 8 and ask: *Is this story fiction* or *non-fiction?* (Fiction.) *Why?* (It is a story, not fact.) Make a note of the children's responses.

Whole-class shared work
● Ask: *What genre of story is 'Pandora's Box'?* (Myth.) Write this on page 8 and discuss the term's meaning. Find a definition in an online encyclopaedia.
● Go to page 9. Ask: *What features do you expect in a myth?* Write a list, going back and highlighting relevant text in 'Pandora's Box'.
● Pull out features of myths from the box on page 9.
● Go to page 10 and ask: *Who was Zeus?* (The highest god in Greek mythology.) Use a website to find names of other Greek gods and goddesses. There are many more myths that involve different Greek gods.
● Read the story again, asking the children to think about the characters.
● Go to page 11. Place an adjective inside the discussion circle (for example: *sensible*).
● Ask a child to choose and place the appropriate character to join this word, and to justify the choice. For example, *'Sensible describes Epimatheus because he left the box alone.'*
● Let another child make a change – person, adjective or both – and explain their choice. Encourage reference to the text.
● Vary the use of the discussion circle. For example, both characters could be inside with the same adjective(s) applicable.
● Our opinions of the characters have been moulded by the writer's approach. The writer could have told the story differently, yet still kept the same facts. If Pandora was the narrator, she might have emphasised the importance of knowing the contents of the box.

Independent work
● Display or print page 12 of the Notebook file.
● Ask the children to read the text on the page, and then rewrite it in their own words.
● They should retain facts, but treat Pandora sympathetically.
● They can write as the author, or let Pandora narrate.
● Provide less confident learners with a list of useful adjectives.
● Challenge more confident learners to do the same with the third part of the story (see page 5 of the Notebook file).

Plenary
● Invite the children to read their new versions of the second part of the story. Ensure that they can distinguish between an author's and a narrator's voice.
● Discuss new reactions to Pandora. Note down the children's responses on page 13.

Learning objectives

PNS: Speaking
● Tell a story using notes.
PNS: Understanding and interpreting texts
● Compare different types of narrative texts and identify how they are structured.
● Infer writer's perspectives from what is written and from what is implied.

Resources 💿

'Fables' Notebook file; writing materials.

Links to other subjects

Speaking and listening
Objective 48: To tell a story using notes designed to cue techniques, such as repetition, recap and humour.
● Encourage children to design their storyboard pictures as cues for telling their stories aloud.

Whiteboard tools

Use the Fill Colour tool to reveal hidden text. Upload scanned images by selecting Insert, then Picture File, and browsing to where you have saved the image.

🖳 Pen tray

⌨ On-screen Keyboard

✐ Highlighter pen

🖰 Select tool

🖻 Page Sorter

🏳 Fill Colour tool

Spoken and written language

Starter

Open page 2 of the Notebook file. Tell the fable 'The Tortoise and the Hare'. Use effective intonation, dramatic pauses, and voice changes to suit how or what is said. As you say the six cue words on the Notebook page, move them into the box. Point out how the cue words remind you of the key incidents. Ask: *How is listening to a story different from reading it?* (Intonation and pauses help you to understand what is happening.)

Whole-class shared work

● Read page 3 and ask: *What does this story have in common with the Starter story?* (They are both fables.) Fables began as oral stories and many are attributed to Aesop, a Greek storyteller. Centuries later, these oral stories were put into writing.
● Ask: *What helps you understand this written story?* (Written words and punctuation.)
● Highlight where punctuation guides the reader: for example, speech marks and exclamation marks.
● Ask: *What does this story teach us?* Press the button to reveal the moral.
● Discuss the list of features of fables on page 4, identifying examples in the story on page 3.
● Go to page 5. Discuss the moral of the story on page 3. Reveal one feature of a moral at a time (by using the Fill Colour tool 🏳 to fill each box with a light colour) and discuss each feature in turn.
● Return to page 2 and experiment with writing a moral for 'The Tortoise and the Hare'.
● Go to page 6 and read the moral. Discuss ideas for an appropriate fable to go with it. Ask: *What animals would you use? What plot?*
● Add the children's suggestions for animals and plots to the Notebook page.
● Press the button to view some story suggestions. These can be selected and dragged to page 6 in the Page Sorter.

Independent work

● The children should create a pictorial storyboard of their fable, to act as a prompt for oral storytelling.
● Allow less confident learners to work in pairs.
● As an extra challenge, encourage more confident learners to repeat the task with a new moral.

Plenary

● Add the scanned storyboards to page 7 of the Notebook file. Allow the children to talk the class through their storyboards.
● Hold a storytelling session, with the children using their storyboards for their cues.

Imagery

Learning objective
PNS: Understanding and interpreting texts
● Infer writer's perspectives from what is written and from what is implied.

Resources 💿
'Imagery' Notebook file; writing materials.

Links to other subjects
History
QCA Unit 11 'What was it like for children living in Victorian Britain?'
● Make a comparison between school life in the past and now.

Starter
Go to page 2 of the Notebook file and ask the children to look around the classroom: at the room, the people in it, and what is happening. Ask: *What descriptive word comes into your mind?* Note the children's responses.

Start combining and adding to words to create some descriptive lines of poetry or prose. Ask the children to shut their eyes as you read lines aloud. Ask: *How vivid are the visual images?*

Whole-class shared work
● Go to page 3. Tell the children that these poems have been written in the same way as in the Starter. Point out that both poems are called 'Our Classroom'. Read them aloud.
● Ask the children to identify words that may have been starting points: *wintry, steamy, noisy, rushing, busy, lunch.* Highlight them.
● Ask: *How do the poems differ in their language?* (The first poem describes the classroom in straightforward language; the second poem describes the classroom as a kitchen.)
● Define 'literal language' and 'figurative language'. Ask the children to vote on which poem uses which type of language. (Poem (a) uses literal language: words are used with their normal meanings. Poem (b) uses figurative language: words do not have their usual meanings.)
● Investigate poem (b). Ask: *Who is the rushing, harassed cook?* (The teacher.) *What is the meal?* (The lesson.) *What is the gong?* (The bell.)
● Point out that the metaphor of the classroom as a kitchen is carried throughout the poem. The figurative language creates a strong visual image.
● Look at the picture on page 4. Discuss when and where the scene is set. (An Edwardian schoolroom.) Working in pairs, give the children time to think of and suggest words to describe the room, atmosphere, people, or feelings shown. Annotate the picture with the children's suggestions.
● Suggest that some of these words could be the starting point for a poem or descriptive passage about the lesson shown in the photograph.

Independent work
● Ask the children to write their poetry or prose about the classroom scene, making initial rough drafts.
● Emphasise using figurative language to bring the picture to life.
● Less confident learners could be given starting lines, and be allowed to work in pairs.
● As an extra challenge, ask more confident learners to write a poem or prose passage about their school.

Plenary
● Invite children to read their work to the rest of the class. Display the image on page 4 of the Notebook file. How well do the words match the scene?
● If a microphone is available, record the children's readings and add the sound files to page 4.
● Pages 5 and 6 offer an opportunity to assess the children's understanding of literal and figurative language.

Whiteboard tools
Use a Highlighter pen to identify key words. If a microphone is available, use Windows® Sound Recorder (accessed through Start> Programs>Accessories> Entertainment) to record the children's readings. Upload sound files by selecting Insert, the Sound, and browsing to where you have save the sound.

⌨ Pen tray

🔖 Select tool

🖊 Highlighter pen

Homophones

Starter

Say this sentence and ask the children to write it on their individual whiteboards: *Last night I went to see a film.* Then write this sentence on the whiteboard: *Last knight eye went to sea a film.*

Ask: *Is this right?* Use a computer spellchecker on your sentence to 'prove' that your sentence is correct. Ask: *Where did I go wrong?* Discuss the need to consider context and meaning of words, as well as sound, when spelling them. Write the correct words above the incorrect ones. Identify the disputed pairs of words as homophones. Define 'homophones': words with the same sound but different meanings or spellings.

Whole-class shared work

- Go to a new Notebook page. Introduce *there* and *their* as homophones. Make sure that the children know how to use them.
- Give the children *there* and *their* cards. Say a *there/their* sentence out loud and ask the children to show you the correct card before you write it on the Notebook page. Vary this with writing sentences on the Notebook page, leaving a gap for the *there* or *their*. Ensure that each homophone's meaning is clear.
- Open your prepared Notebook file of the following text (hide the underlined words by drawing over them with a Pen from the Pen tray, set to draw a thick line):
  - Farming is a <u>great</u> (grate/great) life, but a hectic one. A farmer can be <u>too</u> (two/too/to) busy. There is <u>cereal</u> (serial/cereal) to <u>sow</u> (so/sow/sew) and every <u>piece</u> (peace/piece) of land <u>to</u> (two/too/to) think about. The amount of <u>rain</u> (reign/rein/rain) or <u>sun</u> (son/sun) matters. A farmer is <u>not</u> (knot/not) even <u>allowed</u> (aloud/allowed) to get up late: a cow or <u>ewe</u> (you/ewe) wakes <u>him</u>! (hymn/him).
- Explain that the spaces should be filled by one of the homophones in brackets.
- Work through the text, asking the children to write the correct words on their individual whiteboards. Compare results before you use the Eraser to reveal the correct word.
- If the children struggle, discuss helpful memory tips. For example: *Write needs a **w** to make words.* Discuss any misconceptions – for example, neither rain nor rein describes a monarch's time on the throne (reign).
- Give the children a homophone riddle to solve, such as:
  - What is put in a cake and sits in a vase? (Answer: *flour* and *flower.*)

Independent work

- Provide each child with a copy of photocopiable page 49.
- The children should list the answers to each of their riddles on a separate piece of paper.
- Less confident learners could work in pairs.
- Encourage more confident learners to repeat the activity with different homophones.

Plenary

- Use the scanner to display the children's riddles on the Notebook page.
- Invite the children try out their riddles on one another.

Learning objective
PNS: Word structure and spelling
- Group and classify words according to their spelling patterns and their meanings.

Resources ▣
Photocopiable page 49 'What's what?' for each child; individual whiteboards and pens; sets of cards with *there* and *their* written on them; saved Notebook page (see whole-class activity).

Links to other subjects
ICT
PoS (2a) To develop and refine ideas by bringing together, organising and reorganising text, tables, images and sound as appropriate.
- Ask the children to use computers to type their riddle poems for display. They should list the answers and incorporate graphics to illustrate meanings.

Whiteboard tools
Add text to the page with the On-screen Keyboard, accessed through the Pen tray or the SMART Board tools menu. Write quick annotations using a Pen from the Pen tray. Use the Eraser from the Pen tray to reveal hidden text. Upload scanned images by selecting Insert, then Picture File, and browsing to where you have saved the image.

🖥 Pen tray

🖱 Select tool

⌨ On-screen Keyboard

Explanations

Starter
Read page 2 of the Notebook file. Ask: *What text type is this?* (An explanation.) On page 3, pull the different features of an explanation out of the box, arrange them as a list, and discuss them.

Whole-class shared work
● Return to page 2. Use a Highlighter pen 🖊 to point out:
  ● correct technical terms *(refinery, drill bit)*
  ● sequential connectives *(once, then, after that)*
  ● hypothetical language *(**If** the presence and location of oil are established, **then**...)*
  ● impersonal style with the passive voice *(loose soil **is carried**)*
  ● some complex sentences *(As the mud flows back up to the surface, loose soil is carried with it.)*
● These (and diagrams) are all typical features of explanations. Add them to the list on page 3.
● Explain that *How* and *Why* questions are often used as titles. Look for examples in science and geography textbooks.
● Refer to the children's recent science writing. Ask: *Did you use an explanatory style? Did a supporting diagram help? Can you think of a suitable title?*
● Tell them that you want to write an explanation of the water cycle. Agree on a title: 'How does the water cycle work?'
● Suggest that you now need accurate information to make notes from. Press the hyperlink on page 4 to open the Canterbury Environmental Education Centre's Nature Grid website. From the home page you can navigate to the Water Cycle Explorer page.
● Move through the pages, pointing out:
  ● step-by-step order
  ● correct technical terms: *evaporation, water vapour* (Evaporation)
  ● causal language: *due to* (Evaporation)
  ● hypothetical language: ***If** the air is very cold* (Precipitation).
● Model note-making on page 5 of the Notebook file. If necessary, refer back to the website to check spelling of technical terms or sequential order. Use words and phrases rather than sentences. Point out that you are using abbreviations and symbols, but being careful with facts and technical terms.
● An example of how notes could be written is given on page 6.

Independent work
● Give out copies of photocopiable page 50. Ask the children to make notes in preparation for writing an explanation of the water cycle. Tell them to include one diagram.
● When the children are satisfied with their notes, provide sheets of paper for them to write their explanations.
● Give less confident learners a writing frame with sentence openers.
● Challenge more confident learners to set themselves a new *How* or *Why* question (linked to their work in science or geography) to research.

Plenary
● Use the scanner to view some of the children's explanations.
● Compare the ways in which the children have written their explanations and the diagrams they have chosen. Use page 7 to make relevant notes.
● Point out where and how diagrams can support writing.
● Save the Notebook file to use with a later lesson (see Lesson 20).

Letter strings

Learning objective
PNS: Word structure and spelling
● Group and classify words according to their spelling patterns.

Resources
Individual whiteboards and pens; writing materials.

Links to other subjects
History
QCA Unit 6C 'Why have people invaded and settled in Britain in the past? A Viking case study'
● Ask the children to create a letter string chart of place names, using a map of the United Kingdom.

Starter
Randomly type up these words: *eight, pear, cook, fried, mood, niece, height, learn.* Ask the children to find ways to pair them. If necessary, advise them to look carefully at the letters. Agree on: *eight, height; cook, mood; fried, niece; learn, pear.* Ask: *Why are the words paired like this?* (They have the same letter strings.) *What is strange about the pairs?* (Different pronunciation of letter strings.) Agree on two words to add to each group. Investigate if they match the pronunciation of one of the original words, or have a different pronunciation. If a microphone is available, use Windows® Sound Recorder to record how the words are spoken.

Whole-class shared work
● Open a new Notebook page. Use the Shapes tool 🖻 to add a square to the page. Select Infinite Cloner from the dropdown menu to create multiple squares behind the original one. Drag a further ten squares randomly onto the page.
● Type the following words on the page: *favour, eight, shield, cool, cried, search, piece, pour, light, soot, weight, niece, fight, hour, lied, field, learn, flour, colour, your, good, pool.*
● Tell the children to work in pairs to match words with the same letter string and pronunciation. They could record these on their individual whiteboards.
● Ask different children to pair words. They should read the pairs aloud and highlight the matching letter strings. Ask: *Are they a match?*
● Go to a new Notebook page and use the Lines tool 🖊 to create a ladder on the page. Write a word at the top (for example, *cough*). To move down a rung, a new *ough* word must be made by changing one letter of *cough.* Ask the children to write a new word on their individual whiteboards.
● Let someone add a word below yours. Then repeat with another rung. For example: *cough - rough - bough.*
● Widen the rules of the game, allowing a letter to be changed or added. For example: *cough - rough - bough - bought - brought.*
● Read the word ladders aloud. Ask: *How many ways is the letter string pronounced as it moves down the ladder?*
● On a new page, create a chart with these six headings: *ight; ear; oo; ough; ie; our.*
● Explain that these are common letter strings that are likely to change pronunciation.

Independent work
● Ask the children to copy the chart into their books and to list eight to ten different words in each column.
● At the bottom of each column, they should record the number of pronunciations used.
● Support less confident learners with shorter lists. Encourage them to pronounce the words aloud to a partner.
● As an extra challenge, ask more confident learners to create letter string ladders with the same pronunciations.

Plenary
● Let the children help complete the chart on the whiteboard.
● Play 'Letter string pairs' with the columns.
● Work out which letter string is most likely to vary in pronunciation.

Whiteboard tools
Use the Lines and Shapes tools to add shapes and create tables.

🖾 On-screen Keyboard

🖈 Select tool

🖻 Shapes tool

🖊 Lines tool

🖉 Highlighter pen

Note-making

Learning objective
PNS: Understanding and interpreting texts
● Make notes on and use evidence from across a text to explain events or ideas.

Resources 💿
'Making notes' Notebook file; printouts of pages 10 and 11 of the Notebook file, one for each child; copy of page 15 of the Notebook file; prepared Notebook page of your own notes based on this information; notes on the Water Cycle Explorer web pages, from Lesson 18.

Links to other subjects
Science
QCA Unit 5A 'Keeping healthy'
● Link the independent work to the need for an adequate and varied diet.

Starter
Read out the scurvy passage from page 15 of the Notebook file, without letting the children see the text (press the red box at the bottom of the page to go to page 15). Ask them to make quick notes on their individual whiteboards. Share the notes, and write up on page 8 the key information that they all identified.

Whole-class shared work
● Explain that notes should be short and quick to write, using words and phrases, not sentences. Go to page 9 and discuss the list of important features of notes.
● Refer to the last point in the list. Point out that the children wrote notes for themselves in the Starter activity.
● Show the children your own notes on the passage. Ask: *What would you do differently?* Demonstrate any changes they suggest.
● Ask the children to compare their Starter notes with a partner's. Ask: *Does your partner understand your notes?*
● Go to page 15, allowing the children to compare this with their notes and with yours.
● Display page 5 of the Notebook file, which shows notes made in an earlier lesson from information on the Water Cycle Explorer web pages. Ask: *Do you find the notes clear? Would you use a different layout or different abbreviations?* Share opinions, demonstrating possible changes.
● Go back to page 2. Make notes on the passage about oil, working on a paragraph at a time and identifying essential information and words. Demonstrate using your own words (unless deliberately copying names or technical vocabulary).
● Discuss possible problems when writing notes for other users. Remind the children that notes must be written with the user in mind.

Independent work
● Ask the children to read the report 'Modern eating' on pages 10 and 11 of the Notebook file. Give a printout of the two pages to each child.
● Ask them to write two sets of notes:
  1. personal notes for their own use
  2. notes suitable for someone else.
● Provide a list of essential and technical vocabulary for less confident learners.
● Ask more confident learners to make notes on another report.

Plenary
● Use the scanner to view the children's notes.
● Investigate the changes made between the first and second sets of notes.
● Make a note of these differences on page 12 of the Notebook file.

Whiteboard tools
Press a page thumbnail in the Page Sorter to navigate the different pages in the Notebook file. Upload scanned images by selecting Insert, then Picture file, and browsing to where you have saved the image.

🖿 Pen tray

✐ Highlighter pen

▨ Select tool

▦ Page Sorter

Prepositions

Learning objective
PNS: Sentence structure and punctuation

Resources 💿 🅿
'Prepositions' Notebook file; individual whiteboards and pens; photocopiable page 51 'The second half' for each child.

Links to other subjects
PE
QCA Unit 29 'Athletic activities' (3): To understand the basic principles of warming up.
● Ask the children to write a set of warm-up activities for an ice-hockey team, using a range of prepositions.

Starter
Go to page 2 of the Notebook file. Explain that Darren has lost his mobile phone. Ask the children to jot down five phrases (not sentences) on their individual whiteboards of where it could be. Compare answers, and use the Creative pen ✎ to mark five suggested places with a star. Beside each star write an appropriate phrase given by the children (for example, **behind** the car, **in** the post box; **under** his foot). Select phrases that begin with different prepositions. Press on the car's rear bumper to reveal that the phone is behind the car and in front of the lamp post.

Go to page 3 of the Notebook file and repeat the exercise, this time guessing the location of items in the classroom (for example, your glasses). Make notes on the Notebook page.

Whole-class shared work
● Investigate the phrases on page 2. Highlight the prepositions and ask: *What word class are they?*
● Explain that a preposition is usually followed by a noun phrase (for example, *his pocket*). Ask: *What are all these prepositions about?* (They indicate position.)
● Go to page 4 of the Notebook file. Allow thinking or partner discussion time before taking suggestions for prepositions from the children. Annotate each gap with a possible preposition.
● Ask someone to read the story using a preposition in each gap. Let someone else read a different version, making different selections. (Use the Eraser from the Pen tray to clear the page to add different prepositions.) Point out how different prepositions affect meaning (for example, *before sunrise* or *after sunrise*).
● Use the Eraser to clear the page and pull the tab across the screen to reveal the author's choices.
● Highlight *after sunrise*. Ask: *Does **after** indicate position?* (No, it indicates time.)
● Go to page 5. Prepositions may indicate position, time, direction, possession, instrument, purpose and accompaniment. Use a Highlighter pen to colour-code each type.
● Investigate and highlight the author's choices in the story: *What is indicated by each preposition?* Colour-code them appropriately.

Independent work
● Give out copies of photocopiable page 51 for the children to complete. They should use between 10 and 15 prepositions with noun phrases.
● Display page 5 of the Notebook file to remind the children of the different uses of prepositions.
● Give less confident learners a list of prepositions to use.
● Encourage more confident learners to investigate the prepositions on a page of their current reading book.

Plenary
● Select one of the children's story endings and discuss it. Ask the writer to explain what is indicated by the prepositions they used. Do the class agree?
● Go to page 6, and enter prepositions next to the correct headings.
● Repeat this with some other story endings.
● Use the voting question on page 7 to discuss the differences between prepositions for direction, purpose and position.

Whiteboard tools
Use the Creative Pen to add stars to highlight parts of the picture on page 2. Use the Eraser from the Pen tray to remove any unsaved changes. Upload scanned images by selecting Insert, then Picture File, and browsing to where you have saved the image.

🖥 Pen tray

✎ Highlighter pen

🔖 Select tool

✎ Creative pen

Empathy

Learning objective
PNS: Engaging with and responding to texts
● Compare the usefulness of techniques such as visualisation and empathy in exploring the meaning of texts.

Resources 💿
'Point of view' Notebook file; individual whiteboards and pens; writing books or paper and pens.

Links to other subjects
Speaking and listening
Objective 55: To analyse the use of persuasive language.
● Ask the children to identify the words that made them empathise with a character.

Starter
Discuss the main events of the story 'Cinderella' and list them on page 2 of the Notebook file. (Press on the red box to see an example list on page 9.) Ask: *Which character(s) do you feel sympathy with? Why?*

Whole-class shared work
● Go to page 3. Choose one incident from 'Cinderella' (for example, the day after the Ball). Write up the facts: palace courtier arrives with slipper; stepmother and two sisters try on; Cinderella kept out of way; finally sent for.
● Introduce and define the word *empathy*: the ability to identify with someone else. Most readers empathise with Cinderella, so they are likely to see things from her point of view. If parts of the story were told from another point of view, readers might empathise with a different character.
● Demonstrate how the stepmother would tell the story: *In my opinion, Cinderella should be grateful for... From my point of view, she is lucky...*
● Point out the use of persuasive phrases *(in my opinion; from my point of view)* and their appropriate prepositions.
● Divide the class into groups of four. Each member takes the role of a different character and has one to two minutes to retell part of the story from their own point of view, ensuring that the facts are correct, but trying to gain sympathy for themselves.
● Move among the groups, making oral contributions. Afterwards let the class listen to good examples. Discuss how and why these characters persuaded listeners to empathise with them *(vocabulary; emphasis on one aspect of the situation; insight into feelings)*.
● Go to page 4. Investigate how the nursery maid gains audience empathy by mentioning:
  ● how long she has waited for one day off (four weeks);
  ● the length of the walk home;
  ● vocabulary (*whole, first*);
  ● her feelings (excitement and then disappointment).

Independent work
● Ask the children to write about the same incident from another character's point of view (for example, Nanny or the Mistress). They should retain facts, but emphasise new details, additional information, or a different perspective.
● Provide useful phrases for less confident learners.
● Ask more confident learners to repeat the task with a third character.

Whiteboard tools
Write on the Notebook page using the Pen tool. Use a Highlighter pen to point out key words and phrases. Upload scanned images by selecting Insert, then Picture File, and then browsing to where you have saved the image.

🖥 Pen tray

🔲 Select tool

⌨ On-screen Keyboard

📝 Highlighter pen

Plenary
● Scan some of the accounts and add them to page 5 of the Notebook file. Ask the writers to perform them.
● Ask listeners: *How much empathy do you have for the character? Which words affect you?* Annotate and highlight words on the Notebook file.
● Go to page 6. Ask a volunteer to read the speech bubble. How far do the children agree with Cinderella's point of view? Can they give reasons for their choices?
● Hold a class vote to give Cinderella an 'empathy' rating.

Performance poetry

Learning objective
PNS: Drama
● Use and recognise the impact of theatrical effects in drama.

Resources 🅿
Photocopiable page 52 'School days' for each child; individual whiteboards and pens; an extract from 'Part III: Hiawatha's Childhood' in the *Song of Hiawatha* by Henry Wadsworth Longfellow (from 'At the door on summer evenings' to 'Ere in sleep I close my eyelids!'), copied into a Word document or a Notebook page.

Links to other subjects
Speaking and listening
Objective 56: To understand different ways to take the lead and support others in groups.
● Ask the children to work with others to rehearse and perform a poem.

Whiteboard tools
Annotate the children's ideas and responses with a Pen from the Pen tray. If a microphone is available, use Windows® Sound Recorder (accessed through Start> Programs>Accessories> Entertainment) to record sounds. Upload scanned images by selecting Insert, then Picture File, and browsing to where you have saved the image.

🖳 Pen tray

🔖 Select tool

📝 Highlighter pen

Starter
Say these sound words to the children: *buzzing; whining; screech; squeal*. Ask the children to write on individual whiteboards the first word they associate with each sound. Compare answers, making notes on a new Notebook page.

Now say these words: *chalk; pencil; children; puppy*. Ask the children to write the first sound word they think of. Compare answers and make notes on a new Notebook page.

Finally, make some sounds – hum, whistle, gasp, hiss. Ask the children to write on individual whiteboards a phrase linking each sound with a person, object or animal.

Share the children's answers. Ask: *Can you hear the noise in the words?* Write the most popular phrases on a new Notebook page. If a microphone is available, record the sounds to accompany the phrases.

Whole-class shared work
● Display the extract from the *Song of Hiawatha*. Immediately, without reading aloud, ask: *What form of writing is this?* (A poem.) *How do you know?*
● Point out the use of new lines and a capital letter at the start of each line. Stress that rhyme is not a requirement.
● Ask the children to read the text silently. Then read it aloud to them. Ask: *Which way is better? Why?*
● Discuss viewpoints and suggest that the poem is improved by oral performance. Identify rhythm as the main reason.
● Ask the children to read lines to a partner. Ask: *Did you easily find a rhythm? Which words are improved by being said aloud?* (Minne-wawa; Mudway-aushka). *What do the words mean?* (They reproduce sounds made by the trees and water.)
● Investigate how the sound of a poem's words can matter as much as their meaning. Identify and highlight:
  1. onomatopoeia *(whispering, lapping)*
  2. alliteration (**b**rakes and **b**ushes; **w**ords of **w**onder; **s**ang the **s**ong; **f**ire **f**ly … **f**litting)
  3. repetition *(heard, sang the song, little … white-fire)*.
● Divide the class into small groups. Give each group a section of the poem to rehearse and then perform.
● Try out a class performance, maintaining the poem's rhythm.

Independent work
● Provide copies of photocopiable page 52 for the children to complete.
● Emphasise the importance of rhythm and sound.
● Encourage the children to try out phrases and lines on a listening partner.
● Less confident learners should work orally with a partner before writing.
● Challenge more confident learners to add a new section to the poem.

Plenary
● Scan in the poems and ask the poets to perform them for the rest of the class.
● Pick out effective phrases.
● If a microphone is available, record the readings.

Spelling rules

Learning objective
PNS: Word structure and spelling
● Group and classify words according to their spelling patterns.

Resources 💿
'Spelling rules' Notebook file; individual whiteboards and pens; computers, if available.

Links to other subjects
ICT
PoS (3b) To be sensitive to the needs of the audience and think carefully about the content and quality when communicating information.
● Encourage children to think carefully about how to present their information for their audience when they are designing their spelling posters on the computer.

Starter
Go to page 2 of the Notebook file. Tell the children to write on individual whiteboards one thing that the words have in common, and one thing that they don't. They should compare answers with a partner. Encourage them to look closely at spelling and to say the words to each other. Share ideas as a class and identify the common feature (they all contain *ie*) and the difference (*ie* has a different pronunciation each time). Pull out the tabs to check that the children are correct.

Whole-class shared work
● The letters *i* and *e* are often next to each other in words. Ask: *Which order is more common - ie or ei?* (*ie*.)
● Ask the children to write any *ie* word (not a Starter example) on their individual whiteboards. Count the number of different words.
● Go to page 3 and remove the box covering the heading of the first column, *ie*, using the Delete button or selecting the Delete option from the dropdown menu. List the children's words underneath.
● Ask: *Which letter makes words break the ie spelling rule?* (c)
● Tell the children the spelling rule: *i before e except after c.*
● Delete the box covering the heading of the second column, *cei*. Six words are listed but concealed in the column. Reveal each word's letters gradually by pulling back the box covering them, encouraging the children to predict spelling and words.
● Say the word *vein*. Emphasise its long *ay* sound. Explain that *ei* makes this sound. Delete the box over the next column heading, *ei (long ay sound)*, and give clues to allow the children to predict words and their spelling. Reveal the words in the column.
● Some words simply break the rules and these are best memorised. Delete the box over the final heading, *ei (other sounds)*, and gradually reveal the words in the column. Set these words as homework.

Independent work
● Ask the children to design and create a poster advertising the *i* and *e* spelling pattern. Suggest that each poster concentrates on one or two rules.
● Some children could design and complete their poster on the computer.
● Allow less confident learners to work in pairs.
● Ask more confident learners to find *ie* words on three pages of their reading book. They should group the words they find according to the way *ie* sounds.

Plenary
● View the posters on page 4 of the Notebook file.
● Ask children to explain the information to the rest of the class. Encourage constructive feedback.
● Play the spelling game on pages 5 and 6.

Whiteboard tools
If a microphone is available, use Windows® Sound Recorder (accessed through Start>Programs>Accessories> Entertainment) to record any slogans or rhymes to help the children to remember the spelling rules. Upload scanned images by selecting Insert, then Picture File, and browsing to where you have saved the image.

🖳 Pen tray

↖ Select tool

✗ Delete button

🔲 Fill Colour tool

Longer sentences

Learning objective
PNS: Sentence structure and punctuation
● Punctuate sentences accurately.

Resources 🄿
Photocopiable page 53 'Longer sentences' for each child; individual whiteboards and pens; prepared Notebook file (see whole-class shared work).

Links to other subjects
Geography
PoS (1e) To communicate in ways appropriate to the task and audience.
History
PoS (5c) To communicate their knowledge and understanding of history in a variety of ways.
● Encourage the children to use complex sentences when they write reports for other subjects. They should be able to identify the main clause in the sentence when reading about other subjects, to identify the main fact or issue.

Whiteboard tools
Use the On-screen Keyboard to add text to the page. Use a Highlighter pen to draw attention to parts of sentences. Hide and reveal the page with the Screen Shade. Upload scanned images by selecting Insert, then Picture File, and browsing to where you have saved the image.

🖥 Pen tray

▣ Select tool

⌨ On-screen Keyboard

✏ Highlighter pen

▣ Screen Shade

Starter
Type two simple sentences on the whiteboard: *The team played football. It started to snow.* Ask the children, on individual whiteboards, to show two different ways to join the sentences without using *and*. Compare results, recording some on the whiteboard. Add the following example: *The team played football until it started to snow,* and label it (a).

Repeat the task with these sentences: *Charley was fed up. She trudged off the pitch.* Encourage adventurous links. Compare results, recording some on the whiteboard. Add the following example: *Charley, who was fed up, trudged off the pitch,* labelling it (b).

Whole-class shared work
● Remind the children of sentence types:
   1. simple sentence: contains one clause;
   2. complex sentence: contains two or more clauses, one being the main clause.
● Identify the original pairs of sentences from the Starter as simple sentences. Identify the complex sentences that were made using the simple sentences.
● Explain that complex sentences always have a main clause. Ask: *Which is the main clause in sentence (a)?* (The team played football.) Highlight and label the main clause.
● Highlight and label the other clause (until it started to snow) as subordinate. Ask: *Which word creates the join?* (until)
● Analyse sentence (b) in the same way. The main clause here is *Charley trudged off the pitch.*
● Explain that a subordinate clause often begins with a conjunction (for example, *until it started to snow).* It may also begin with a relative pronoun: ***who** was fed up.*
● Point out that sentence (b) uses commas. Ask: *How can you tell whether a comma is needed?* Suggest reading the sentence aloud to hear when a comma is needed (where there is a pause). Enable the Screen Shade 🔲 and open a prepared Notebook page with this text:
   Once she was changed, she set off. Although it was still early, Charley was anxious to get home. The snow, that had only started falling an hour ago, was looking menacing. Charley, who had a good memory, knew about snowdrifts. This road had once been blocked until the next day's thaw.
● Read the text aloud and ask where commas should be. Reveal one sentence at a time to check.

Independent work
● Hand out copies of photocopiable page 53 for the children to complete. They should try to use all 12 sentences, planning the links before writing.
● Finished sentences could be given to a response partner, to check that the punctuation makes the meaning clear.
● Provide support for less confident learners by giving them some pairs of simple sentences.
● As an extra challenge, ask more confident learners to re-do the exercise with alternative longer sentences.

Plenary
● Use the scanner to view answers.
● Read some of the sentences aloud and ask the children to verify the punctuation.

Prefixes

Learning objective
PNS: Word structure and spelling
● Know and use less common prefixes, such as *im-* and *ir-*.

Resources 💿 ▣
'Prefixes that mean *not*' Notebook file; photocopiable page 54 'Using prefixes' for each child; individual whiteboards and pens.

Links to other subjects
Design and technology
QCA Unit 5C 'Moving toys'
● Ask the children to write a criticism of the design of a moving toy. They must use ten words with a prefix meaning 'not'.

Starter
Remind the children of the terms *synonym* (a word of the same meaning) and *antonym* (a word of the opposite meaning). Go to page 2 of the Notebook file. Use the Delete button ☒ to uncover a word hidden behind an oval. Say the word out loud. Give the children ten seconds to write a synonym on their whiteboards. Do this for five words, then ask the children to hold up their whiteboards. Compare answers and repeat the exercise for the antonyms.

Whole-class shared work
● Read the words on page 3. Ask the children to use them orally in sentences. Discuss what the words mean.
● Ask the children to write an antonym for each word on their individual whiteboards. Compare results. Check to see if any children have used a prefix in front of the original word.
● The most accurate antonyms can be made with prefixes. Reveal the antonyms on page 3. Highlight the prefixes.
● Ask: *What do the prefixes mean?* (not) *Can you think of other prefixes that mean 'not'?* (ir-, im-, un-, dis-, de-, anti-)
● Return to your Starter words. Add relevant prefixes in front of the words to form antonyms.
● Go to page 4. Form antonyms by using one of the prefixes shown. Allow time for the children to decide and write answers on their individual whiteboards. Ask them to hold up their answers before you drag and drop the word into its correct circle where the appropriate prefix is attached.
● Investigate the words in each circle. Point out patterns:
   1. *il-* is used in front of words starting with *l*
   2. *im-* goes before words starting with *m* or *p*
   3. *ir-* goes in front of words starting with *r*.
● Emphasise the spelling patterns of double letters. Point out that words can show the same spelling patterns, but not have the root meaning of *not*. For example: *illuminate, illustrate, irritate, irrigate*.

Independent work
● Give out copies of photocopiable page 54 for the children to complete.
● Suggest checking spelling in a dictionary.
● Simplify some of the clues for less confident learners.
● As an extra challenge, ask the children to make a new crossword for more words beginning with prefixes.

Plenary
● Point out that many of the clues relate to the prefix by using the word *not*. Talk about the meanings of other prefixes, such as *sus-* and *pro-*.
● Ask: *Can you think of words beginning in this way?* List some answers (for example: *suspicion, suspend, projection*). Choose some of the words and ask the children to define them to a partner. Ask: *Have you worked out what the prefixes mean?* (*sus* [like *sub*] means 'under'; *pro* means 'ahead').
● Pages 5, 6 and 7 offer an opportunity to assess the children's understanding of prefixes that mean *not* (page 5 also includes the answers to the crossword puzzle on photocopiable page 54).

Whiteboard tools
Use the Fill Colour tool to reveal the answers on pages 6 and 7.

🖥 Pen tray

☒ Delete button

▣ Fill Colour tool

▨ Select tool

Connecting ideas

Learning objectives
PNS: Listening and responding
● Analyse the use of persuasive language.
PNS: Creating and shaping text
● Adapt non-narrative forms and styles to write factual texts.
PNS: Sentence structure and punctuation
● Adapt sentence structure to different text-types, purposes and readers.

Resources
'Connecting ideas' Notebook file; a local traffic issue for discussion (for example, a proposed, possible or recent change, such as a one-way system, cycle lanes, speed ramps near school or a pedestrian crossing); individual whiteboards and pens; pens and paper.

Links to other subjects
Geography
QCA Unit 20 'Local traffic – an environmental issue'
● Use the independent work to help children identify different points of view.

Starter
Introduce and outline the local traffic issue on page 2 of the Notebook file. Give out pens and paper. Working in pairs, the children should consider both sides of the issue - one arguing for the change, the other against. They should each write two or three points supporting their view, compare ideas, and take turns to argue their case. Ask: *Can you reach a conclusion?* Tell the children that they will be learning how to connect their ideas to construct a balanced argument. They will need their notes later on in the lesson.

Whole-class shared work
● Go to page 3. Type short sentences and link them with connectives. Highlight the connectives and explain that these can be used within sentences, between sentences and between paragraphs, to link ideas. The connectives may be single words *(later)* or adverbial phrases *(later in the day)*.
● Go to page 4. Connectives can link cause and effect. Ask the children to add a sentence to precede *I was late this morning because of this.* (For example, *I missed the bus.*)
● Ask: *What is the connective?* (because of this.) *What type of information does it introduce?* (The effect of the first sentence.)
● Repeat with different sentences, and the connective as a consequence.
● Read the text on page 5. The children should listen for and write down connectives linked to cause and effect and then show you the answers: *Therefore; Consequently; In consequence; As a result.*
● Work together identifying and highlighting adverbial connectives in the text: *Therefore; On the one hand; In addition; Furthermore; On the other hand; Meanwhile; Conversely; Consequently; In addition; Nevertheless; In consequence; As a result.*
● Read the third paragraph. Focus on this adverbial connective: *On the other hand.* Ask: *What does this connective link do?* (It introduces the other side, the counter-argument to a point.)
● Ask the children to identify other counter-argument links in paragraphs 4 *(Conversely)* and 5 *(Nevertheless).*
● Go to page 6. Discuss the children's points from the Starter and note some on the whiteboard.

Independent work
● The children should write a newspaper article about the traffic issue that includes points on both sides of the argument.
● Emphasise the need for connective links between sentences.
● Give less confident learners a list of connective sentence openers.
● Challenge more confident learners to write a 'For and Against' article about another issue.

Plenary
● Invite the children to share their work.
● Identify adverbial connectives and make a note of good examples of connecting ideas on page 7 of the Notebook file.
● Display page 8. Encourage the children to vote on whether they agree or disagree with the issue.

Whiteboard tools

Pen tray

Select tool

On-screen Keyboard

Highlighter pen

Persuasive letters

Learning objectives
PNS: Listening and responding
● Analyse the use of persuasive language.
PNS: Creating and shaping texts
● Adapt non-narrative forms and styles to write factual texts.
PNS: Sentence structure and punctuation
● Adapt sentence structure to different text-types, purposes and readers.

Resources 💿
'Dear Sir' Notebook file; individual whiteboards and pens; writing materials. (Microsoft Word is required to view the embedded text document in the Notebook file.)

Links to other subjects
Geography
QCA Unit 20 'Local traffic – an environmental issue'
● Link the independent work to a relevant local traffic issue.

Starter
Open page 2 of the Notebook file. Present this scenario:
There are two clubs after school today. You and a friend have agreed to go together to one of them. However, each of you prefers a different club.
In pairs, the children should take turns to persuade each other, in one or two minutes, that their choice of club is better. Take feedback from the children. Ask: *Were you persuaded? How?* Let the class listen to some successful persuaders.

Whole-class shared work
● Go to pages 3 and 4 of the Notebook file and explain the context of the letter page of the village magazine. There has been talk of installing a pelican crossing in the village. Although this letter is written to the Editor, the magazine readers are the intended audience.
● Open the Microsoft Word document on page 4. Point out the layout, the opening of *Dear Sir* and the ending of *Yours faithfully.* (*Yours sincerely* is used when the person is addressed by his/her actual name.)
● Read the letter aloud and discuss its content. Ask: *Is the letter writer for or against a crossing?* (Against.) Identify the points in the letter writer's argument: *traditional charm of street; tourism; ugliness of lights.*
● Focus on the language. Ask the children to close their eyes as you read the letter aloud. They should choose a word or phrase they find effective in persuading them to support the writer's views, and write it on their individual whiteboards. Compare results.
● Point out that the writer uses words to manipulate, persuading others to her viewpoint. Identify and list some of persuasive devices, copying relevant words from the text onto page 2 of the Notebook file:
   1. persuasive words: *obviously...*
   2. rhetorical questions: *Where will our future visitors come from? Are we expected to...?*
   3. concession: *Naturally, people are concerned about...*
   4. persuasive definitions: *No one in this village is a careless driver.*
   5. deliberate ambiguities: *probably the best in England.*
● Keep this list on display.
● Refer to a local traffic issue, perhaps the one used in lesson 27.
● Agree on some points that could be made in letters to the local authority about the issue.

Independent work
● Ask the children to write a letter to the Council authority. Remind them about letter layout, and the use of persuasive language and devices. The letter should argue a clear point of view.
● Give less confident learners a writing frame and a list of points to use.
● Encourage more confident learners to write a letter to the headteacher arguing the case for a new school club.

Plenary
● Ask the children to read their letters aloud. Encourage listeners to identify persuasive words and devices.
● Use the voting question on page 5 to find out whether the children were persuaded by the arguments presented in the letters.

Whiteboard tools
Minimise Notebook and use the Floating tools to annotate the Microsoft Word document.

🖥 Pen tray

▐ Select tool

🖉 Highlighter pen

Word transformations

Learning objective
PNS: Word structure and spelling
● Know and use less common prefixes and suffixes.

Resources ℗
Photocopiable page 55 'Word transformations' for each child; PDF of 'Word transformations' (provided on the CD-ROM); individual whiteboards and pens. Prepare a Notebook file with the following text:
It was a longish walk. Carl longed for a drink. The café was open longer on Fridays – it was their longest day of the week. He was still longing for a drink when he reached the closed café!

Links to other subjects
History
QCA Unit 11 'What was it like for children living in Victorian Britain?'
● The independent work links well to this unit.

Starter
Read the text on your prepared Notebook page. Ask: *Which words belong together?* (longish, longed, longer, longest, longing.) *What do they have in common?* (They are all formed from the word 'long'.)

Whole-class shared work
● Explain that a base word can often be transformed in a number of ways. This can change the word's meaning or its role in a sentence.
● List likely word transformations:
  ● negation
  ● changing word class: verb to noun (or noun to verb)
  ● tense
  ● comparatives.
● Discuss the changes in detail. Ask:
  ● Which prefixes add the meaning 'not'? (*un-, dis-, il-*)
  ● Which suffixes can make a verb, such as 'educate' or 'like', into a noun? (*-tion* and *-ness*)
  ● Which suffixes can make a noun, such as 'length' or 'class', into a verb? (*-en* and *-ify*)
  ● Which suffix makes the past tense? (*-ed*) The continuous tense? (*-ing*)
  ● Which suffixes transform adjectives into comparatives? (*-er, -est, -ish*)
● Type the 12 suffixes and prefixes separately on the whiteboard.
● Divide the class into small groups. Give each group one or two of the prefixes or suffixes to write on their individual whiteboards.
● Type a base word on the whiteboard. If groups decide their letters can transform it, they hold up their whiteboards. Demonstrate the word transformations by duplicating base words and dragging and dropping prefixes or suffixes.
● Use these base words for the bracketed transformations:
  ● small (small**er**, small**est,** small**ish**)
  ● press (**im**press, press**ed**, press**ing**)
  ● legal (**ill**egal)
  ● like (**dis**like, lik**ing**, lik**ed**)
  ● compose (composi**tion**, compos**ed**, compos**er**, compos**ing**)
  ● happy (happi**er**, happi**est**, **un**happy)
  ● decide (decid**ed**, decid**er**)
  ● please (**dis**please, pleas**ing**, pleas**ed**)
  ● educate (educa**tion**, educat**ing**, educa**ted**)
  ● trust (**en**trust, trust**ing**, trust**ed**)
  ● fine (fin**ing**, fin**ed**, fin**er**, fin**est**, fin**ish**).
● Point out the spelling changes in some words (happy → happier; decide → decided). Emphasise that words ending in **y** change the **y** to **i** when a suffix is added; words ending in **e** lose the **e**.

Independent work
● Give out copies of photocopiable page 55 for the children to complete.
● Support less confident learners by reducing the number of options.
● Challenge more confident learners to create as many words as possible from each base word.

Plenary
● Display the PDF of 'Word transformations' on the whiteboard. Go through possible answers for the first question, pointing out spelling changes.
● Ask the children to read out some of their sentences. Discuss whether the transformed words have been used correctly.

Whiteboard tools
Double-press on existing text and overtype with the On-screen Keyboard. Select Infinite Cloner from the dropdown menu, then press and drag to create as many copies of the word as needed.

🖥 Pen tray

🖈 Select tool

⌨ On-screen Keyboard

🖊 Highlighter pen

Persuasion

Learning objectives
PNS: Listening and responding
● Identify different question types and evaluate their impact on the audience.
● Analyse the use of persuasive language.
PNS: Sentence structure and punctuation
● Adapt sentence structure to different text-types, purposes and readers.

Resources 💿
'What do YOU want?' Notebook file; individual whiteboards and pens; printouts of page 7 of the Notebook file, one for each child; writing and drawing materials.

Links to other subjects
PE
QCA Unit 30 'Outdoor and adventurous activities'
● Link the independent work to research on the safety measures that need to be followed in adventure activities.

Whiteboard tools
Highlight interesting sections of the poster using a Highlighter pen. Take screenshots of examples of the class posters with the Capture tool.

🖳 Pen tray

✏️ Highlighter pen

⌨️ On-screen Keyboard

🖱 Select tool

📷 Capture tool

Starter
Go to page 2 of the Notebook file. Ask the children to think of a food advertisement that they like and to write on individual whiteboards the name of the product and what sticks in their mind about the advertisement. Share results and work together to list three important ingredients for a successful advertisement.

Whole-class shared work
● Go to page 3. Ask: *What information does this poster give?* Discuss ideas. For example, the spread contains fruit and can be used in different ways.
● Ask: *What is the poster's aim?* (To get more people to buy the spread.)
● Ask: *What does it not tell us?* (For example, perhaps the spread contains a lot of sugar or is expensive.)
● Explain that persuasive texts often inform readers about things that will attract them but leave out information that could put them off.
● Ask: *How else does the poster persuade us?* For example:
1. persuasive words: *sunshine, brighten*
2. word play: *jam-packed*
3. rhetorical question: *Boring sandwiches?*
4. presentation features: slanting text
5. interesting layout: speech bubble
6. font variation: large capitals to catch attention
7. effective illustration
8. symbols
9. colour
10. quotes to support claims.
● Highlight these devices in the text and make a list of them on page 4.
● Go to page 5, making notes on the language used. For example, information is quick and easy to read, alliteration *(Sunshine Spread)* and rhyme *(spread/bread)* are used, and there is a dramatic use of exclamation marks.
● Go to page 6 and think of suitable quotes. Emphasise that the aim is to persuade people to buy the spread.

Independent work
● Open page 7. Ask the children to imagine that the school is organising an adventure holiday. Their task is to design a poster to win parental support.
● Provide the children with printouts of page 7, and resources to design the poster. Working individually or in pairs, encourage them to experiment with different picture positions and different ways of presenting the information.
● Give less confident learners some persuasive words and phrases to start them off.
● Challenge more confident learners to design a poster persuading parents to protest against the adventure holiday.

Plenary
● Ask the children to present their designs. Discuss which parts of each one work particularly well.
● As a class, build up a poster design on page 8 using some of the best ideas.
● Use the Capture tool 📷 to take a screenshot of the poster and save it to a new Notebook page.
● If you have time, make another poster, using different ideas, and add this to a new page.
● Take a class vote on which poster is most persuasive, and discuss why.

Complex sentences

■ Make eight different sentences. Begin each sentence with a subordinate (less important) clause.

Clause	Clause	Conjunction	Comma
you start athletic activities	you need cool-down exercises	although	,
take greater responsibility for your safety	an accident could occur	because	,
record results on a spreadsheet	you move something heavy	in case	,
you want to improve your skills	you are in Year 5	whenever	,
you finish a PE session	warm-up exercises are important	after	,
vary your activities	you want to judge progress	before	,
have somebody to assist	you may have special interests	as	,
use equipment carefully	practise regularly	if	,

1. _____

2. _____

3. _____

4. _____

5. _____

6. _____

7. _____

8. _____

A tour of tastes

■ Use the words around the page to write a poem.

avocados   pizzas   macaroni

tomatoes

Pastas are pressed into pretty shapes

kiwis

_____

_____

_____

tunas

_____   potatoes

_____

_____

paellas

_____

_____

sultanas

_____

_____   mangoes

_____

_____   risottos

papayas

_____

_____

_____

spaghetti   chapattis

samosas   ravioli

tagliatelle

Illustrations © Andy Keylock/Beehive Illustration

☀ SCHOLASTIC
w w w . s c h o l a s t i c . c o . u k

Mapping texts

Story title:

Character names:

1.	2.
3.	4.
5.	6.
7.	8.

9.

Using adverbs

■ Cinderella's stepsisters and stepmother are getting ready for the ball.
Finish the dialogue and put adverbs in the gaps. Then finish writing the scene.

"Get my other shoes," said one stepsister _____ .

"Fetch me more jewels," called the other stepsister _____ .

Then Cinderella's stepmother shouted _____ , "_____".

Cinderella _____

_____

_____

_____

_____

_____

_____

_____

_____

_____

_____

_____

Illustrations © Andy Keylock/Beehive Illustration

Keeping healthy

■ The school nutrition advisor is watching what children are eating. For speed, she writes a commentary on what she sees (using the present tense).

The cook serves school meals very quickly. She puts too many chips on each plate. She does not notice whether everyone takes a balanced meal. Some children avoid the vegetables. There are pieces of fruit. Most children choose cake instead. The first children get most of the protein food; the rest of the children take too many fatty foods. Cook piles one plate with carbohydrates.

Some lunch boxes do not contain a balanced meal. I can see one boy with a chocolate bar and crisps in his lunchbox. Most sandwiches are good. They contain protein foods. Some children drink two fizzy drinks. The school needs a healthy eating campaign.

1. Highlight all the verbs.

2. Write the past tense version of each verb above the present tense version in the extract.

3. Write a recount for the advisor's report, based on these notes. Write the recount in the past tense. Continue on the back of this sheet if you need to.

_____

_____

_____

_____

_____

_____

_____

_____

Reading journal

■ Complete the reading journal entry below.

Date: _____

Title of book: _____

Author: _____

The cover

Where I am up to in the book

My thoughts at the moment

What I think will happen

School life

By the school gates, mums and dads, chatting cheerfully,

In the cloakroom, noisy children, hanging coats up,

_____

_____

_____

_____

_____

_____

_____

_____

_____

_____

_____

_____

_____

_____

_____

Same sound – different suffixes

■ Identify two base words for each suffix. Use lines or colours to match them.

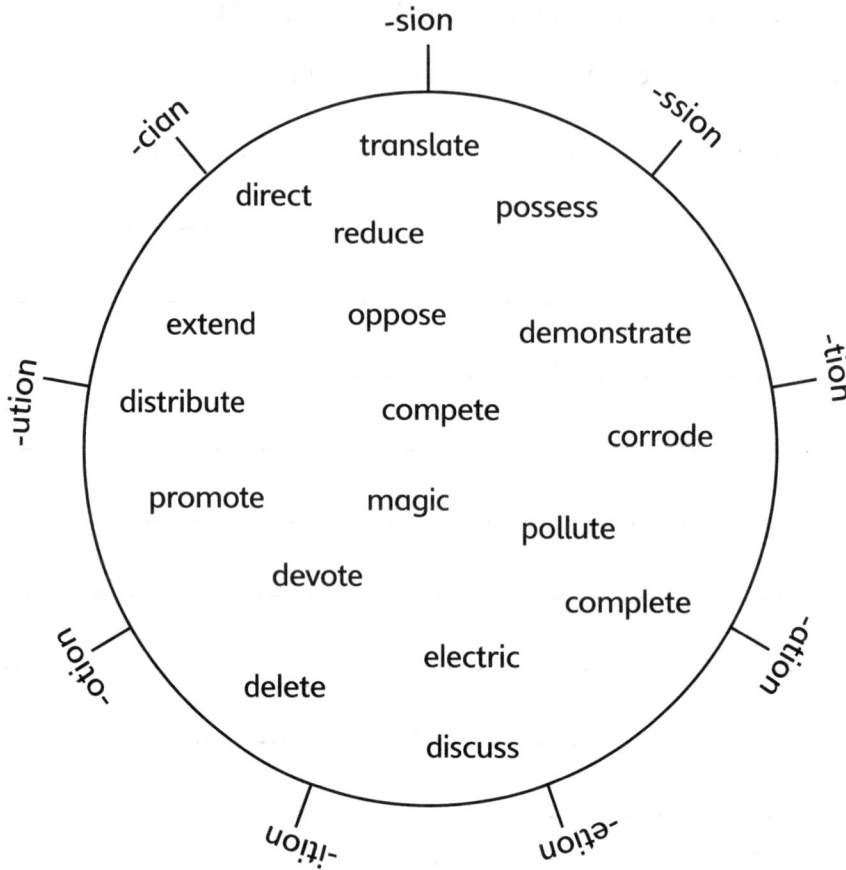

-sion

-cian

-ssion

translate

direct

possess

reduce

extend   oppose

demonstrate

-tion

distribute   compete

corrode

-ution

promote   magic

pollute

devote

complete

-otion

electric

delete

-ation

discuss

-ition

-etion

Write the 'shun' words below.

1. _____   _____ -cian

2. _____   _____ -sion

3. _____   _____ -ssion

4. _____   _____ -tion

5. _____   _____ -ation

6. _____   _____ -etion

7. _____   _____ -ition

8. _____   _____ -otion

9. _____   _____ -ution

■ S C H O L A S T I C
w w w . s c h o l a s t i c . c o . u k

What's what?

■ Write some homophone riddles, using the words included at the foot of this page.

What is eaten at breakfast and watched in episodes? _____

What is a story and _____ ?

_____

_____

_____

_____

_____

_____

_____

_____

_____

him/hymn

tail/tale

beech/beach

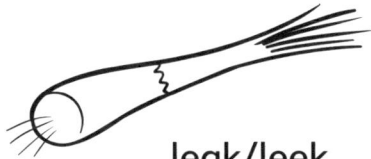

leak/leek

flour/flower

sun/son

pane/pain

serial/cereal

hair/hare

rain/rein

knight/night

right/write

key/quay

Note-making

- ◾ Notes should be short and quick to write.
    - ☐ Write important words and short phrases instead of whole sentences.

- ◾ Notes should:
    - ☐ have clarity
    - ☐ a helpful layout
    - ☐ include important information
    - ☐ use correct facts
    - ☐ use correct names and technical words
    - ☐ be mainly written in your own words (don't try to copy exactly what is said)
    - ☐ use quick methods of writing (such as abbreviations, symbols)
    - ☐ be understood by the intended reader (yourself).

- ◾ Make notes below for an explanation of the water cycle.
  Remember to include a diagram.

The second half

1. Complete the story. Remember to include prepositions.

_____

_____

_____

_____

_____

_____

_____

_____

_____

_____

_____

_____

_____

_____

_____

_____

_____

2. Highlight each preposition and noun phrase and give it a number. Then decide which column each phrase goes into in the table below, and write in its number.

Position	Time	Direction	Possession	Instrument	Purpose	Accompaniment

School days

■ Use these lines for your performance poem:

Into school on summer mornings

Raced the barging, bright-eyed children;

Heard the pounding of the footsteps,

Heard the _____

_____

_____

_____

Saw the busy bee, the teacher,

Darting, dashing round the sports pitch;

With the _____

_____

_____

_____

Longer sentences

Helpful subordinating words

when		before
	although	
despite		unless
	who	
once		because
	while	
that		

Simple sentences

Albert strolled down the street.

He was lost in thought.

Albert had a school project.

The project was unfinished.

It was on protected wildlife.

Albert was wearing his striped football kit.

He reached the park gate.

There was a large notice.

The writing was large.

It was difficult to read.

One of the words ended in '-ger'.

The notice was covered in graffiti.

1. Make five longer sentences out of the simple sentences above. Remember to use a subordinating word!

_____

_____

_____

_____

_____

2. Highlight the main clause in each longer sentence.

Using prefixes

■ All the answers use prefixes that mean 'not' (ir-, il-, im-, in-).

Across

4. Has no sense of responsibility

6. Do not give this answer a tick?

7. Not according to the law

8. Not the proper way to act

9. Not very likely

Down

1. Cannot be read

2. At no fixed time

3. Does not like to be active

5. Not able to read or write

6. Cannot be done?

Name _____

Word transformations

What it does	Prefix	Suffix
Negation	un-, de-, dis-, anti-, il-, ir-, im-, in-	
Verb to noun		-tion, -ism, -ness, -ity, -ist
Noun to verb		-ise, -ify, -ate, -en
Tense		-s/es, -e/ed, -ing, -en
Comparatives		-er, -est, -ish, -like

1. Create a transformation for each base word. Use the prefix and suffix chart to help you.

Base words	Transformations
strict	
teach	
educate	
kind	
happy	
responsible	
small	
like	
possible	

2. Use the transformed words in sentences about a child's life in Victorian Britain.

_____

_____

_____

_____

_____

_____

Mathematics

This chapter provides 30 lessons based on the objectives taken from the Primary National Strategy's *Primary Framework for mathematics*, covering a range of strands and objectives. The curriculum grids below are also provided on the accompanying CD-ROM, in editable format, to enable you to integrate the lessons into your planning.

The lessons in this unit use two types of interactive teaching tools. The first of these is the Notebook file. Within some of the Notebook files are Interactive Teaching Programs (ITPs). These programs were initially designed by the National Numeracy Strategy (NNS) to support teachers in class who did not have access to interactive whiteboard Notebook file programs. They are simple programs that model a small range of objectives, such as data presentation. Their strength is that they are simple and easy to read (all of the programs have a standard blue background enabling children, often boys, who find it hard to distinguish between colours or who find a white screen very bright). The interactive whiteboard is an ideal medium for making the most of these exciting resources.

Lesson title	PNS objectives	NNS objectives	Expected prior knowledge	Cross-curricular links
Lesson 1: The 24-hour day	**Measuring** • Read time using 24-hour clock notation.	• Use units of time; read the time on a 24-hour digital clock and use 24-hour clock notation, such as 19:53.	• What the parts of an analogue clock face represent and how to read a digital clock.	**Geography** QCA Unit 25 'Geography and numbers' **Science** QCA Unit 5E 'Earth, Sun and Moon'
Lesson 2: World time zones	**Measuring** • Read timetables and time using 24-hour clock notation.	• Use units of time; read the time on a 24-hour digital clock, and use 24-hour clock notation, such as 19:53.	• That time zone changes are made in hourly steps.	**Geography** QCA Unit 25 'Geography and numbers'
Lesson 3: Flight films	**Measuring** • Read timetables and time using 24-hour clock notation.	• Use units of time.	• That there are 60 minutes in an hour.	**Geography** QCA Unit 20 'Local traffic – an environmental issue'
Lesson 4: Setting the TV recorder	**Measuring** • Read timetables and time using 24-hour clock notation.	• To use units of time and 24-hour clock notation.	• How to read a TV schedule.	**English** PNS Drama: Use and recognise the impact of theatrical effects in drama.
Lesson 5: Ruler rules	**Measuring** • Draw and measure lines to the nearest millimetre.	• Measure and draw lines to nearest millimetre.	• How to accurately use a ruler and how to orientate it.	**English** PNS Drama: Reflect on how working in role helps to explore complex issues.
Lesson 6: Ruler express	**Measuring** • Read, choose, use and record standard metric units to estimate and measure length to a suitable degree of accuracy (eg the nearest centimetre); convert larger to smaller units using decimals to one place (eg change 2.6kg to 2600g).	• Use, read and write standard metric units including their abbreviations and relationships between them. Convert larger to smaller units of length.	• That there is a relationship between millimetres, centimetres, metres and kilometres.	**Art and design** PoS (3a) Compare ideas, methods and approaches in their own and others' work and say what they think and feel about them.
Lesson 7: Distance decisions	**Measuring** • Read, choose, use and record standard metric units to estimate and measure length.	• Suggest suitable units and measuring equipment to estimate or measure length.	• How to make reasonable estimates for distances under a kilometre.	**Design and technology** QCA Unit 5C 'Moving toys' **Geography** QCA Unit 25 'Geography and numbers'
Lesson 8: Triangle terrors	**Understanding shape** • Identify, visualise and describe properties of triangles.	• Classify triangles (isosceles, equilateral, scalene) using criteria such as lines of symmetry.	• Know what attributes make a triangle.	**Design and technology** PoS (4b) How materials can be combined and mixed to create more useful properties (for example, using cardboard triangles on the corners of a wooden framework to strengthen it).

Mathematics ⬚ Chapter 2

Lesson title	PNS objectives	NNS objectives	Expected prior knowledge	Cross-curricular links
Lesson 9: Fraction machines	**Counting and understanding number** • Express a smaller whole number as a fraction of a larger one (eg recognise that 5 out of 8 is $^5/_8$).	• Use fraction notation, including mixed numbers, and the vocabulary *numerator* and *denominator*.	• Know that a fraction is part of a number.	**ICT** PoS (2b) Pupils should be taught how to create, test, improve and refine sequences of instructions to make things happen and to monitor events and respond to them.
Lesson 10: Fraction pizzas	**Counting and understanding number** • Express a smaller whole number as a fraction of a larger one (eg recognise that 5 out of 8 is $^5/_8$).	• Change an improper fraction to a mixed number.	• Know that a fraction is part of a number.	**Design and technology** QCA Unit 5D 'Biscuits'
Lesson 11: Show me the line!	**Handling data** • Answer a set of related questions by collecting, selecting and organising relevant data; draw conclusions, using ICT to present features, and identify further questions to ask.	• Solve a problem by presenting and interpreting data in tables, charts, graphs and diagrams, including those generated by a computer, for example: bar line charts, vertical axis labelled in 2s, 5s, 10s, 20s or 100s.	• That the vertical axis generally represents the total on a line graph.	**ICT** PoS (2c) Pupils should be taught to use simulations and explore models in order to answer 'What if...?' questions, to investigate and evaluate the effect of changing values and to identify patterns and relationships.
Lesson 12: Questionnaire	**Handling data** • Answer a set of related questions by collecting, selecting and organising relevant data.	• Represent data in tables and charts.	• That a database can be made from the results of one or more questions.	**English** PNS Creating and shaping texts: Adapt non-narrative forms and styles to write factual texts.
Lesson 13: Representing data	**Handling data** • Answer a set of related questions by collecting, selecting and organising relevant data; draw conclusions, using ICT to present features, and identify further questions to ask.	• Solve a problem by presenting and interpreting data in tables, charts, graphs and diagrams.	• Where and how they have seen or used questionnaires in the past (eg pupil questionnaires).	**ICT** PoS (2c) To use simulations and explore models in order to answer 'What if...?' questions, to investigate and evaluate the effect of changing values and to identify patterns and relationships.
Lesson 14: Power graphs	**Handling data** • Answer a set of related questions by collecting, selecting and organising relevant data; draw conclusions, using ICT to present features, and identify further questions to ask.	• Use and compare charts and graphs that have been generated by a computer.	• Where and how they have seen or used questionnaires in the past (eg pupil questionnaires).	**ICT** QCA Unit 5B 'Analysing data and asking questions: using complex searches'
Lesson 15: Crazy quads	**Measuring** • Use the formula for the area of a rectangle to calculate its area.	• Understand area measured in square centimetres. • Understand and use formula in words for the area of a rectangle.	• What a quad is.	**Design and technology** PoS (1a) To generate ideas for products after thinking about who will use them and what they will be used for, using information from a number of sources, including ICT-based sources.
Lesson 16: Find the shape!	**Understanding shape** • Read and plot coordinates in the first quadrant.	• Recognise positions and directions, read and plot coordinates in the first quadrant.	• How to read a coordinate in its most simple form.	**Geography** PoS (2e) To draw plans and maps at a range of scales.
Lesson 17: What's my coordinate?	**Understanding shape** • Read and plot coordinates.	• Recognise positions, read and plot coordinates in all four quadrants (preparation for Year 6 work).	• How to read a coordinate in its most simple form.	**Geography** PoS (2e) To draw plans and maps at a range of scales.
Lesson 18: Nets	**Understanding shape** • Identify, visualise and describe properties of rectangles, triangles, regular polygons and 3D solids; use knowledge of properties to draw 2D shapes and identify and draw nets of 3D shapes.	• Visualise 3D shapes from 2D drawings and identify different nets of an open cube.	• The attributes of simple 2D and 3D shapes.	**Design and technology** PoS (1c) Plan what they have to do, suggesting a sequence of actions and alternatives, if needed.
Lesson 19: Mirror shapes	**Understanding shape** • Complete patterns with up to two lines of symmetry and draw the position of a shape after a reflection or translation.	• Recognise reflective symmetry in regular polygons.	• The attributes of simple 2D shapes.	**English** PNS Word structure and spelling: Group and classify words according to their spelling patterns and their meanings.

Lesson title	PNS objectives	NNS objectives	Expected prior knowledge	Cross-curricular links
Lesson 20: Angle madness ⬤ P	**Understanding shape** • Estimate, draw and measure acute and obtuse angles using an angle measurer or protractor to a suitable degree of accuracy.	• Understand and use angle measure in degrees.	• How to read the divisions on a protractor and understand how to use it.	**Science** Sc4 (2b) Pupils should be taught that objects are pulled downwards because of the gravitational attraction between them and the Earth.
Lesson 21: At the airport ⬤ P	**Measuring** • Read timetables and time using 24-hour clock notation.	• Use timetables.	• That timetables are to be read across from left to right.	**Geography** QCA Unit 25 'Geography and numbers' PoS (2c) To use globes, maps and plans at a range of scales.
Lesson 22: Polygon puzzles ⬤ P	**Measuring** • Measure and calculate the perimeter of regular and irregular polygons; use the formula for the area of a rectangle to calculate its area.	• Understand, measure and calculate perimeters of rectangles, and regular polygons. • Use and understand formula in words for the area of a rectangle.	• That a polygon is a straight-sided shape with three or more sides.	**Design and technology** PoS (1a) To generate ideas for products after thinking about who will use them and what they will be used for.
Lesson 23: Superheroes (single-stage problems) ⬤ P	**Using and applying mathematics** • Solve one-step and two-step problems involving whole numbers and decimals and all four operations, choosing and using appropriate calculation strategies.	• Use all four operations to solve simple word problems based on 'real life' or money.	• Simple operations (+, –, ×, ÷).	**English** PNS Creating and shaping texts: Adapt non-narrative forms and styles to write fiction texts.
Lesson 24: More superheroes (double and multi-stage problems) ⬤ P	**Using and applying mathematics** • Solve one-step and two-step problems involving whole numbers and decimals and all four operations, choosing and using appropriate calculation strategies.	• Use all four operations to solve simple word problems based on 'real life' or money.	• Simple operations (+, –, ×, ÷).	**English** PNS Creating and shaping texts: Adapt non-narrative forms and styles to write fiction texts.
Lesson 25: My superhero ⬤	**Using and applying mathematics** • Solve one-step and two-step problems involving whole numbers and decimals and all four operations, choosing and using appropriate calculation strategies.	• Use all four operations to solve simple word problems based on 'real life' or money.	• Simple operations (+, –, ×, ÷).	**Design and technology** PoS (1d) To communicate design ideas in different ways as these develop.
Lesson 26: Budget fliers ⬤ P	**Using and applying mathematics** • Solve one-step and two-step problems involving whole numbers and decimals and all four operations, choosing and using appropriate calculation strategies, including calculator use.	• Simple conversions of pounds to foreign currency.	• That there are 100p in a £.	**Geography** PoS (2c) To use atlases and globes, and maps and plans at a range of scales.
Lesson 27: Holiday gifts ⬤ P	**Using and applying mathematics** • Solve one-step and two-step problems involving whole numbers and decimals and all four operations, choosing and using appropriate calculation strategies.	• Simple conversions of pounds to foreign currency.	• That there are 100p in a £.	**Geography** PoS (3a) To identify and describe what places are like (for example, in terms of weather, jobs).
Lesson 28: Currency complications ⬤ P	**Using and applying mathematics** • Solve one-step and two-step problems involving whole numbers and decimals and all four operations, choosing and using appropriate calculation strategies.	• Use all four operations to solve simple word problems based on 'real life' or money.	• Simple operations (+, –, ×, ÷).	**PSHE** PoS (4a) Pupils should be taught that their actions affect themselves and others.
Lesson 29: People percentages ⬤	**Counting and understanding number** • Understand percentage as the number of parts in every 100.	• Begin to understand percentage as the number of parts in every 100.	• That a fraction is part of a number that can be translated into a percentage.	**Science** QCA Unit 5A 'Keeping healthy'
Lesson 30: Angle challenge ⬤ P	**Understanding shape** • Estimate, draw and measure acute and obtuse angles using an angle measurer or protractor to a suitable degree of accuracy.	• Identify, estimate, and order acute and obtuse angles. Use a protractor to measure and draw acute and obtuse angles to the nearest 5°.	• The divisions on a protractor and understand how to use it.	**Design and technology** PoS (3c) To recognise that the quality of a product depends on how well it is made.. **Geography** PoS (2c) To use maps and plans.

The 24-hour day

Learning objective
PNS: Measuring
● Read time using 24-hour clock notation.

Resources ● P
'Time around the world' Notebook file; individual whiteboards and pens; class clock; digital clock (a sports stopwatch or your own watch); photocopiable page 89 'Digital and analogue clocks' for each child.

Links to other subjects
Geography
QCA Unit 25 'Geography and numbers'
● Discuss why there is the need for time differences (spin of the Earth).
Science
QCA Unit 5E 'Earth, Sun and Moon'
● Show how the Earth spins and that during any 12-hour difference one half of the world is light and the other half is dark. Discuss why sunrise and sunset times change.

Starter
Go to page 2 of the Notebook file. Ask the children to count up in 6s to 72. Ask a volunteer to write the numbers on the line. Then challenge the children to count up in 60s until they reach 720. Tell the children this is the number of minutes in half a day. In pairs, the children should work out how many minutes there are in one day, ten days and one hundred days.

Whole-class shared work
● Go to page 3. Ask the children to look at their partner's watch. Some will be digital and some will be analogue. They should write or draw on their individual whiteboards how the time is displayed.
● Share results and ask: *Why are there differences? Which do you prefer?* Note their preferences on page 3 of the Notebook file.
● The day is separated using am and pm. Ask: *How can we do that using a digital clock?* Guide the children towards the idea of 24-hour time.
● Go to page 4 and press the interactive teaching program link. Use the ITP to model 24-hour time. Show both clock faces. Then hide the analogue clock face (both types of face can be revealed or hidden by pressing on their button). By default, it will show the computer's time. Press Set and choose 24-hour time. Set the time to four hours ahead. Press Set again. Discuss what has changed.
● Show the analogue clock face and discuss what has changed.
● Repeat this, moving the 24-hour clock face on four hours, and then checking the analogue clock face, until you reach the start time again.
● Ensure that the children understand that 11.59pm is shown as 23:59 on the 24-hour clock face, and that 12 o'clock midnight is shown as 00:00.

Independent work
● Ask the children to complete photocopiable page 89.
● If children need support, work with them using the ITP. Show them what happens at 11.59pm/am, and discuss these changes. Ask the group to show the times given on the photocopiable sheet using the ITP.
● More confident learners could work out a timetable for their day, written in 24-hour time.

Plenary
● Hold a voting session using pages 5 and 6 of the Notebook file. Ask the children to vote on the correct box for each answer by writing the voting letter on their individual whiteboards. Take a tally of their votes before revealing the correct answer on the Notebook page.
● Go to page 7 of the Notebook file. Explain that in the next lesson the children will be looking at world time.
● Ask: *Which countries have you been to? Were there time differences? If so, what time differences were there?*
● List these on the whiteboard in preparation for the next lesson. Discuss GMT and BST.

Whiteboard tools
Use a Pen from the Pen tray to write numbers on the number line.

⌨ Pen tray

🔧 Select tool

World time zones

Starter
Go to page 8 of the Notebook file. Roll the two on-screen dice and ask the children to multiply the two numbers. Write the answer on the board and show the class. Repeat this several times, making it faster as the children understand how to play the game.

Whole-class shared work
● Ask the class where the world's time centre is. (Greenwich.) Review the countries that members of the class have visited (listed in the previous lesson's Plenary) and discuss the changes in time.
● Display page 9, which shows a world map with ten major cities highlighted. Invite two children to select a city. Set the clock to the current time. Ask: *What time is it now in the two selected cities?* (Numbers along the top and bottom of the map show the difference in time between the different zones. For example, New York is '-5' hours, so whatever time it is in the United Kingdom, New York will be five hours behind.)
● Discuss how to find out the difference using a number line. Take particular care when crossing 00.00 and highlight what other changes have taken place - one city is Tuesday, the other Wednesday. Emphasise that it is only the hours that change, not the minutes.
● Go to page 10 to ask specific questions of the children using the timer. They should work out the times using number lines on their individual whiteboards. Ask them to show some of their results and, importantly, how they came to them. They can write the times on the map.
● Do this several times with other cities. Identify that the further west they go, the further time is behind, and the further east, the further they are ahead of GMT.

Independent work
● Ask the children to create a chart for different times of day in different cities. Choose times of day that are meaningful to them, such as the times they wake up and go to school.
● Less confident learners should include London and one other city.
● More confident learners could extend their chart to include cities in the Far East and West, and to note down the time difference. For example:

	Wake up	Go to school	Lunch	Go home	Dinner	Bedtime
New York	7.30am	9.00am	12.00 noon	3.30pm	6.00pm	8.00pm
London	12.30pm	2.00pm	5.00pm	8.30pm	11.00pm	1.00am
Tokyo	9.30pm	11.00pm	2.00am	5.30am	8.00am	10.00am

Plenary
● Share results: what do the children notice?
● Go to page 11 of the Notebook file. Explain that supersonic aircraft travel fast enough to beat time. Until recently, Concorde was able to beat the clock when travelling to New York from London. Ask the children why this would not work in reverse.

Flight films

Learning objective
PNS: Measuring
● Read timetables and time using 24-hour clock notation.

Resources 💿
'Flight films' Notebook file; individual whiteboards and pens; some examples of film time, from DVDs or videos, or taken from TV listings (you will need about ten, in minutes).

Links to other subjects
Geography
QCA Unit 20 'Local traffic - an environmental issue'
● Discuss the impact that larger airports have on a community. Consider the expanding London airports and discuss the pros and cons.

Starter
Use page 2 of the Notebook file to practise counting on and back from 0 to 1 in steps of 0.1, from different start points. Annotate the line, using different colours, to illustrate different jump sizes. Point to various places on the line, and ask: *If this is 0.3, what will this be? If we jump in steps of 0.3, which numbers will be in the sequence?* Use the Delete button ☒ to remove the circles to reveal the decimal numbers 0.1, 0.2, 0.3, and so on.

Whole-class shared work
● Display page 3 of the Notebook file. Help the children to order the films from shortest to longest.
● Ask the children how these times have been presented. (In minutes only, for example, 90 minutes.)
● Ask the children: *How could we translate these times from minutes to hours and minutes? What do we need to know?*
● Guide them towards identifying that 1 hour = 60 minutes. Therefore, each number of minutes is a multiple of 60, and whatever is left over are the remaining minutes, or part of one hour.
● Let the children work in pairs to change the film times into hours and minutes. They should write the answers on their individual whiteboards. Share results, and check answers.
● Press the red box to reveal the converted film times on the next page. To view the two versions together, use the Dual Page Display (select View from the top taskbar, then Zoom, then Dual Page Display).
● Go to page 5. Work through the examples of films that you have brought in, converting the lengths from minutes into hours and minutes.
● Now go to page 6. Tell the children to imagine that they are members of the flight crew. Their job is to select films that will, as near as possible, match the flight time (seven and a half hours).

Independent work
● In pairs, the children should choose which films they think will fit the flight time. They can use whatever method they like but it must be linked to time and not preference.
● Less confident learners can add together pairs of times. They can then estimate how many films the flight attendants could realistically put together for one flight.
● Challenge more confident learners to carry out the activity for different flight lengths.

Plenary
● Ask the class if anybody got near to the flight time. Using page 7 of the Notebook file, ask different pairs to write up which films they chose and how they got to their answer.
● Discuss other reasons for choosing films. For example, trying to show the maximum number of films in one flight might not be a good idea, as longer films may be more absorbing and make the flight seem shorter.

Whiteboard tools
Use a Pen from the Pen tray to write on the page. Convert handwritten words to text by selecting them and choosing the Recognise option from the dropdown menu. Use the Delete button to reveal the decimal numbers.

🖥 Pen tray

☒ Delete button

🖱 Select tool

Setting the TV recorder

Learning objective
PNS: Measuring
● Read timetables and time using 24-hour clock notation.

Resources 💿
'Setting the TV recorder' Notebook file; calculators.

Links to other subjects
English
PNS: Drama
● Ask children to write the script and perform/hot-seat as a link presenter between programmes. Consider what sort of witty links they might use, what sort of information they might want the viewers to consider, what tone of voice they might use.

Starter
Open the 'Setting the TV recorder' Notebook file and display page 2. Give each pair of children a calculator. The first child enters a number between 1 and 10,000 and shows it to the second child. The first child then either multiplies or divides the number by 10 or 100. He/she hands the calculator to the second child, who then has to tell the first child which operations and number he/she used. Swap roles, and play the game again.

Whole-class shared work
● Go to page 3 of the Notebook file. Discuss what information you need to record a television programme. Write suggestions on the board.
● Go to page 4 and tell the children that the first programme is 30 minutes long and starts at 7.00pm. Discuss what time the programme will finish.
● Lower the Screen Shade 🖳 to reveal the row of start times, and the empty row of finish times, at the bottom of the page. Ask: *What would the finish times be for a 30-minute programme if it started at these times?* Ask volunteers to write the correct finish time underneath each start time. Ensure that all the children are able to change the time if it crosses into a new hour.
● Look at the final row. What would the finish times be in 24-hour time? Ask volunteers to write these under each finish time.
● Ask the class to imagine that they work for a TV network. They have the lengths of time for a number of programmes and have to organise when programmes start.
● Display page 5. Explain the fixed points: the news at 10.00pm and the soap opera at 7.30pm. Ask: *If a film starts at 9.00pm, what will happen half way through?* (The news.) *What will you have to do?* (Split the film into two sections.)

Independent work
● Ask the children to organise the programme schedule.
● Challenge more confident learners to include commercial breaks, following these rules: a 30-minute programme has one break, a 45-minute programme has two, and a 60-minute programme has three.
● Less confident learners will need help to fill in the fixed points of their schedule first, and then consider which programmes will 'fit' before and after these points.

Plenary
● Discuss the children's answers, asking volunteers to move the programmes on the board and add in their timings.
● Display page 6 of the Notebook file. Explain that your recorder has broken. You set it to record a 30-minute programme on Monday at 7.30pm but it started recording for 90 minutes starting at 8.00pm on Monday. Ask: *What programmes were recorded?* Ask a child to come up and highlight these on the Notebook page.
● Set similar problems for different days of the week.

Whiteboard tools
Move the Screen Shade to reveal the lower half of page 4 of the Notebook file.

🖳 Pen tray

🖳 Screen Shade

🖈 Select tool

🖊 Highlighter pen

Ruler rules

Learning objective
PNS: Measuring
● Draw and measure lines to the nearest millimetre.

Resources 💿 🅿️
'Ruler rules' Notebook file; individual whiteboards and whiteboard markers; assortment of everyday class items: pencil, pen, eraser, pencil sharpener, book, stationery case, reading book, homework diary; rulers (15 and 30cm); photocopiable page 90 'Measuring table' for each child.

Links to other subjects
English
PNS: Drama
● Ask children to use drama to teach younger children the differences between kilometres and centimetres, making the explanation as fun and visual as possible.

Starter
Go to page 2 of the Notebook file. The children have to re-arrange the digits to make numbers that are greater than, then less than, then as close as possible to the number on the board. Ask one or two children to read the number out loud each time. Invite a volunteer to re-arrange the numbers on the board. Use the Random Number Generator to create a four-digit number. Ask the children to create a greater than/less than/as close as possible number to the one on the board.

Whole-class shared work
● Give the children rulers and ask them to place their fingers on any millimetre line. Ask: *What is a millimetre a division of?* (A centimetre, a metre and a kilometre.)
● Display the ruler on page 3 of the Notebook file. Ask: *What do the divisions stand for?* Explain that although this metric ruler is enlarged, it measures centimetres and millimetres (show the divisions).
● Move the Screen Shade 🖵 to reveal the lower half of the page. Demonstrate placing the ruler accurately on the end of the square, over the 0, to ensure an accurate measurement. Ask for a volunteer to come up and read the answer. Repeat with the other shapes.
● Discuss how the measurements would be different if a centimetre ruler were used.
● Display page 4. Ask the class to write an estimate for the length of the recorder on their whiteboards, using the interactive whiteboard ruler as the guide. Note down answers. Measure the recorder. Congratulate the person with the nearest estimate. Repeat with the other objects. (The objects are all movable and the ruler can be rotated.)

Independent work
● Display page 5. Ask the children to find, estimate and measure the items listed in the table.
● Give each child a copy of photocopiable page 90. Working in pairs, they should choose five more items to estimate and measure.
● The children should estimate the length of an object to the nearest millimetre, keeping their estimates hidden from their partners. They should then measure the object, deduct their estimated length from the actual measurement and enter this as their score.
● When all of the items have been measured, the person with the lowest score is the winner.
● Ensure that less confident learners choose smaller items to estimate.
● Challenge more confident learners to estimate and measure larger items, such as the length of a bookcase.

Plenary
● Ask volunteers to write up their estimated and actual measurements for each item on page 5 of the Notebook file. Discuss the differences between the estimated and actual measurements.
● Compare everyone's scores and celebrate the success of the person with the lowest score.
● Ask: *What happened to your estimates as you measured more items?* (They should have improved with practice.)
● Discuss where people got estimates very wrong - usually with larger objects - and reflect that it is harder to estimate larger objects accurately, and that another unit of measurement is needed in those cases.

Whiteboard tools
To rotate the ruler, select it, press the green dot and drag to rotate.

🖳 Pen tray

🖰 Select tool

🖵 Screen Shade

Ruler express

Learning objective
PNS: Measuring
● Read, choose, use and record standard metric units to estimate and measure length to a suitable degree of accuracy (eg the nearest centimetre); convert larger to smaller units using decimals to one place (eg change 2.6kg to 2600g).

Resources
'Ruler express' Notebook file; individual whiteboards and pens; rulers (15 and 30 centimetres); millimetre-squared graph paper and drawing materials.

Links to other subjects
Art and design
PoS (3a) Compare ideas, methods and approaches in their own and others' work and say what they think and feel about them.
● Invite groups to review each others' work. Encourage them to identify strengths and explain that designers redraft their work in the same way that writers redraft stories. Ask children to work in pairs to redraft their designs, and create a gallery of architectural blueprints of children's studies.

Starter
Open the 'Ruler express' Notebook file and go to page 2. Ask the class to read out the number. Highlight the place value of each digit and point out that there is no comma or space between the hundreds and thousands. Ask: *What would you need to subtract to get 76,049?* (200.) *Which digit has changed?* (The hundreds digit.) *What if you took away 300? Which digits would change this time?* Repeat with another six- or seven-digit number.

Whole-class shared work
● Revise measuring accurately with a millimetre ruler. Ask: *What items would you expect to measure in millimetres? What items would not be suitable to measure in millimetres? Why not?*
● Go to page 3 and ask volunteers to move the items into the correct box.
● Explain that architects work in millimetres. Tell the children to imagine that they are architects designing a prototype child's study.
● Display page 4, and talk about what might be in the study (some items are shown on the page).
● A sample plan of a study is given on page 5. Let the children experiment with moving things around within the room.
● Show them some millimetre-squared paper and explain that, when they draw their plans, every millimetre will represent ten centimetres, or one hundred millimetres.
● Measure the items on page 6, writing their dimensions in millimetres and then converting to centimetres.

Independent work
● The children should design their study, deciding on the dimensions of the room, and what furniture and other items they will put into it.
● They should measure each dimension of the room, and convert the measurement into centimetres (1mm = 10cm), and do the same for each item in the room. They can record this information as a chart.
● Less confident learners could work on the whiteboard, using the furniture and squared paper on page 5.
● Challenge more confident learners to use different items other than those shown in the example.

Plenary
● Discuss the children's study plans, scanning a few into the computer to view on page 7 of the Notebook file. Invite feedback, asking questions such as: *Do you think the furniture is a reasonable size? Would a computer fit on this table?*
● Discuss other standard units of measurement, and where they might be best used (kilometres for long distances, for example, rather than metres).
● Explain that all of these units are interchangeable, and that they can be expressed either in mm, cm or km.

Whiteboard tools
To rotate the ruler, select it, press the green dot and drag to rotate. Upload scanned images by selecting Insert, then Picture File, and browsing to where you have saved the image.

🖥 Pen tray

↖ Select tool

⌨ On-screen Keyboard

Distance decisions

Learning objective
PNS: Measuring
● Read, choose, use and record standard metric units to estimate and measure length.

Resources ● P
'Distance decisions' Notebook file; photocopiable page 91 'Map of the United Kingdom' for each child; individual whiteboards and pens; rulers (15 and 30 centimetres).

Links to other subjects
Design and technology
QCA Unit 5C 'Moving toys'
● Encourage children to use their knowledge of scale when they design and make their toy.
Geography
QCA Unit 25 'Geography and numbers'
● The unit's objective of drawing plans and maps links well with the work in this lesson, particularly if children are studying the local area.

Starter
Go to page 2 of the Notebook file. Use the Random Number Generator to create a two-digit number. Ask the class to think of a three-digit target number ending in zero (for example, 780). What number do they need to add to the two-digit number to make the target number? Demonstrate this on the number line, using no more than four jumps (for example, 35 + 5, 40 + 10, 50 + 30, 80 + 700). Repeat with a new two-digit number. Ask the class to draw an empty number line on their individual whiteboards, and show their jumps on this.

Repeat the activity, this time using the Random Number Generator to create a three-digit starting number.

Whole-class shared work
● Display page 3. Ask the children to discuss, in pairs, how they would measure each of these items and what equipment they would use. Consider each item in turn, discussing appropriate units of length and appropriate measuring equipment. Can the class list any other examples where units of measurement need to be changed? (For example, a journey to Mars, the distance to the headteacher's office.)
● Display page 4. Ask the children to suggest what units of length might be reasonable to measure between the major cities marked on the map.
● Explain that on maps the distances have to be compressed, otherwise the maps would be too large to carry. On this map, every millimetre is the equivalent of ten kilometres. Demonstrate measuring a distance and converting it into kilometres.

Independent work
● Give out copies of photocopiable page 91 and ask the children to measure the distances between the cities in millimetres. They then have to convert their measurements to kilometres, and enter the distances into the table.
● Work with less confident learners on the whiteboard, using page 4 of the Notebook file and the on-screen ruler.
● Challenge more confident learners to use a road atlas or other map to help them locate other towns or cities, and to measure the distances between these. Alternatively, they could work out the distances in miles.

Plenary
● Ask for volunteers to demonstrate measuring on the whiteboard.
● Go to page 5, and ask volunteers to fill in the distances in the chart. Press the red answer box to reveal the correct answers, and discuss any misunderstandings that may have arisen.
● Ask the class for other examples where sizes or distances have been reduced (A–Z maps, models of vehicles). Explain that with models, the size difference is usually shown as a ratio (for example, 6:1) and that the real object is six times longer than this one. So, if a car model (at a ratio of 6:1) was 40cm long, how long is the real vehicle?

Whiteboard tools
Use the Random Number Generator to generate numbers. To rotate the ruler, select it, press the green dot and drag to rotate. Edit existing text with the On-screen Keyboard, accessed through the Pen tray of the SMART Board tools menu.

⬚ Pen tray

➤ Select tool

⬚ On-screen Keyboard

Triangle terrors

Starter
Go to page 2 of the Notebook file, showing just the first row of numbers: 2, 4, 8, 16, 32, 64. Discuss what is happening in the number sequence. (The numbers are doubling.) Now move the Screen Shade ⬚ to reveal the second line. Ask for the relationship in this sequence. (They are squared numbers.) Finally, reveal the third line and ask for the relationship. (They are triangle numbers.) Draw the numbers on the board in the shape of a triangle to show this. For example:

$$1$$
$$1 + 2$$
$$1 + 2 + 3$$
$$1 + 2 + 3 + 4$$

Whole-class shared work
● Go to page 3 and read the question at the top of the page. Tell the children that they will be investigating the properties of different types of triangles and their lines of symmetry.
● Discuss with the children the names of different types of triangles. Write a separate 'definition' text box for each type of triangle, listing its name, the number of equal sides and the number of equal angles. (Simple definitions can be accessed by pulling out the Definitions tab.)
● Drag triangles out of the box at the bottom of the page. Ask: *Which definition goes with which triangle?* Ask volunteers to match them.
● Look at pages 4 and 5. Ask volunteers to come to the whiteboard and show where the lines of symmetry are for each triangle, using the Lines tool ⬚. (They can rotate the triangles and the line.) Each time, encourage the children to agree that the lines are correct, and ask them to suggest what type of triangle this is. Refer back to the names they agreed on earlier to check. Then use the Eraser from the Pen tray to erase the black marks to reveal the names of the triangles.

Independent work
● Give each child a copy of photocopiable page 92.
● Divide the class into ability groups. Ask less confident learners to look for isosceles triangles, and to find one line of symmetry in each. Confident learners can name and find lines of symmetry in all the triangles.
● Challenge more confident learners to draw their own triangles with different numbers of lines of symmetry, using a mirror to check. They could also draw a triangle for another child to draw lines of symmetry.

Plenary
● Ask for a volunteer from each group to come up to the whiteboard and show where different types of triangle are on page 6, and to draw in the lines of symmetry.
● Refer back to the class definitions to agree the groupings, and add the information about lines of symmetry for each type of triangle.

Fraction machines

Learning objective
PNS: Counting and understanding number
● Express a smaller whole number as a fraction of a larger one (eg recognise that 5 out of 8 is $5/8$).

Resources
'Fractions' Notebook file; individual whiteboards and pens.

Links to other subjects
ICT
PoS (2b) Creating and testing sequences of instructions.
● In Excel, key 8 into A1 and 4 into B1. Write the formula =(A1/B1) into C1. Press return: C1 now shows a quarter of A1 (2). Now type 12 into A1. C1 will change to 3. Type 3 into B1 (to represent a third) and C1 will change to 4 (dividing A1 by 3).

Starter
Display page 2 of the Notebook file. Ask: *What pairs of factors make the number in the circle?* Use the Eraser from the Pen tray to reveal the factors in the smaller circles. Repeat for pages 3 and 4. There are only two factors for the final number because 51 is a prime number and can only be divided by 1 and itself.

Whole-class shared work
● Go to page 5 and ask a volunteer to say a fraction. Create it on the Notebook page using the Fraction Maker. Repeat two or three times. Ask the class to think of as many different fractions as they can, writing them on their whiteboards. Warn them that they must be able to read the fraction correctly to their partner for the next part of the exercise.
● Go to page 6. Can the children remember the names of the two number parts of a fraction? Discuss before revealing the names and definitions by pressing the box at the top of the page.
● Ask one child in each pair to select a fraction from the other child's list. The other child has to name it. If the answerer can't name it, the questioner gets a point; if the answerer can name it, the answerer gets a point.
● Move around the classroom as the children play, spotting problems (for example, a quarter being referred to as a 'fourth').
● Discuss any common disagreements and make general class rules. Ask volunteers to write a fraction on the board and challenge the whole class to say it.
● Go to page 7. The fraction machine converts mixed-number fractions into top-heavy fractions (vulgar fractions). Remind the class of the definition for a denominator. As an example, show the children that $3^1/_3$ is equal to the sum:

$$\frac{(3 \times 3) + 1}{3} = \frac{10}{3}$$

● Ask the children to work out what the top-heavy fraction is for the first example. Drag the fraction over to the other side of the machine to reveal the answer. Repeat for the other fractions.

Independent work
● The children should randomly select a whole number and match it to one of the common fractions on the board. They should then express this mixed fraction as a vulgar fraction.
● More confident learners can choose two whole numbers (such as 3 and 5 making 35) and partner it with a common fraction. For example:
$$35¼ = \frac{141}{4}.$$

Whiteboard tools
Reveal hidden numbers with the Eraser from the Pen tray. To use the Fraction Maker, write the numerator and denominator using a Pen from the Pen tray and then press the arrow to create the fraction.

🖥 Pen tray

🔖 Select tool

Plenary
● Go to page 8 of the Notebook file and ask the children to show how they created their fraction from the mixed-number fraction that they started with.
● Review the terms *denominator* and *numerator* and identify any misconceptions.

Fraction pizzas

Learning objective
PNS: Counting and understanding number
● Express a smaller whole number as a fraction of a larger one (eg recognise that 5 out of 8 is $^5/_8$).

Resources
'Fractions' Notebook file; individual whiteboards and pens.

Links to other subjects
Design and technology
QCA Unit 5D 'Biscuits'
● Link the work in this lesson to this Unit, looking at ways of adapting a recipe to make more or fewer biscuits, or of dividing the mixture to make bigger or smaller biscuits.

Starter
Write six whole numbers on page 9 of the 'Fractions' Notebook file. Ask: *What totals can you make by multiplying pairs of these numbers together?* The children should write calculations and answers on their individual whiteboards. Use the timer to impose a time limit.

Ask volunteers to write one multiplication and its answer on the board for the rest of the class to check. If the class is not sure, use the Calculator 🖩 to confirm the answers.

Whole-class shared work
● Remind the children of their definitions for a numerator and a denominator.
● Display page 10. Ask: *How many quarters of pizza are there?* (Twelve slices in three whole pizzas.)
● Explain that $^{12}/_4$ is an improper fraction (one that is top heavy). Copy and paste another pizza cut up into quarters. Ask: *How many quarters are there now?* ($^{16}/_4$) Repeat this with another pizza.
● Go to page 11. Discuss methods to work out the pizza problems. (Suggestions may include adding four, counting on, or multiplying by four.)
● Write up suggestions. Say that you want to test the multiplying rule.
● Display page 12. The pizzas have now been cut into three equal pieces. Ask: *How many thirds will there be in total? How can you check this answer?* (There are 12 thirds because $4 \times 3 = 12$.)
● Check the answer by doing the sum in reverse: divide 12 by 3 to work out that there are four whole pizzas.
● Display page 13 and ask the children to work out the fraction number sentence for these pizzas. Repeat the activity for pages 14 and 15.
● Go to page 16. Ask: *What happens if the answer is not a whole number? How could we find out how many whole pizzas there are in $^{11}/_5$ slices?* Compare answers and discuss. Extra copies of the pizza are available underneath the top image. The pizza can be divided into five equal slices by pressing on the image and dragging each slice away from the centre.

Independent work
● Display page 17. The children have to choose one number from each column to create an improper fraction ($^{12}/_5$ for example).
● They then have to put the class method to the test, by using it to change the improper fraction back into a mixed-number fraction.

Plenary
● Ask the children to use page 18 of the Notebook file to explain their work. Highlight good strategies.
● Explain that 'chunking' can be used for large numbers, such as $^{523}/_5$. For example, there are 100 5s in 500, 4 in 20, which leaves $^3/_5$. The answer is therefore $120^3/_5$.

Whiteboard tools
Use the Calculator, accessed through the SMART Board tools menu, to check multiplications if necessary.

🖥 Pen tray

▚ Select tool

🖩 Calculator

Show me the line!

Learning objective
PNS: Handling data
● Answer a set of related questions by collecting, selecting and organising relevant data; draw conclusions, using ICT to present features, and identify further questions to ask.

Resources ⊙ ℗
'Data-handling' Notebook file, with the Interactive Teaching Program 'Data handling'; photocopiable page 93 'Database and bar chart' for each child; drawing materials.

Links to other subjects
ICT
PoS (2c) Pupils should be taught to use simulations and explore models in order to answer 'What if...?' questions, to investigate and evaluate the effect of changing values and to identify patterns and relationships.
● Input the table of hair colour data into Excel or a similar spreadsheet program. Highlight the table by pressing and dragging over it. Select 'Chart' from the 'Insert' menu. This will bring up the Chart Wizard. Create a simple bar chart of the data. The data and the chart are now linked – if you alter the data in the table, the chart will alter accordingly. This demonstrates that changes in the data affect its representation in the chart.

Whiteboard tools
Use the Shapes tool to add a triangle to page 2. Use the Spotlight tool to explore the triangles in the Starter.

🖳 Pen tray

🔖 Select tool

🖳 Shapes tool

🖳 Spotlight tool

Starter
Go to page 2 of the Notebook file. Ask the children to name a triangle. Using the Shapes tool 🖳 draw and label it, and describe its properties. Ask the class to put their heads down. Select either the round or square Spotlight tool 🖳 and then go to page 3. (Increase or decrease the size of the Spotlight by dragging it.) Ask the class to lift their heads. Slide the Spotlight slowly around a triangle, asking: *What could this shape be? Look at the angle, what shape isn't it?* Repeat this with the other triangles.

Whole-class shared work
● Go to page 4 of the Notebook file and press the thumbnail image to open the 'Data handling' ITP.
● Use the preset database for eye colour to make a chart. Identify the title of the chart, the content of each column and the horizontal and vertical axes. Note that the vertical axis goes up in fours.
● Explain the importance of an appropriate set of divisions for the numbered axis. Ask: *Why is going up in ones not always practical?* (Large numbers would make the chart very long and hard to read.)
● Reset the data and show the preset database for 'our favourite drinks'. Discuss what a suitable set of division might be. Show the chart and explain that is only a suggestion: the key objective is to come up with a range that is useful and easy to read.
● Reset the data and show the preset database for a village population. This is in the hundreds, so the range is likely to be wider than 2, 5 or 10. Ask the class to discuss why, reinforcing the objective of presenting data that can be interpreted. Ask for suggestions for divisions, then show the vertical chart and discuss.
● Repeat this exercise with 'Olympic gold medals'. Point out that the bars do not touch. Point out the colour coding. Explain that with most computer-generated charts the database will have a colour-coded key to match the chart.

Independent work
● Select the preset data for hair colour. The data in the white boxes can be altered by double-pressing on it and typing into the box. Collect and type in data for hair colour for the class.
● Give out copies of photocopiable page 93. The children should copy the data for hair colour from the board onto the database, and then represent it on the chart. They will need to decide on a suitable set of divisions for the numbered axis.

Plenary
● Ask volunteers to show their charts and explain how they decided on their sets of divisions.
● Show how data can be presented either vertically or horizontally by selecting the different options on the ITP.

Questionnaire

Starter
Go to page 5 of the Notebook file. Use the Random Number Generator to create a two-digit number and ask the class to halve it and double it. The children should write down the answer as quickly as they can on their individual whiteboards. Draw out the link between halving and dividing by two, and doubling and multiplying by two. Repeat with different numbers, ensuring that some odd numbers are halved.

Whole-class shared work
● Split the class into small groups and give each group a set of photocopies taken of the completed questionnaires (see Resources).
● Ask each group to number their questionnaires, to ensure that none is counted twice. Emphasise that knowing how many questionnaires there are is important for checking the final total of data (this should tally with the number of photocopies).
● Display page 6 and open the ITP 'Data handling'. Explain that you are only going to use the database section of the chart. Choose one part of the questionnaire (shoe sizes, for example) and explain that this is the information that you are going to collect for your database.
● Create a rough database on an individual whiteboard. Ask for a volunteer to help you, and start to collect the data from the questionnaires using a tally system. When you have collected the data, transfer it to the ITP database. Explain that the data is the same but that it is presented in a clearer format on the ITP.

Independent work
● Give each group a set of questionnaires. Ask the groups to select one part of the questionnaire, ensuring that all parts of the questionnaire are covered across the class.
● The children should collect the data and choose a way of presenting it in a database so that it can be easily understood by other people.
● Set some ground rules about the physical handling of questionnaires, and how the groups should conduct their discussions about the way they will select, collect and present their data. Ask: *How will you check your work?*
● Most of the class time will need to be allocated for this part of the lesson.

Plenary
● Ask groups to explain how they collected the data and what strategies they used. Use page 7 of the Notebook file to make notes if required.
● The groups should then take turns to share their databases with the class. If another group made the same database, explore whether both groups got the same results.
● Tell the children that in the next lesson they will use the databases to create charts.

Representing data

Learning objective
PNS: Handling data
● Answer a set of related questions by collecting, selecting and organising relevant data; draw conclusions, using ICT to present features, and identify further questions to ask.

Resources ⊙ P
'Data-handling' Notebook file including the 'Line graph' ITP; individual whiteboards and pens; computers (one for each pair or group), with Excel software; photocopiable page 93 'Database and bar chart' for each child; coloured pencils; a set of continuous data (for example, the temperature of a particular corner of the playground during the course of a day, or a week); paper and pencils.

Links to other subjects
ICT
PoS (2c) To use simulations and explore models in order to answer 'What if...?' questions, to investigate and evaluate the effect of changing values and to identify patterns and relationships.
● Use Microsoft Excel's Chart Wizard to create a pie chart. Press one of the segments and drag it away from the pie chart to highlight one specific piece of information.

Starter
Go to page 8 of the Notebook file. Using the Random Number Generator, record six two-digit numbers on the board (for example, 25, 34, 61, 44, 58 and 23). Write a number that is the sum of two of the numbers on the board (for example, 102). Ask the children to discuss which two numbers you used to make your total and to record this on their individual whiteboards. Repeat with one or two more totals. In pairs, children take turns to give totals, partners identifying the pair of numbers chosen.

Whole-class shared work
● Go to page 9 of the Notebook file. Revise what is needed to create a useful chart – for example, a title and appropriate divisions.
● Explain that the same things are needed for a line graph. However, the line graph conveys a different sort of information because it shows how something changes over time.
● Use the 'Line graph' ITP on page 9 to see some examples of line graphs.
● Go to page 10 and press the bar at the top of the page to open a blank Excel file. Ask the class what functions they know. Explain that Excel has many similarities with the word-processing programs, with buttons such as font, colour, size and underline. However, Excel's main task is to analyse data, not produce and format text.
● Explain that in today's lesson the class will be using the Chart Wizard, a tool that allows the user to create quick graphs and charts. Demonstrate Chart Wizard: enter some data, select it by right-pressing, go to the insert menu, select Chart to bring up the Chart Wizard, and follow the instructions to make a chart from the data.

Independent work
● Divide the children into small, mixed-ability groups and assign each group a computer.
● The groups should then use Excel to create graphs, using the data you have provided.
● Ask the children to fill in photocopiable page 93, showing the data and a line graph.
● Encourage more confident learners to support less confident learners in their work.

Plenary
● Use page 11 of the Notebook file to summarise what the children have learned about line graphs.
● Ask the children to show their graphs. Do the graphs reflect the data in their database? Ask questions about the graphs, such as: *What was the temperature at this point on the line?*
● Explain that data can be represented in a range of ways, for different purposes. Press the link to the ITP 'Data handling' and select the 'favourite drinks' data. Show the data as a pie chart. Ask: *Why might a pie chart be useful?* (To show visually what share of the whole each part represents.)

Whiteboard tools
To enter data in a spreadsheet, select the cell and use the On-screen Keyboard, accessed through the Pen tray or the SMART Board tools menu, to type.

🖥 Pen tray

🔖 Select tool

🖼 On-screen Keyboard

Power graphs

Learning objective
PNS: Handling data
● Answer a set of related questions by collecting, selecting and organising relevant data; draw conclusions, using ICT to present features, and identify further questions to ask.

Resources P
Photocopiable page 93 'Database and chart' for each child; individual whiteboards and pens; various examples of data (from previous lessons or from books and the internet); computers with Excel software; coloured pencils; databases.

Links to other subjects
ICT
QCA Unit 5B 'Analysing data and asking questions: using complex searches'
● Link this work to searching the internet for data to use.

Starter
Explain that you are going to roll three dice to play a game. The aim of the game is to add the numbers on the first two dice together and take away the number on the third dice from this total. Point out that the total may be a negative number, for example, $(1 + 2) - 5 = -2$. Use dice from the Gallery. Ask the children to write the answer on their individual whiteboards, then show their answers. Gradually speed up the game.

Whole-class shared work
● Review the work on databases, charts and graphs from the previous two lessons. Explain that computers can manipulate data and produce high-quality charts and graphs very quickly. Explain that during this lesson the children will be investigating the types of graph that a computer can create from class data.
● Upload Excel, revise what the children remember from using it in the previous lesson and open Chart Wizard. Demonstrate by inputting some quickly gathered data (for example, shoe sizes) and pressing the Finish button.
● Explain that the type of graph can be altered (3D, line, scatter, pie, bar, doughnut, area, radar). Discuss how different types of graph and chart are used to show different types of information – for example, bar charts show how much is in each column, pie charts show the relative proportions of the various parts to the whole, and line graphs show changes over time.
● Tell the children that they will be creating a graph or chart using Chart Wizard. Give each group a set of data, from previous lessons or from the internet or books: for example, temperatures in a particular part of the world during the course of a year.

Independent work
● Get the children to input the data into Chart Wizard to create a graph or chart.
● Emphasise that they must choose the best type of chart or graph for their data, and be ready to explain the reasons for their choices.
● The charts can be copied into a Word document by pressing on the edge of the chart, pressing the Copy button, pressing on the Word document and pressing the Paste button.
● Ensure that the data you give to the children is suited to their level of ability. Less confident learners could be given data suitable for bar charts, while more confident learners could be given data suitable for line graphs or pie charts.

Plenary
● Display the children's charts and graphs.
● Ask groups to explain where their data came from, and why they chose to represent it in this way.
● Encourage discussion from the rest of the class. Has the data been presented in an appropriate way?

Whiteboard tools
Use dice from the Gallery to roll a virtual dice on the board. To enter data in a spreadsheet, select the cell and use the On-screen Keyboard, accessed through the Pen tray or the SMART Board tools menu, to type.

⌨ Pen tray

▢ Select tool

▢ On-screen Keyboard

▢ Gallery

Crazy quads

Learning objective
PNS: Measuring
● Use the formula for the area of a rectangle to calculate its area.

Resources ●
'Area and perimeter' Notebook file; photocopiable page 95 'Quads' for each child; individual whiteboards and pens.

Links to other subjects
Design and technology
PoS (1a) To generate ideas for products after thinking about who will use them and what they will be used for, using information from a number of sources, including ICT-based sources.
● Look at and discuss blueprints or architectural drawings of the school. Produce blueprints for the 'ideal classroom', using an accurate scale.

Starter
Open the 'Area and perimeter' Notebook file and go to page 2. Split the class into two groups. Choose a child from the first group to say a simple fraction: some examples are given on page 2, or different fractions can be added using the Fraction Maker. The other group have to call out the percentage equivalent. Repeat this and then alter the game by picking a child from the percentage group to say a percentage. The fraction group have to call out the fraction equivalent.

Whole-class shared work
● Display page 3 of the Notebook file. Ask the class to discuss how they would find the area of the quadrilateral. Explain that it has to be measured accurately and that in this case they will be using centimetres.
● Demonstrate measuring the shape using the on-screen ruler (one square on the grid represents 1cm) and note the lengths of each side on the board. To find the area, use a formula: multiply length by width ($L \times W = A^2$) ($7 \times 5 = 35cm^2$).
● Point out that area is given in centimetres squared, which is shown using the squared symbol (^{2}).
● Go to page 4 and choose one of the shapes. Repeat the process using the formula. Then ask a volunteer to count up the squares to show that the number of squares in the quad is the same as the answer that was achieved using the formula.
● Repeat the activity for the other quadrilaterals.

Independent work
● Give each child a copy of photocopiable page 95. They should use the agreed formula to measure the quadrilaterals and give the areas in centimetres squared.
● Less confident learners could draw the shapes onto squared paper first.
● Extend the activity for more confident learners by asking them to cut out two quads and group them to create a new shape. What is the total surface area of this new shape?

Plenary
● Ask children to show their working out on the whiteboard.
● Display page 5 of the Notebook file. Ask: *How would you measure the area of these shapes?* Use the Lines tool ◥ to cut one of the new shapes into two, creating two quadrilaterals. Measure both these parts of the shape and then add the two areas together for the final total. Repeat for the second shape.
● Explain that if the quad is square, the formula that could be used is x^2. The result will therefore be a square number.

Whiteboard tools
Use the Lines tool to cut the complex shapes into two on page 5 of the Notebook file. Use the on-screen ruler to measure the sides of the shapes.

⬜ Pen tray

◥ Select tool

◥ Lines tool

Find the shape!

Learning objective
PNS: Understanding shape
● Read and plot coordinates in the first quadrant.

Resources 💿
'Build your own' file; 'Coordinates' ITP from My Content in the Gallery (this ITP allows the user to show coordinates in all quadrants, with or without a grid, with preset markers and with a cross-hair finder tool); individual whiteboards and pens; squared paper.

Links to other subjects
Geography
PoS (2e) To draw plans and maps at a range of scales.
● Look at two maps drawn to different scales. Focus on one coordinate (4D, for example). What information is located in that square on both maps? What are the differences between the two? How can each map be of use?

Starter

Open the 'Build your own' file, which consists of a blank Notebook page and a ready-made Gallery collection of resources located in My Content 🖼. Ask volunteers to give six negative numbers between −20 and 0. Record them randomly with a space between each. Ask for six positive numbers between 0 and 20. Record them among the negative numbers. Draw a number line on the board and label the positions −20, 0 and 20. Ask a child to indicate the position of −10. Repeat with other numbers to confirm that the children can identify key markers. Then ask them to write the 12 numbers in order on their whiteboards, starting with the lowest, using the number line for reference.

Whole-class shared work

● Display the ITP 'Coordinates' from the Mathematics folder under My Content. Explain that you will be focusing on the first quadrant, which has positive numbers on both axes.
● Add a cross-hair by pressing the cross-hair button.
● Explain the golden rule for coordinates: horizontal before vertical. (Use the alphabet as a way to remember this – H before V.)
● Repeat two more times. Then hide the coordinates by pressing on the (x,y) button.
● Drag the cross-hairs to new positions.
● Ask the children to write down the coordinates on their individual whiteboards. Press the (x,y) button to reveal the coordinates. Repeat this until the class becomes familiar with how to plot coordinates.

Independent work

● Ask the children to draw a 10×10 quadrant on squared paper, draw a shape and plot its coordinates. They can check the coordinates with another person on their table.
● The children should then work in pairs, taking turns to read out the coordinates to the other child, who attempts to draw the shape. Encourage the children to discuss and make corrections if needed.
● Less confident learners may need a pre-drawn 10×10 grid in order to get them started.
● More confident learners could work on shapes that take up the first two quadrants, using negative and positive coordinates.

Plenary

● Discuss how the children drew and plotted their shapes, and what challenges they faced.
● Using the 'Coordinates' ITP again, demonstrate using the on-screen pencil to draw shapes on the board. (Press on the Pencil and select the Pencil and Shape icon. Press on the Pencil icon that appears on the screen and drag it to a position on the graph. Now press and drag the Pencil to another position on the graph. A line should now appear to link the two positions. Continue to do this until you end up at the start position. A shape is automatically created to fill the joined-up lines.)
● Use the cross-hair to check the coordinates.
● The children can draw their own shapes, and shapes using other children's coordinates.
● Save the shapes the children have created for use in Lesson 17.

Whiteboard tools
Use a Pen from the Pen tray to write the numbers in the Starter.

🖥 Pen tray

🖱 Select tool

🖼 Gallery

What's my coordinate?

Starter
Open the 'Build your own' file, which consists of a blank Notebook page and a ready-made Gallery collection of images located in My Content 📷. Use the Random Number Generator to create a number between 1.1 and 9.9, such as 3.4. Ask the children to round up to the nearest whole number and write the answer on their individual whiteboards. Ask them to show their answers. Repeat this activity several times.

Whole-class shared work
● Use the ITP 'Coordinates' to review how to plot coordinates in the first quadrant. Recap the alphabetical method of remembering which coordinate should be plotted first. (H for horizontal comes before V for vertical.)
● Tell the children that they are going to test that method, plotting in all four quadrants.
● Show on the ITP that coordinates can be plotted in one, two or four quadrants. Explain to the children that they will do more work on this in Year 6.
● Show a grid with all four quadrants revealed and ask the class to discuss what they see on the various axes. Conclude that there are negative numbers as well as positive.
● Using the cross-hairs, show how the coordinates change as plots are moved clockwise around the board. Focus on where negative numbers are used. When you get to the third quadrant, remind the children that coordinates do not change alignment but stay the same.
● Draw a shape in the first quadrant and demonstrate that you can repeat this shape in any quadrant, but that the coordinates change each time. (To draw a shape, press on the Pencil and select the Pencil and Shape icon. Press on the Pencil icon that appears on the screen and drag it to a position on the graph. Now press and drag the Pencil to another position on the graph. A line appears to link the two positions. Continue to do this until you end up at the start position. A shape is automatically created to fill the joined-up lines.)

Independent work
● The children should draw a grid that goes from -10 to +10 on both axes.
● Give them the shapes that they drew for Lesson 16. They should draw their original shape in the first quadrant of the new grid, then choose another quadrant to repeat the shape and plot the new coordinates.
● They should ask a partner to check their coordinates, using the alphabetical guide learned earlier.
● Less confident learners may need a pre-drawn grid.
● More confident learners could plot in all four quadrants.

Plenary
● Ask the children to discuss their work and any challenges it presented.
● Demonstrate using the on-screen pencil on the ITP. Invite one volunteer to dictate their coordinates and another to draw these on the board. Check their coordinates using the cross-hair. Do this a number of times, with different children.

Nets

Learning objective
PNS: Understanding shape
● Identify, visualise and describe properties of rectangles, triangles, regular polygons and 3D shapes; use knowledge of properties to identify and draw nets of 3D shapes.

Resources 💿
'Nets' Notebook file; individual whiteboards and pens.

Links to other subjects
Design and technology
PoS (1c) Plan what they have to do, suggesting a sequence of actions and alternatives, if needed.
● Investigate flat pack furniture, exploring what items can be bought in this way and why flat pack furniture is popular with retailers and consumers. Some modern houses are made from flat packs.

Starter
Give the children these instructions:
1. Close your eyes.
2. Imagine a square.
3. 'Draw' a diagonal line from one corner of the square to another.
4. Visualise the triangles that are created by the diagonal line.
5. Open your eyes.
6. Draw the triangle on your whiteboard.
7. In pairs, discuss what type of triangle you have drawn, and things you can say about it.

Take feedback from the children, encouraging them to use the correct vocabulary. Make a note of key words on page 2 of the Notebook file. Repeat the activity with a rectangle and discuss the differences.

Whole-class shared work
● Explain to the class that they will be looking at how to make 3D shapes from 2D nets.
● Display page 3 of the Notebook file. Ask: *What is a net?* Write correct definitions on the board (the children should have been introduced to nets in Year 4). Explain that they will be designing their own net for a cube, and that this is the most common net they are likely to come across.
● Use the squares on page 4 to create the standard cross design for a cube net. Discuss whether the children have seen this net before – they may have used it to make dice, for example.
● Break up the net and ask a volunteer to reconstruct it.
● Demonstrate another possible net by moving one of the squares one place.
● Display page 5 of the Notebook file, and ask if these nets would produce a cube. Tell the children that there are over a dozen different nets for a cube using six squares.
● Move one of the squares so that it would not be possible to make a cube from the net. Ask: *Why won't this net make a cube?*

Independent work
● The children should investigate drawing nets for a cube, in order to identify as many variations as possible.
● They should work in pairs and put a question mark on any shapes that they think won't turn into nets. This is important for the Plenary, as the shapes will be used, along with the correct nets, to identify common errors and strategies.

Plenary
● Invite the children to recreate their nets on the whiteboard by moving the squares on page 6. Ask them to show a net that they think is correct and explain why it would work, and then another that they think is incorrect and to explain why. Try to fit both nets on one page.
● Draw conclusions about the right way to make a net. Formulate rules, such as: *The sides that are joined together should be the same size.* Print out the pages and model making up the nets if necessary.

Whiteboard tools
🖵 Pen tray

🖱 Select tool

Mirror shapes

Learning objective
PNS: Understanding shape
● Complete patterns with up to two lines of symmetry.

Resources 🔘 📁
'Lines of symmetry' Notebook file; photocopiable page 96 'Polygon shapes' for each child; individual whiteboards and pens; small plastic mirrors, one for each child; large mirror.

Links to other subjects
English
PNS: Word structure and spelling
● Link this work to palindromes. Challenge children to identify palindromes and find palindromes that are symmetrical in the strictest sense (for example, MUM and TUT-TUT). Compile a class dictionary of symmetrical words and shapes. The internet has sites that are dedicated to palindromes.

Starter

Remind the children about the rules for rounding to the nearest 10, and then the nearest 100. Display page 7 of the Notebook file. Ask volunteers to move the numbers that would round to 370 into the box. Repeat the activity for the second question, which deals with rounding to the nearest 100. Go to page 8 of the Notebook file. Ask the children to write up numbers next to the numbers shown.

Whole-class shared work

● Display page 9 of the Notebook file. Ask the class to discuss, in pairs, what properties the shape has (corner, side, parallel sides and so on). Label these properties.
● Explain that in this lesson they will be looking at another property that many polygons have: symmetry. In pairs, ask the children to come up with a definition for symmetry. Invite them to explain their definitions and write them on page 10 of the Notebook file. As a class, they should agree on the most correct definition.
● Go back to page 9 and explain that this regular quadrilateral (not square) has two lines of reflective symmetry. Draw these on the shape. Use a large mirror to show the lines of symmetry (some dedicated maths programs may have a tool that will allow you to do this without using a real mirror).
● Display page 11 and ask the class to discuss where they think the lines of symmetry will appear on the first shape. Ask for a volunteer to draw these lines in, and then check them with the mirror. Repeat this with the other polygons. (The shapes can be rotated, if required.)

Independent work

● Give out copies of photocopiable page 96 and plastic mirrors. Ask the children to explore the symmetry of each of the regular shapes, writing beneath each how many lines of symmetry it has (an equilateral triangle has three lines of symmetry, for example).
● Early finishers could continue the investigation by finding the lines of symmetry to words (see Links to other subjects).

Plenary

● Display page 12 of the Notebook file, which includes the same shapes as on the photocopiable sheet. Review the work done by the children by asking for volunteers to draw the common lines of symmetry onto the shapes on the board.
● Ask the children if there were any shapes that they found unusual. Direct the conversation towards circles, which have an infinite number of lines of symmetry. Illustrate this, using page 13 of the Notebook file.
● Return to the class definition and ask if it needs editing. Make any suggested changes.

Whiteboard tools
Use the Lines tool to indicate the lines of symmetry. Use a Pen from the Pen tray to write on the page.

🖳 Pen tray

🔲 Select tool

✎ Lines tool

Angle madness

Learning objective
PNS: Understanding shape
● Estimate, draw and measure acute and obtuse angles using an angle measurer or protractor to a suitable degree of accuracy.

Resources 💿 🅿
'Angle madness' Notebook file; photocopiable page 97 'Triangle sorter' for each child; individual whiteboards and pens; protractors.

Links to other subjects
Science
PoS Sc4 (2b) Pupils should be taught that objects are pulled downwards because of the gravitational attraction between them and the Earth.
● Using a toy car and a ramp, set up a fair test to show that the smaller the angle is on the ramp the slower the car will descend, and that the higher the angle (up to 90°) the faster the car will descend.

Starter
Display page 2 of the Notebook file and point out the fractions 2½, 2¾, 4½, 2¼, ¼, above the number line. Ask the children to draw the number line on their own whiteboards, representing a scale from 0 to 5, and order the fractions in their correct positions. Ask volunteers to move the fractions into position on the board. Repeat with the following fractions at the bottom of the page: $^{25}/_{100}$, $^{50}/_{100}$, $^{3}/_{2}$, $2^{5}/_{10}$.

Whole-class shared work
● Share the children's ideas about angles and the different types of angle, making notes on page 3.
● Go to page 4 and model how to use the protractor to measure the bottom left angle of the triangle. Align the protractor so that its cross-hairs meet the tip of the angle and its base-line is flat against the bottom line of the shape.
● Show that the numbers move in both directions on the protractor. Ask: *Why is that useful?* Show that by moving the protractor to the opposite side of the triangle, in order to measure the new angle you now have to read from the opposite direction.
● Ask for volunteers to measure the angles of the triangle on page 5. Ask the class to give each volunteer a thumbs-up or thumbs-down, to show whether they think that the angle has been correctly measured and read.
● Show how the protractor can be moved and rotated to fit next to the new side to meet the new angle. To do this, press on it and then press and drag the green circle at the top of the box to rotate the protractor
● Demonstrate this by measuring the angles at the top of the triangles on pages 4 and 5. Ask the class to read these new angles.
● Model this process with the triangles on page 6, inviting the children to measure angles that are not horizontal.

Independent work
● Hand out copies of photocopiable page 97 and protractors. Tell the children that all three angles make 180° and ask them to test this rule.
● Challenge more confident learners by not giving them the rule. Ask them to investigate what the three angles of each triangle have in common.
● Less confident learners could be given some of the angles. Ask them to measure only the horizontal edges, so they don't have to rotate the protractor.

Plenary
● Ask groups to report back on their findings. If anybody found that the rule did not work, replicate a similar triangle on the whiteboard and measure it again to prove the rule.
● Display page 7 and show that other family shapes have similar angle rules: for example, the angles of quadrilaterals add up to 360°. Demonstrate with the regular square and rectangle, and then with the rhombus and trapezium.

Whiteboard tools
Use a Pen from the Pen tray to write in the angles measured.

🖥 Pen tray

🔖 Select tool

At the airport

Starter
Go to page 2 of the Notebook file. Count in steps of 20 and stop at any given point (for example, 160). Ask: *What multiple of 20 equals 140?* Move to page 3 and repeat with steps of 30 and 15 (common intervals for minutes).

Whole-class shared work
● Recap the time changes between different countries (covered in Lessons 1 to 3).
● Explain that airport terminals need to show the local time of either departure or arrival (depending on whether the plane is coming to or leaving the UK) and the flight time in hours. Although the flight to Paris is two hours, it appears to be three hours because of the time difference.
● Display page 4 and show that if the destination is behind our time (for example, New York), it may appear from the arrival time that the flight is far shorter than it actually is. (New York is five hours behind, a flight takes seven hours, so local time of arrival in New York is only two hours later than the departure time in London.)
● Display page 5. The first column shows the city the plane is travelling from, the second column the local departure time, and the third column the duration of the flight. Explain that the fourth column is blank because of a computer fault – the UK arrival times have been omitted.
● Ask the children to use their whiteboards and the 'World time zones map' (photocopiable page 134) to work out when each plane should arrive, local time. They will need to take into consideration flight duration and time changes. Ask for volunteers to drag and drop the correct answers from the foot of the page into the appropriate place on the board.

Independent work
● Leave the colour version of the flight zones map on the board.
● Give each pair of children copies of photocopiable pages 98 and 134. Each pair should fill in the table of arrival times on page 98.
● Encourage more confident learners to complete the second chart on page 98, working out the flight times from the departure and arrival times.

Plenary
● Ask the children to show how they filled in the arrivals board. Ask volunteers to fill in the answers on pages 6 and 7 of the Notebook file.
● Investigate how it is possible to find the total flight time when given just the local departure and local arrival times. (Take one from the other and then either add or subtract the time difference.)

Polygon puzzles

Learning objective
PNS: Measuring
● Measure and calculate the perimeter of regular and irregular polygons; use the formula for the area of a rectangle to calculate its area.

Resources ● 𝗣
'Area and perimeter' Notebook file; photocopiable page 95 'Quads' for each child.

Links to other subjects
Design and technology
PoS (1a) To generate ideas for products after thinking about who will use them and what they will be used for.
● Investigate the perimeter of the building, class or playground. Discuss how the perimeter could be enlarged, or whether the use of the space is poor and could be more efficient.

Starter
Display page 6 of the Notebook file. Ask the children for equivalent fractions of ½ and write them on the board. Repeat this for ¼ and ¾. Now ask for ten random fractions and write these on the board. Ask the children to write them down in order, from the smallest to the largest.

Whole-class shared work
● Ask: *What does 'perimeter' mean?* (The measurement of the outside edge of a shape or polygon.)
● Go to page 7 of the Notebook file and discuss how to measure these shapes. Measure the shape in centimetres, writing the measurements next to each edge. Add the measurements together to calculate the perimeter. Explain that perimeter is measured in centimetres, not centimetres squared, like area.
● Repeat the activity on page 8, asking the children to make the measurements.
● Display page 9: each of these new shapes has been made with two quadrilaterals. Although the original quads had parallel edges that were the same length, this is no longer the case. Use the Lines tool ◺ to show the divisions. Show the children how to measure each edge, and point out that the sum of these edges is the perimeter.
● Use the six squares on page 10 to make different shapes. Show that the perimeter of each new shape can be greater or smaller, even though you are using the same number of blocks.

Independent work
● Give each child a copy of photocopiable page 95 to cut out quads and create irregular polygons. They should then measure the shapes to find the perimeter, using centimetre rulers.
● Less confident learners could measure the perimeter of the quads on the sheet, rather than cutting them out and re-arranging them. (Turn back to page 9 of the Notebook file if this is helpful.)
● More confident learners could choose three shapes from the sheet and investigate how the perimeter of a shape changes depending on how the three shapes are combined. What are the largest and smallest perimeters possible?

Plenary
● Let the children show and discuss their work. Children in the extension group can show their work about longest and shortest perimeters using the same three shapes.
● Use page 10 to demonstrate that because all the sides are the same length it is possible to count the number of squares to work out the perimeter.
● Discuss why this would be important for architects and builders working on a site. Discuss the difference between area and perimeter - that the area can be the same but the perimeter alters. Show this with the six blocks again.

Whiteboard tools
Use the Lines tool to show the divisions of the combined quadrilaterals on page 9.

⌨ Pen tray

▣ Select tool

◺ Lines tool

Learning objective
PNS: Using and applying mathematics
● Solve one-step and two-step problems involving whole numbers and decimals and all four operations, choosing and using appropriate calculation strategies.

Resources ◉ 🅟
'Superheroes' Notebook file; photocopiable page 99 'Superhero problems' for each child; individual whiteboards and pens.

Links to other subjects
English
PNS: Creating and shaping texts
● Ask the children to write a biography of a superhero. Where were they born/created? What are their super powers? What is their one weakness? Do they have an alias, or a regular job? What is their deep, dark secret?

Superheroes (single-stage problems)

Starter
Display page 2 of the Notebook file. Play 'Guess my number': you think of a number and tell the children which times table it is in; the children ask questions to which you can only answer 'yes' or 'no'. Encourage questions that narrow down the possible answers (*Is it odd or even? Is it less than 20?*). The winner chooses the next number.

Whole-class shared work
● Go to page 3 and ask volunteers to order the statements by dragging and dropping them into the correct sequence.
● Read the problem on page 4. Explain that reading the problem is the first stage of answering it. Ask: *How should we begin to work this out?*
● Discuss what mathematics is required and ask volunteers to highlight the key maths points in the sentence on the board.
● Ask: *Is there any information missing?* (The top temperature of an average oven, which is 200°C.) Explain to the children that they have now completed the second stage.
● Next, the children should organise this information onto their individual whiteboards to begin solving the problem in pairs. This is the third stage.
● The fourth stage involves completing the problem and answering it. Invite children to explain their solutions to the rest of the class, or to write their workings and solutions on the board.
● Check these solutions together, explaining that this is the fifth and final stage.
● Try this sequence again with the next problem on page 5 of the Notebook file.

Independent work
● Give out copies of photocopiable page 99. The children should complete these using the five-stage method. They can choose which problems they want to tackle and in which order they do them.
● Less confident learners could highlight what information is needed to solve the problems on the worksheet and what mathematics is needed to solve them.
● Encourage more confident learners to complete the sheet, working through all the problems.

Plenary
● Review the children's solutions, investigating the maths they have used. Make notes on page 6 of the Notebook file.
● Explain that the problems are challenging because there is so much maths involved. Following a simple five-stage system helps to keep things clear.
● Go to page 3, which should now show the five stages in the correct order, and ask the class to chant the five stages to maths problem paradise!
● For their homework, invite the children to make a list of four of their favourite superheroes for the next lesson.

Whiteboard tools
Use a Highlighter pen to identify key information and a Pen from the Pen tray to annotate the methods of working out.

🖥 Pen tray

✏️ Highlighter pen

🔖 Select tool

Learning objective
PNS: Using and applying mathematics
● Solve one-step and two-step problems involving whole numbers and decimals and all four operations, choosing and using appropriate calculation strategies.

Resources ● P
'Superheroes' Notebook file; photocopiable page 100 'More superhero problems' for each child; individual whiteboards and pens; calculators.

Links to other subjects
English
PNS: Creating and shaping texts
● Ask the children to use the information from their superhero biography as the basis for a cartoon (graphic novel), explaining how their superhero met a prime enemy. The children should make the enemy as opposite to the hero as possible and give them an evil name.

Whiteboard tools
Use the On-screen Keyboard to add numbers to the page in the Starter activity. Use a Highlighter pen to identify key information and a Pen from the Pen tray to annotate the methods of working out.

- Pen tray
- On-screen Keyboard
- Select tool
- Highlighter pen

More superheroes (double and multi-stage problems)

Starter
Display page 7 of the Notebook file. Establish that 0 is in the middle of the number line. Ask the children to draw the same line on their whiteboards. Then ask them for three positive and three negative numbers between –20 and +20. Write these numbers randomly on the board.

Ask the children to order the six numbers on their number lines. Collect answers and ask for a volunteer to move the numbers into order on the board. Extend the activity by telling the children that you have reversed the signs, so negative numbers are now positive and vice versa. Ask a child to re-order the numbers on the board.

Whole-class shared work
- Review the five stages to solving a problem from the previous lesson (refer back to page 3 of the Notebook file).
- Display page 8 and read out the problem.
- Discuss what information the class needs and invite volunteers to highlight the parts of the problem that supply the information.
- Ask the class to break the problem into two parts and invite children to explain each part.
- Identify that the first part is 14 × 8, and that the second part is (14 × 8) × 7. Demonstrate the solution.
- Look at the problem on page 9. This problem involves different maths. Invite the children to highlight the key maths parts and ask the class to discuss what different types of maths are being used with this problem (addition and division), and how they could be used together to solve the question.
- If the children need more practice, work through the third example on page 10.

Independent work
- Give out copies of photocopiable page 100 for the children to complete, using the five-stage method. All the problems are multi-stage. The children can choose which problems they want to do, and in which order they do them.
- Less confident learners could highlight what information is needed to solve each problem, and what mathematics is needed to solve it.
- Encourage more confident learners to work through all the problems.

Plenary
- Review the solutions from a number of children. Ask them what maths they used and make a note of this on page 11. Discuss how, with multi-stage problems, a wider range of maths is needed in order to work out the answer.
- Explain that in the next lesson the class will be writing their own problems and presenting them to their friends to solve.

My superhero

Learning objective
PNS: Using and applying mathematics
● Solve one-step and two-step problems involving whole numbers and decimals and all four operations, choosing and using appropriate calculation strategies.

Resources
'Build your own' file; individual whiteboards and pens; completed 'Superhero problems' from previous two lessons; calculators.

Links to other subjects
Design and technology
PoS (1d) To communicate design ideas in different ways as these develop.
● Design a super-vehicle for your hero. On the design, explain how the vehicle works, labelling the materials used to make it, any special functions and any security devices (it will only open for the superhero, for example).

Whiteboard tools
Type the problems on the Notebook page using the On-screen Keyboard, accessed through the Pen tray or the SMART Board tools menu. Use a Highlighter pen to identify key information.

⬚ Pen tray

⬚ Select tool

⬚ On-screen Keyboard

⬚ Highlighter pen

⬚ Gallery

Starter
Open the 'Build your own' file, which consists of a blank Notebook page and a ready-made Gallery collection of images located in My Content ⬚.

Play 'Halves bingo'. Ask the children to draw a 2×3 grid on their individual whiteboards. Use the Random Number Generator from the Mathematics folder under My Content to generate ten two-digit numbers, or multiples of 10 between 100 and 1000, on the blank Notebook page. Each child chooses six numbers, halves them, and writes down the answers in their grid. Call out numbers from the board. The children have to halve the numbers mentally, in order to cross them out. The first child to cross out all six numbers is the winner.

Whole-class shared work
● Review the five stages to solving a problem (from Lesson 23).
● Discuss the heroes that the children prepared for homework, making a list on the board. Use the superhero images located in the Mathematics folder under My Content folder to illustrate, if required.
● Tell the children that they will be writing single or multi-stage problems about these heroes (or other heroes that they have made up).
● Advise them to choose everyday scenarios, such as shopping, but to give these activities a 'super' twist: a shopping list may contain kryptonite, for example!
● Remind them to provide clues to solve the problem: show one of the Notebook file problems to the class to illustrate this. For example:
  ● Mack 1 can fly to Australia in 18 hours. How long will the return journey take in total?
  ● The one-way journey is 18 hours and this number must be doubled to find the length of the return journey.
● Emphasise that problems should be clear and easy to read.

Independent work
● Most children should write a simple, single-stage problem.
● More confident learners may want to write a multi-stage problem.
● Break the task into steps for less confident learners. They should choose a scenario first (for example, the superhero goes to buy some sweets). Then they should build a problem into this (for example, the sweets cost 18p each and the superhero buys a packet of six). Once the child has the basic problem, he or she can add 'super' twists (for example, the sweets are super-strong flying mints).
● Some children might consider building in bogus information, which has nothing to do with the question but acts as a red herring.

Plenary
● Invite a volunteer to read out a problem. Type it on a new Notebook page as they do so.
● Ask them to explain what sort of problem it is and how their friends could begin to solve it. Don't ask for the answer (unless someone is very persistent).
● Do this with several other problems, emphasising the five stages to answering a problem and how to look for clues in the questions. Invite other children to come up and highlight the relevant clues.
● Demonstrate solving the problems.

Budget fliers

Starter
Display page 2 of the Notebook file. Ask the children to draw a nine-square grid (like a noughts-and-crosses grid) on their whiteboards, and to fill each square with a total from the multiplication grid. When they are ready, start calling out pairs of factors. One child should write these pairs on the board as you say them. The winner is the first person to match all their totals with the factors called out.

Whole-class shared work
● Open a new Notebook page. Ask the children what countries they have visited outside of the United Kingdom. Ask what currency they used in the countries they visited, and make a note of the different currencies on the board. Select images of a dollar, a euro and a pound coin from the Mathematics folder under My Content in the Gallery 🖼 . Ask the class to discuss what the differences are between these currencies.
● Explain that different currencies often have varying rates against the pound, and that this is known as their 'exchange rate'. Go to the market data web page on the BBC site (see Resources), and find the currencies chart on this page.
● Make a note of the exchange rates for the currencies of popular countries: for example, American dollars, euros, yen and so on. Make the notes on paper and then annotate the rates directly in the Notebook page.
● Demonstrate how to convert pounds into dollars, euros or yen by multiplying the number of pounds by the appropriate exchange rate. Use the Calculator 🖩 to work out the foreign currency price of a meal (£14.50), a flight (£120) and a day trip (£25).

Independent work
● Hand out copies of photocopiable page 101. Ask the children to imagine that they are going on holiday, and have to budget for a range of activities. They can choose the currency they prefer, and they have £150 for the week.
● The children work in pairs to budget for their week, agreeing on how much to spend on each item.
● Having created the budget, the children should then have to exchange each amount into the new currency.

Plenary
● Ask the children to explain how they have budgeted for their week and which currency they have used, showing the differences between each currency.
● Ask children to come up and demonstrate their workings on the whiteboard.
● Discuss why countries have different currencies. For example: *Does it strengthen a country's identity? Does it create a stronger economic climate?*
● Ask the children which countries have the euro. Debate whether it would be right for the United Kingdom to adopt the euro.

Learning objective
PNS: Using and applying mathematics
● Solve one-step and two-step problems involving whole numbers and decimals and all four operations, choosing and using appropriate calculation strategies.

Resources 💿 🄿
'Currency converter' Notebook file; photocopiable page 102 'Holiday gifts' for each child; individual whiteboards and pens; internet website **www.bbc.co.uk** (select news>business>market data). (Microsoft Excel is required to view the embedded spreadsheet in the Notebook file.)

Links to other subjects
Geography
PoS (3a) To identify and describe what places are like (for example, in terms of weather, jobs).
● Research how much people earn for the same job in different countries. Discuss the results and whether it is fair that the rate varies so widely from country to country. Point out that the cost of living varies, too.

Whiteboard tools
Use the Calculator, accessed through the SMART Board tools menu, to carry out currency conversions.

🖥 Pen tray

🔲 Select tool

🔳 Calculator

Holiday gifts

Starter
Go to page 2 of the Notebook file. Use the Random Number Generator to generate a random three-digit number and mark it on the far left of the number line. The children have to work out the difference by making three jumps to get to 1000. Share different ways of working this out, and model the process. Then use the Eraser from the Pen tray to erase the number and repeat the exercise with a different three-digit number.

Whole-class shared work
● Go to page 3. Revise the work from the previous lesson. Highlight that to convert from pounds sterling to another currency it is necessary to multiply the exchange rate for that currency by the amount of pounds you want to exchange.
● Go to page 4. Ask: *How could euros be changed back into pounds?* (Divide the amount of euros by their exchange rate against the pound.) Test the theory by converting one pound into euros and then reversing the process, modelling the sum on the board. Explain that this is the case for any currency.
● Explain that the children will be looking at a number of common items – a CD, an MP3 player, a digital camera and a DVD – and deciding where would be the cheapest country to buy them. Each item has a sterling, euro, dollar and yen price.
● Give out copies of photocopiable page 102 and work through the first example with the children. Use the 'currency converter' on page 4 of the Notebook file (which uses rates from May 2007), or current exchange rates from the BBC website, to exchange each of the foreign currency prices into sterling. Show how the price varies from country to country. Explain that regional variances and changes in VAT across the world can make certain items cheaper in other countries.

Independent work
● Ask the children to work in pairs to complete the photocopiable sheet. Using calculators, they have to work out which would be the best country to buy each gift, and how much they would save. Keep the currency information up on the board for them to refer to.
● Less confident learners could focus on exchanging one currency only into pound sterling (for example, euros).
● More confident learners could work out which country offers the least value for money for each item and which the best value for money, and work out what the difference in cost would be.

Plenary
● Invite the children to share their results, explaining which country is the best one to buy each gift, and how much they would save. Ask them to show this on the Notebook file.
● End the session by reviewing what the children have learned, making notes on page 5.

Currency complications

Learning objective
PNS: Using and applying mathematics
● Solve one-step and two-step problems involving whole numbers and decimals and all four operations, choosing and using appropriate calculation strategies.

Resources ● ▣
'Currency converter' Notebook file; photocopiable page 103 'Currency exchange problems for each child; individual whiteboards and pens; calculators. (Microsoft Excel is required to view the embedded spreadsheet in the Notebook file.)

Links to other subjects
PSHE
PoS (4a) Pupils should be taught that their actions affect themselves and others.
● Discuss behaviour on holiday. Ask: *How/Why might people behave badly? How might it affect the local community?* Consider a code of behaviour for tourist operators to advertise, to promote positive behaviour. What benefits might there be for tourists if they show positive behaviour abroad?

Starter
Go to page 6 of the Notebook file. Use the Random Number Generator to create a three-digit number. Ask the class to read the number out loud. Change to a four-digit number, explaining that there are now thousands. Count to three (giving the class time to read the number), and ask them to chant the answer. Now create a five-digit number (adding tens of thousands) and, using the same method, ask them to chant the number. (Note: the Random Number Generator cannot be used to create five-digit numbers so you will need to write these on the page using the Pen from the Pen tray.) If there are difficulties, ask pairs to whisper the number to each other before chanting out loud.

Whole-class shared work
● Go to page 7 and revise how to exchange currencies - pound sterling to other currencies and vice versa. Come up with simple rules and write these on the board.
● Explain that the children are going to use the five-step model for solving problems (see Lesson 23) dealing with currency.
● Go to page 8 and open the currency converter. Highlight that the first column shows the name of the currency, and the other shows the amount of that currency that is needed to make one pound sterling.
● The children will be comparing currencies from four major countries. To do this, they will have to convert both currencies into pounds sterling.
● Give an example question:
  ● *Isham has got $100 and the computer game costs 85 euros. Does he have enough money?*
● Ask: *How would you solve this problem?* Model the answer by exchanging the dollars and euros into pounds. The amount produced by the euros figure can be taken away from the amount produced by the dollars figure to find out whether Isham has enough money. Images of money from the Mathematics folder in My Content in the Gallery 🖼 can be used to help to model the problem.

Independent work
● Hand out copies of photocopiable page 103 for the children to complete.
● They should use calculators and the exchange rate grid.
● Answers should be written as fully as possible, showing working.
● Work with less confident learners as a group.
● More confident learners could research other items on the internet, to find out how prices vary.

Plenary
● Go to page 9 and ask the children to demonstrate how they have solved the problems. Ask them to show their working out and encourage them to use the Calculator 🖩 so that the other children can see each problem being modelled.
● Ask: *Is anybody you know going abroad in the near future?* As homework, ask the children to find out which country the person is going to, what currency that country uses and what the current exchange rate is against pounds sterling.

Whiteboard tools
Use the Calculator, accessed through the SMART Board tools menu, to carry out currency conversions.

🖥 Pen tray

🖈 Select tool

✎ Highlighter pen

🖩 Calculator

🖼 Gallery

People percentages

Learning objective
PNS: Counting and understanding number
● Understand percentage as the number of parts in every 100.

Resources
'Data handling' ITP from the 'Build your own' file (by default, the percentage button in the ITP is hidden - reveal it by pressing the last of the four boxes); the data collected in Lesson 12 ('Questionnaire'); coloured pencils.

Links to other subjects
Science
QCA Unit 5A 'Keeping healthy'
● Conduct a Key Stage 2 survey, using a questionnaire with questions such as: *Are chips healthy? Do we need to do exercise to keep healthy?* Use the resulting data to analyse the percentage of children who think chips are healthy, and so on.

Whiteboard tools
Use the Calculator, accessed through the SMART Board tools menu, to work out percentages.

▦ Pen tray

▶ Select tool

▦ Calculator

▦ Gallery

Starter
Give each group a step to count on and back in: 0.1, 0.5, and 5. Lead the groups in counting from any given number, indicating when a new group should start and finish. For example:
● Start at 35.
● First group counts in steps of 0.5.
● Next group continues counting in steps of 0.1.
● Next group continues counting in their given step, and so on.
Change groups to give the children the opportunity to count in different steps.

Whole-class shared work
● Open the 'Build your own' file, which consists of a blank Notebook page and a ready-made Gallery collection of resources located in My Content ▦. Display the ITP 'Data handling' from the Mathematics folder under My Content in the Gallery, and select the preset data for eye colour. Explain that it could be quickly altered to represent the class.
● Say that an element of the data has not been revealed: the column showing the percentages of children who have different eye colours. Reveal this column (press the last of the four rectangles) and discuss the percentages.
● Explain that percentage means 'out of 100' and is, therefore, often a more meaningful number to remember. Explain that percentages can be found by following the formula: 100 divided by the total, multiplied by the group. So if 25 is the total and the group had 10, the percentage would be 100 divided by 25 (4), multiplied by 10, which is 40 per cent. (Many interactive whiteboard calculators do not have percentage buttons.)
● Show the data for hair colour without the percentage column. Ask the children to use the Calculator ▦ to work out the percentages. They can check their answers when they have finished, by displaying the percentages on the ITP.
● Explain that the calculator will give a very accurate answer, and that often it will have several decimal places, making the percentage harder to recall.
● Suggest that only the whole numbers should be taken for the percentages but explain that, when added together, the total will not be 100 per cent, as all of the decimals have been omitted. Explain that this is often common practice: for example, SAT papers state that their totals do not make 100 per cent.

Independent work
● Give the children the data that they collected for Lesson 12 ('Questionnaire'). Ask them to translate the results into percentages, following the formula of 100 divided by total number of children, then multiplied by the number of children in each section.
● They should show this information below each appropriate column.

Plenary
● Explain that percentages can be linked to fractions, making large numbers easier to remember. For example, out of 1000 people surveyed, 250 liked chocolate ice cream: it is far easier to say 25 per cent liked ice cream, or to use the fraction equivalent, ¼. Ask the class why this is easier to remember.
● Return to the ITP, to translate the percentages to fractions.

Angle challenge

Learning objective
PNS: Understanding shape
● Estimate, draw and measure acute and obtuse angles using an angle measurer or protractor to a suitable degree of accuracy.

Resources ⊙ 🄿
'Build your own' file; photocopiable page 104 'Angle challenge' for each child; individual whiteboards and pens.

Links to other subjects
Design and technology
PoS (3c) The quality of a product depends on how well it is made.
● Angles are used to strengthen objects. Investigate which angles are common in buildings and furniture (45°, 60° and 90°).
Geography
PoS (2c) To use maps and plans.
● Test the rule that all corners on the London Underground map must be either 90° or 45°.

Starter
Write a series of two-digit, and then three-digit, numbers on the board. Ask the children to find half, and then a quarter, of the numbers and write the answers on their individual whiteboards. Ask: *What strategies did you use?* Move on to finding half and a quarter of quantities – for example, centimetres, kilometres and kilograms.

Whole-class shared work
● Discuss with the children how to use a protractor (or angle measurer).
● Open the 'Build your own' file, which consists of a blank Notebook page and a collection of resources located in My Content in the Gallery 🖼.
● Use the Lines tool ↘ to draw some angles on the blank Notebook page. Model using the interactive protractor from the Mathematics folder under My Content, showing that the base line has to be aligned to the edge of the angle and the tip of the angle must be in the centre of the cross-hairs of the protractor.
● Show that the protractor can be read either left to right or right to left, and that this depends on the direction of the angle. Explain that it helps to know if the angle is acute (less than 90°) or obtuse (more than 90°).
● Make an angle using two lines. Colour one line red (the lines default to black). Pivot one line to form an angle less than 90°. Explain that this is an acute angle. Then make an angle that is greater than 90° and explain that this is obtuse.
● Play 'Angle challenge': the opponent (in this case the class) has to guess whether the angle is acute or obtuse, and estimate its size. If the player guesses acute or obtuse correctly they get a point. If the estimate is within five degrees, either way, then they get a further point. The winner is the first to reach ten points.
● Create an angle and play a round of the game. Ask the class to show their results on their whiteboards. Assess whether they can correctly differentiate between obtuse and acute. Play another three rounds. By the end of the third round the children should be getting more accurate.

Independent work
● Give out copies of photocopiable page 104 so that the children can play 'Angle challenge' with a partner.
● Less confident learners could play a simplified version, omitting the estimating and measuring.
● Encourage more confident pairs to create angles just slightly bigger or smaller than 90°, to really test their partners.

Plenary
● Ask: *Did anyone create an angle that was exactly 90°? Is that obtuse or acute?* (It has a special name – a right angle.)
● Ask: *Can you see any right angles in the classroom?* (For example, in a table, book or door.) Explain that right angles are always 90°, whether they are in a triangle, quadrilateral or any other shape.

Whiteboard tools
Use the interactive protractor to measure angles. Use the Lines tool to create the angles in the whole-class work.

🖥 Pen tray

🖱 Select tool

🖼 Gallery

↘ Lines tool

Digital and analogue clocks

Write the 24-hour clock time beneath each analogue clock face.

AM	PM	AM
:	:	:
PM	AM	PM
:	:	:
PM	AM	PM
:	:	:

Measuring table

Object	Estimate	Measurement	My score	My partner's score

◀ SCHOLASTIC
w w w . s c h o l a s t i c . c o . u k

Map of the United Kingdom

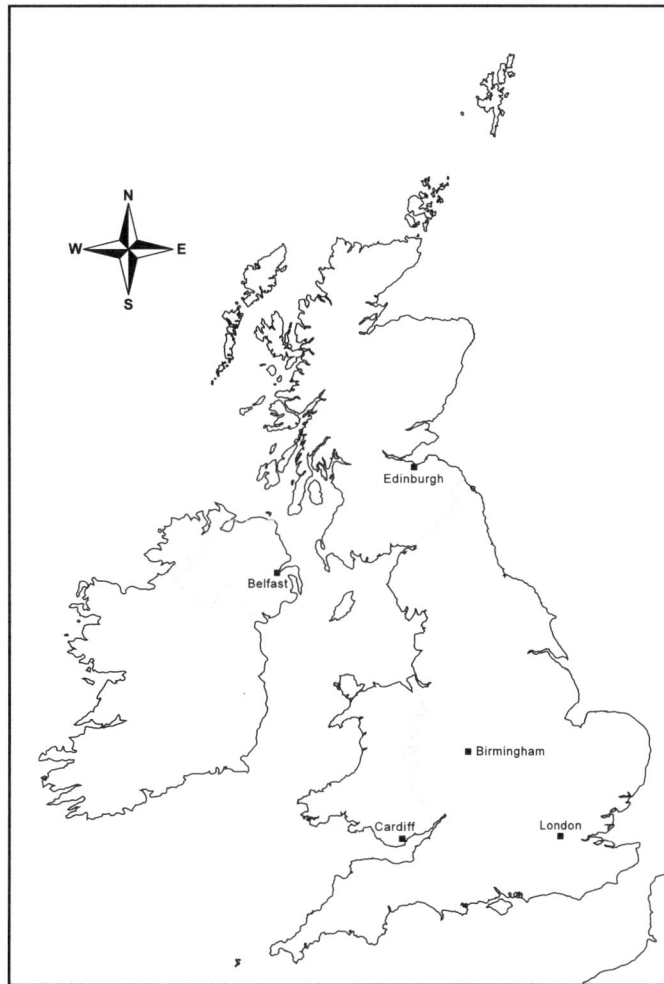

Edinburgh

Belfast

Birmingham

Cardiff   London

Scale
1mm = 10km

◧ Work out the distances between the cities.

	Birmingham	Edinburgh	Cardiff	London	Belfast
Birmingham					
Edinburgh					
Cardiff					
London					
Belfast					

Name _____

Triangles

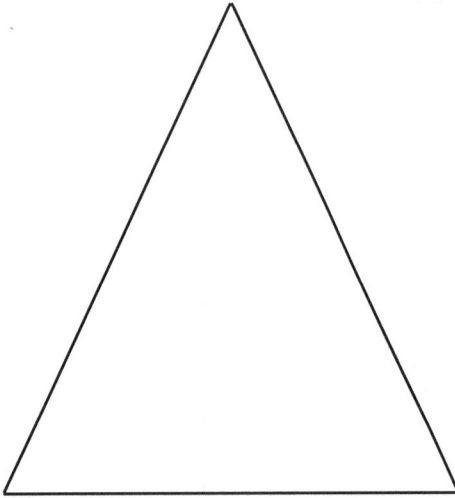
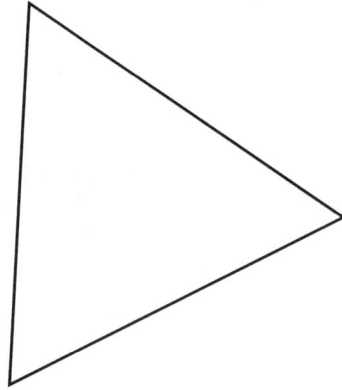
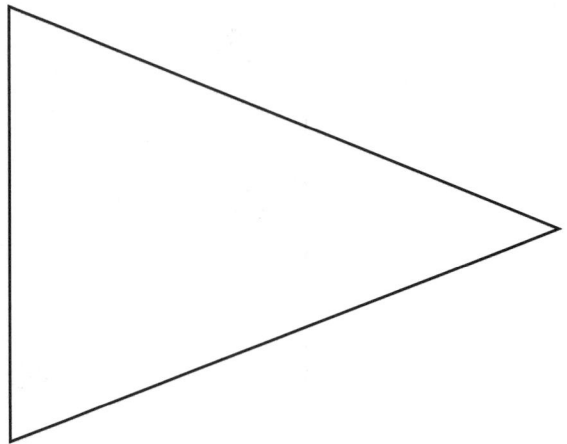
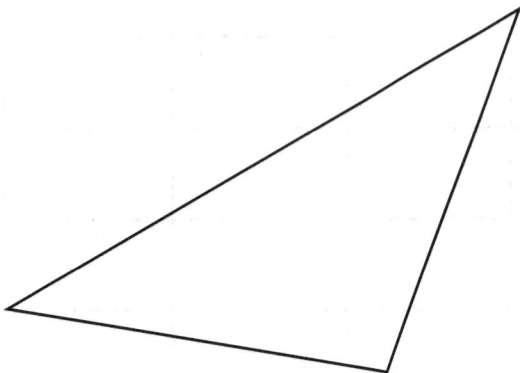
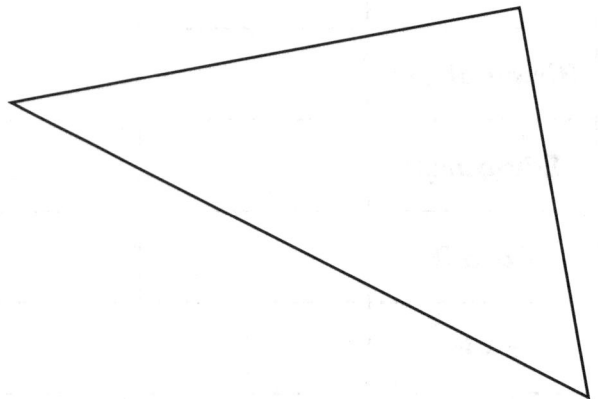

Database and bar chart

■ Complete this database and bar chart using your data.

Criteria					

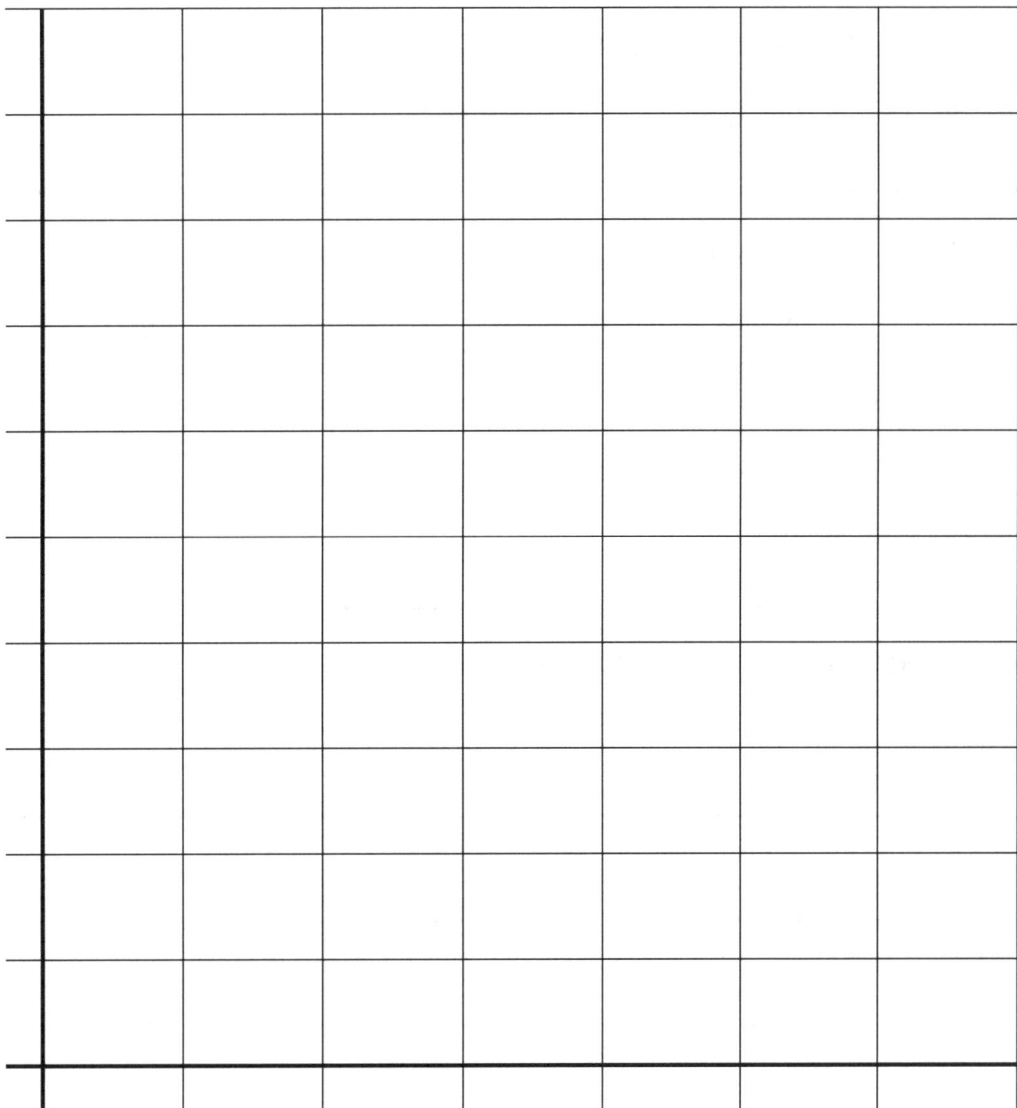

Name _____

Questionnaire

What is your eye colour?
What is your shoe size?
What is your hair colour?
How many people live in your house?
What is your favourite type of film? Comedy ☐   Romance ☐   Adventure ☐   Cartoon ☐
What is your favourite type of book? Romance ☐   Action ☐   True life ☐   Horror ☐   Fantasy ☐
What is your favourite type of writing? Fiction ☐   Non-fiction ☐
How many books have you read this month?
Class question:

Quads

◼ Find the area of each of these quadrilaterals.

Use this formula:

Length x Width = Area in centimetres^2

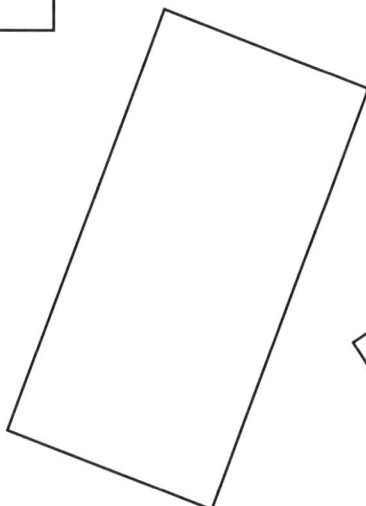
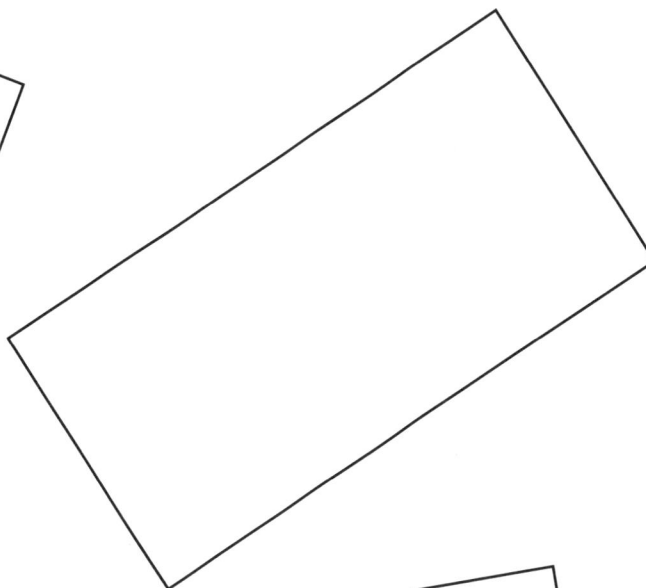
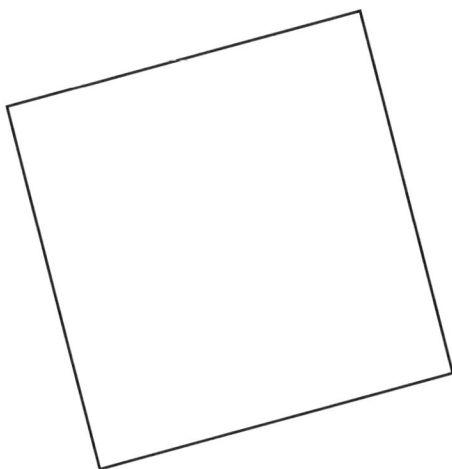

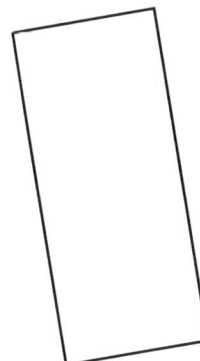

Name _____

Polygon shapes

■ Find out how many lines of symmetry each of the shapes has, and write it beneath the shape.

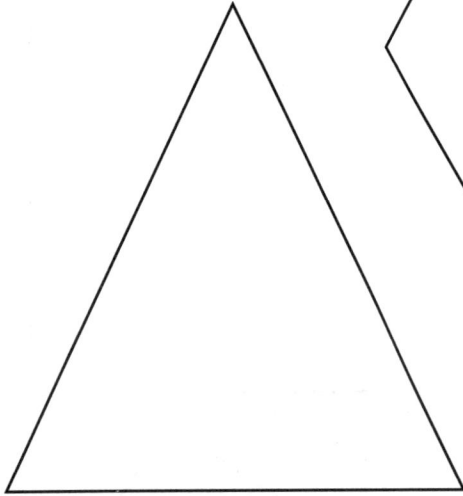

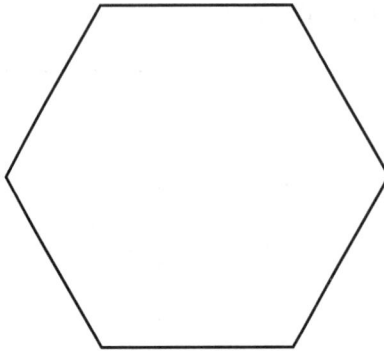

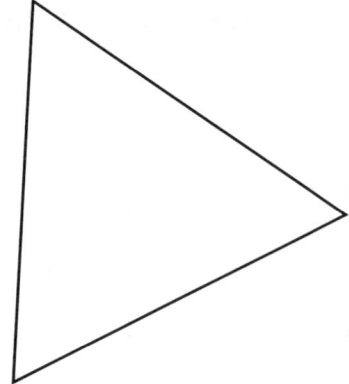

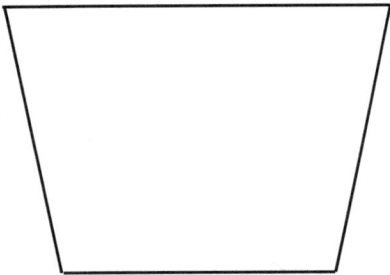

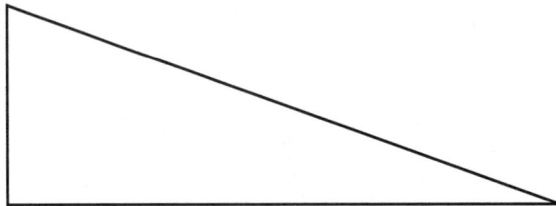

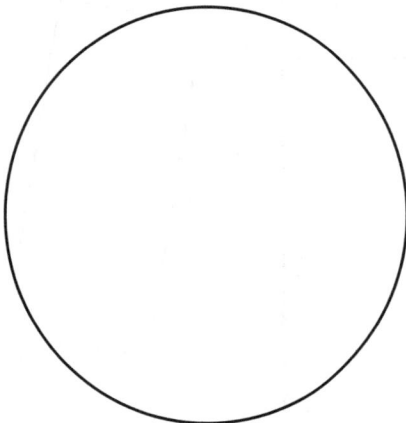

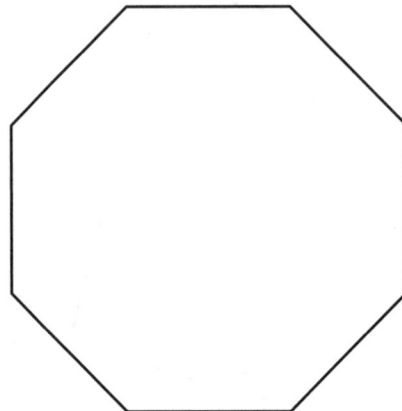

Triangle sorter

◾ For each of the triangles shown below, measure the three angles and add them together. What total do you get?

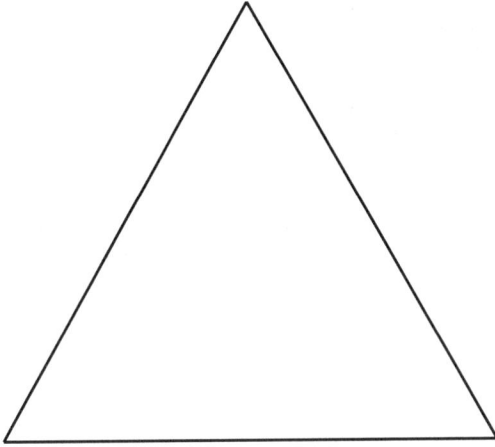

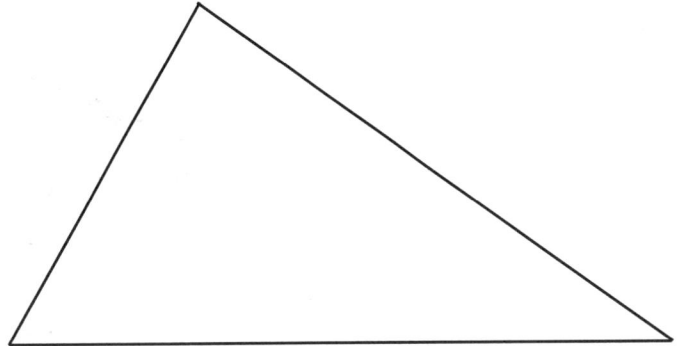

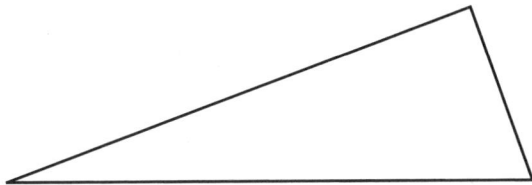

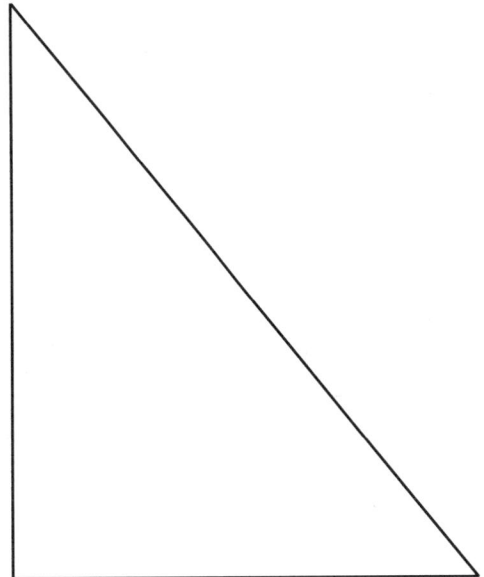

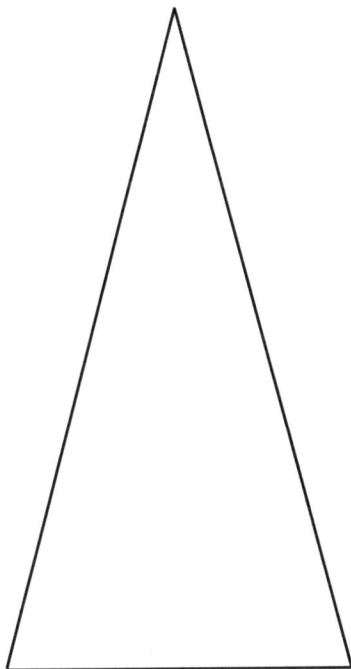

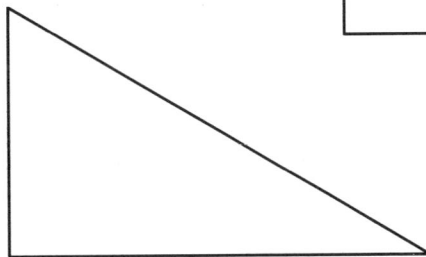

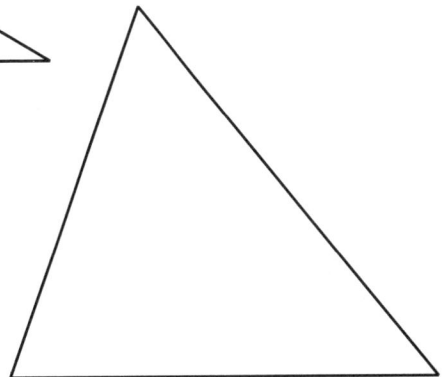

Flight and arrival times

▪ Complete the charts below for flights to London.

Arrival times in London

City	Local Time	Flight Time	Time of Arrival
Paris	12.45pm	2 hours	
New York	9.30am	7 hours	
Nairobi	10.00pm	12 hours	
Tokyo	5.00pm	16 hours	
New Delhi	4.00am	11 hours	

Flight times to London

City	Local Time	Flight Time	Time of Arrival
Madrid	8.00am		10.00am
Chicago	11.00pm		12.00pm
Caracas	9.00am		12.00am
Sydney	10.00am		2.00pm
Hong Kong	5.00pm		8.00pm

Name _____

Superhero problems

1. Red Eyes has set a bomb to go off in 37 minutes.
   You have half an hour to defuse it. Do you have enough time?

   _____

2. In a blink, Super Nova can produce 60,000 watts of light energy,
   a thousand times brighter than the average home bulb.
   How bright is the average home bulb?

   _____

3. Mack 1 can fly to Australia in 18 hours.
   How long will the round trip take in total?

   _____

4. Bolder Boy is fitness mad! Every day he runs for 30 minutes, swims for
   60 minutes and cycles for 90 minutes.
   How long does he spend keeping fit every day?

   _____

5. On Friday, Lizzy Liquid buys 12 litres of water. She drinks 4 litres a day.
   How long will the water she bought on Friday last?

   _____

Illustrations © Andy Keylock/Beehive Illustration

More superhero problems

1. Johnny Stretch keeps his flexibility by stretching three times a day.
   He does this for six months. How many times does he stretch altogether?

   _____

2. The Human Dolphin can hold her breath for thirty-three minutes.
   How many times will she need to take a breath in a twelve-hour period?

   _____

3. Claws uses his giant pincers to climb a 20-storey building. If it takes three
   pincer-grabs to climb each storey, how many grabs will it take to climb the
   whole building and get back down again?

   _____

4. By bouncing off each other, the Bounce Twins can double the height of each
   bounce. If they start bouncing at one metre, how many bounces will they need
   to jump over a 100-metre building?

   _____

5. Captain Kid flew 100km in eight minutes.
   How long did it take him to fly 10km?

   _____

▪ S C H O L A S T I C
w w w . s c h o l a s t i c . c o . u k

Holiday budget

- Imagine you are on holiday. You have £150 to spend so you will need to budget carefully.
- Choose a country and a currency.
- Work out how much £ sterling you will spend on each item in the list below.
- Convert the amounts into new currency.

Item	£ Sterling	New currency
Souvenirs		
Insurance		
Bike hire		
Taxi hire		
Days out		
Snacks and drinks		
Food		
Other		
Total:		

Holiday gifts

	USA	Japan	France
CD Player £9.97	$10.99	¥1200	€20.81
MP3 Player £99.99	$209	¥27,600	€239.99
Digital Camera £149.99	$279.99	¥83,800	€159.00
DVD £14.99	$22.46	¥1260	€19.99

📖 S C H O L A S T I C
w w w . s c h o l a s t i c . c o . u k

Currency exchange problems

1. Chloe is expecting her friend Sarah to visit in Paris. She knows the taxi costs 15 euros from the station. How much will Sarah need to exchange in sterling?

_____

2. Rashid has £20 and wants to buy three DVDs that are priced at $7.99 (US) each. Does he have enough money?

_____

3. The adventure park costs $30 (US) each to enter. Shane wants to know how much to advise both his Australian parents to save if all three want to visit.

_____

4. Isham has got $100 (US) and wants to buy a computer game costing 85 euros. Does he have enough money?

_____

5. Plane tickets to Chicago cost £379 or $741 (US). How much will Coralie save if she buys her tickets in pounds?

_____

Angle challenge

■ Take it in turns to draw an angle that is greater or less than 90°.

■ The other person has to guess whether the angle is acute or obtuse and give an estimate of the size of the angle in degrees.

■ They get one point if they guess correctly whether the angle was acute or obtuse. They get another point if their estimate was within five degrees of the actual measurement.

Acute or obtuse?	Estimate measurement	Actual measurement	Difference in degrees	Points
			Total points	

■SCHOLASTIC
www.scholastic.co.uk

Science

This chapter provides 20 lessons based on the Year 5 units in the QCA Schemes of Work for science. The key objectives from each unit have been deliberately chosen because teaching will be particularly aided and enhanced by the use of an interactive whiteboard. The lessons and associated Notebook files are designed to encourage the whole class to discuss and demonstrate ideas, plan investigations effectively, record and evaluate results and make substantiated conclusions. In this way, many of the lessons actively support teaching and evaluating key scientific enquiry skills (Sc1 National Curriculum). The Notebook files are also designed to enhance the children's ICT skills - for example, creating and manipulating objects on screen, using writing and drawing tools and entering data into tables and spreadsheets.

Lesson title	Objectives	Expected prior knowledge	Cross-curricular links
Lesson 1: Inadequate diets ☉ P	**QCA Unit 5A** 'Keeping healthy' • How a scientific idea about the effect of diet on health can be tested, and the evidence used to support the idea.	• That all animals, including humans, need to feed. • That animals need to feed to grow and to be active. • That sometimes we eat a lot of some foods and not very much of others.	**PSHE** PoS (3a) What makes a healthy lifestyle, including the benefits of exercise and healthy eating. **History** QCA Unit 19 'What were the effects of Tudor exploration?'
Lesson 2: The heart and circulatory system ☉	**QCA Unit 5A** 'Keeping healthy' • That the heart and lungs are protected by the ribs. • That the muscle in the walls of the heart contracts regularly, pumping blood around the body. • That blood vessels carry blood around the body.	• That humans have bodies with similar parts. • That when someone is exercising or moving fast, the muscles work hard.	**PSHE** PoS (3a) What makes a healthy lifestyle, including the benefits of exercise and healthy eating, and how to make informed choices. **ICT** PoS (2b) To monitor events and respond to them.
Lesson 3: Pulse rate investigation ☉ P	**QCA Unit 5A** 'Keeping healthy' • To measure pulse rate and relate it to heart beat. • To identify factors affecting pulse rate and predict the changes. • To plan what evidence to collect (the number of measurements of pulse rate/the number of children to use). • To present results in a bar chart, explaining what these show and whether they support the prediction.	• That humans have bodies with similar parts. • That when someone is exercising or moving fast, the muscles work hard. • How to make and record observations and make simple comparisons.	**PSHE** PoS (3a) What makes a healthy lifestyle, including the benefits of exercise and healthy eating. **ICT** PoS (3a) Share and exchange information in a variety of ways, including email.
Lesson 4: Medicines and safety ☉	**QCA Unit 5A** 'Keeping healthy' • That medicines are also drugs and also affect the way the body functions but the effects are usually beneficial though there may be side effects. • That medicines can be harmful if they are not taken according to instructions.	• That we have five senses, which allow us to find out about the world. • That sometimes we take medicines when we get ill, to help us to get better. • That medicines are useful but are drugs, not foods, and can be dangerous.	**PSHE** PoS (3d) Which commonly available substances and drugs are legal and illegal, their effects and risks. **History** QCA Unit 15 'How do we use ancient Greek ideas today?'
Lesson 5: Seed dispersal ☉	**QCA Unit 5B** 'Life cycles' • That seeds can be dispersed in a variety of ways. • To make careful observations of fruits and seeds, to compare them and use results to draw conclusions. • That many fruits and seeds provide food for animals including humans.	• That plants need healthy roots, leaves and stems to grow well. • How to make and record observations and make simple comparisons.	**PSHE** PoS (3a) What makes a healthy lifestyle, including the benefits of exercise and healthy eating. **English** PNS Creating and shaping texts: Adapt non-narrative forms and styles to write factual texts.
Lesson 6: Pollination investigation ☉ P	**QCA Unit 5B** 'Life cycles' • That insects pollinate some flowers.	• How to make and record observations and make simple comparisons. • How to recognise when a comparison is unfair.	**ICT** PoS (2c) To use simulations and explore models to identify patterns and relationships. **Mathematics** PNS Handling data: Answer a set of related questions by collecting, selecting and organising relevant data; draw conclusions.

Science Chapter 3

Lesson title	Objectives	Expected prior knowledge	Cross-curricular links
Lesson 7: Parts of a flower	**QCA Unit 5B** 'Life cycles' • That plants produce flowers which have male and female organs, seeds are formed when pollen from the male organ fertilises the ovum (female).	• How to make careful observations and present these using drawings. • How to explain observations.	**Design and technology** PoS (4c) How mechanisms can be used to make things move in different ways. **History** PoS (11a) To study the impact of significant individuals.
Lesson 8: The life cycle of a flowering plant	**QCA Unit 5B** 'Life cycles' • To learn about the life cycle of flowering plants including pollination, fertilisation, seed production, seed dispersal and germination.	• That plants can provide food for us and some plants are grown for this. • That plants need water, but not unlimited water, for healthy growth. • That plants need light for healthy growth. • That plants need leaves in order to grow well. • That plant growth is affected by temperature.	**ICT** PoS (2a) How to develop and refine ideas by bringing together and organising text and images. **English** PNS Creating and shaping texts: Adapt non-narrative forms and styles to write factual texts.
Lesson 9: The many gases around us	**QCA Unit 5C** 'Gases around us' • That there are many gases and many of these are important to us.	• How to identify solids and liquids. • That the same material can exist as both solid and liquid.	**Design and technology** QCA Unit 5B 'Bread' **PE** PoS (4a) How exercise affects the body in the short term.
Lesson 10: Air in soil investigation	**QCA Unit 5C** 'Gases around us' • That soils have air trapped within them. • To measure volumes of water carefully. • To recognise whether measurements need to be repeated. • To use their results to compare the air trapped in different soils.	• That there are different kinds of soil, depending on the rock from which they come. • How to use simple apparatus to measure volumes of liquids and to measure time. • How to use what happened to draw a conclusion and to say what they found out.	**Mathematics** PNS Measuring: Read, choose, use and record standard metric units; interpret a reading. **ICT** PoS (1c) To interpret information, to check it is relevant and reasonable.
Lesson 11: Evaporation investigation	**QCA Unit 5C** 'Changing state' • Evaporation is when a liquid turns to a gas. • Investigating ideas, making predictions, deciding what evidence to collect and constructing a fair test. • Making careful measurements, recording them in tables and graphs; identifying trends and drawing conclusions; indicating whether the results support the prediction.	• That melting and solidifying or freezing are changes that can be reversed and are the reverse of each other. • That air has weight and is all around us.	**Mathematics** PNS Measuring: Read, choose, use and record standard metric units; interpret a reading.
Lesson 12: Condensation	**QCA Unit 5C** 'Changing state' • That condensation is when a gas turns to a liquid. • That condensation is the reverse of evaporation. • To make careful observations and draw conclusions, explaining these in terms of scientific knowledge and understanding. • That air contains water vapour and when this hits a cold surface it may condense.	• That gases are formed when liquids evaporate. • That gases flow more easily than liquids and in all directions.	**Geography** PoS (5b) Recognise how and why people may seek to manage environments sustainably, and to identify opportunities for their own involvement. **Music** PoS (2b) Explore, choose, combine and organise musical ideas within musical structures.
Lesson 13: The water cycle	**QCA Unit 5D** 'Changing state' • That water evaporates from oceans, seas and lakes, condenses as clouds and eventually falls as rain. • That water collects in streams and rivers and eventually finds its way to the sea. • That evaporation and condensation are processes that can be reversed. • To interpret the water cycle in terms of the processes involved.	• How to identify and describe differences in properties of solids, liquids and gases. • How to make observations and explain phenomena in terms of scientific knowledge and understanding.	**Geography** PoS (4b) Recognise some physical and human processes and explain how these can cause changes in places and environments. **ICT** PoS (5a) Working with a range of information to consider its characteristics and purposes.

Lesson title	Objectives	Expected prior knowledge	Cross-curricular links
Lesson 14: Day and night 💿 **P**	**QCA Unit 5E** 'Earth, Sun and Moon' • That it is the Earth that moves, not the Sun, and the Earth spins on its axis once every 24 hours. • That it is daytime in the part of the Earth facing the Sun and night-time in the part of the Earth away from the Sun.	• That light is essential for seeing things. • That shadows are formed when light travelling from a source is blocked.	**Geography** QCA Unit 18 'Connecting ourselves to the world'
Lesson 15: Sunrise and sunset 💿 **P**	**QCA Unit 5E** 'Earth, Sun and Moon' • That the Sun rises in the general direction of the east and sets in the general direction of the west. • To make observations of where the Sun rises and sets and to recognise the patterns in these. • To present times of sunrise and sunset in a graph and to recognise trends and patterns in the data.	• That the Sun appears to move across the sky in a regular way every day. • That the Sun appears highest in the sky at midday. • That the Sun does not move, its apparent movement is caused by the spinning of the Earth on its axis.	**Geography** QCA Unit 18 'Connecting ourselves to the world' **RE** PoS (1b) To describe the variety of practices and ways of life in religions.
Lesson 16: The changing faces of the Moon 💿	**QCA Unit 5E** 'Earth, Sun and Moon' • That the Moon takes approximately 28 days to orbit the Earth. • That the different appearance of the Moon over 28 days provides evidence for a 28-day cycle.	• That shiny objects are not light sources. • That shadows are formed when objects block light from the Sun.	**RE** PoS (1b) To describe the variety of practices and ways of life in religions.
Lesson 17: Sound and states of matter 💿 **P**	**QCA Unit 5F** 'Changing sounds' • That vibrations from sound sources travel through different materials to the ear.	• How to identify and describe differences in properties of solids, liquids and gases. • That we hear with our ears. • That there are many different sources of sounds.	**Geography** PoS (1d) Identify and explain different views that people, including themselves, hold about topical geographical issues. **English** PNS Engaging with and responding to texts: Compare how a common theme is presented in poetry, prose and other media.
Lesson 18: Muffling materials investigation 💿 **P**	**QCA Unit 5F** 'Changing sounds' • That some materials muffle sound. • To test how well different materials muffle sound. • To use a prediction to help decide what evidence to collect. • To devise a fair test. • To collect reliable evidence. • To decide whether results support or do not support the prediction.	• That some sounds can be heard from a long distance. • That sounds seem louder the nearer you are to the source. • That sounds get fainter as they travel away from a source.	**Mathematics** PNS Measuring: Read, choose, use and record standard metric units; interpret a reading that lies between two unnumbered dvisions on a scale. **ICT** PoS (5b) Work with others to explore a variety of information sources and ICT tools.
Lesson 19: Vibrating air investigation 💿 **P**	**QCA Unit 5F** 'Changing sounds' • That sounds are made by air vibrating. • To suggest how to alter pitch and to test the prediction. • To listen carefully to sounds made, record results in a suitable table and decide whether these support the prediction. • To describe how pitch can be altered by changing the length of air column in a wind instrument.	• That there are many different sources of sounds. • That there are many different ways of making sounds. • To explain phenomena related to air in terms of scientific knowledge and understanding.	**Design and technology** PoS (4b) How materials can be combined and mixed to create more useful properties. **Music** PoS (4c) How music is produced in different ways and described through relevant established and invented notations.
Lesson 20: Musical instruments presentation 💿 **P**	**QCA Unit 5F** 'Changing sounds' • To relate their understanding of sound to a range of musical instruments. • To explain an application of sound using scientific knowledge and understanding.	• That there are many different ways of making sounds. • How to explore sounds using their sense of hearing.	**Design and technology** PoS (1d) Communicate design ideas in different ways as these develop, bearing in mind aesthetic qualities, and the uses and purposes for which the product is intended. **Music** PoS (1b) Play tuned and untuned instruments with control and rhythmic accuracy.

Inadequate diets

Learning objective
QCA Unit 5A 'Keeping healthy'
● How a scientific idea about the effect of diet on health can be tested, and the evidence used to support the idea.

Resources 🔵 🅿
'Keeping healthy' Notebook file; photocopiable page 128 'Investigation planning sheet' for each child.

Links to other subjects
PSHE
PoS (3a) What makes a healthy lifestyle, including the benefits of exercise and healthy eating.
● Use this lesson as part of work on developing a healthy, safer lifestyle and the five-a-day fruit and vegetable message.
History
QCA Unit 19 'What were the effects of Tudor exploration?'
● Research the effects of scurvy on the great voyages of exploration in Tudor times.

Starter
Display page 2 of the Notebook file. Use different colours to list foods that are considered 'good' and 'bad' for you. Draw out what the children know about eating a balanced, varied diet and about the food pyramid. Ask: *What happens if you eat too much of one certain food type?* (For example, too much fat makes you overweight.) Explain that your body is also affected negatively if you don't eat enough of a certain food type. (For example, too little fibre affects your body's ability to digest food.) Explain that in the past doctors didn't always understand that a poor diet could cause disease.

Whole-class shared work
● Read and discuss pages 3, 4 and 5. Use a Highlighter pen 🖊 to highlight the symptoms and the six 'diets' Lind used.
● Discuss why 12 sailors were used (for repeat measurements and to avoid anomalies) and what the variable was in the investigation (the different diets).
● Ask the children to predict which of the six diets was successful. (Citrus fruits contain ascorbic acid, or Vitamin C, which prevents scurvy.)
● Display page 5 and discuss Lind's results and conclusions. Ask what Lind means by his last line (that further evidence will confirm his results and conclusions).
● Lind's discovery was one of the first that linked a disease directly with diet. It enabled sailors to stay longer at sea. English sailors were known as 'limeys' because of the limes they were given on transatlantic voyages.

Independent work
● Display and read page 6. Draw out similarities and differences with this investigation and James Lind's (they both investigate the link between diet and disease, but Lind was looking for the cure, not the cause).
● Hand out copies of photocopiable page 128. Discuss how the children will tackle the task, then ask them to complete the sheet.
● Less confident learners may need support when they write their question to test, and decide what would need to be recorded as evidence.
● Extend more confident learners by asking them to think of other links between diet and disease (for example, high levels of salt cause high blood pressure) and ways that these links could be tested.

Plenary
● Go to page 7 and ask the children what they would expect to find out from the investigation (sugary drinks are harmful to teeth). Ask: *Why are certain sugary drinks harmful to teeth?* (When sugars come into contact with the bacteria in plaque, acid is produced.) Make notes on the board.
● Emphasise that the children's investigations would provide some evidence to support this idea, just as Lind's work did. Ask them to suggest what could be done to build up greater evidence for this idea. (For example, more studies, larger studies, greater variety of drinks, use real teeth!) Make a note of their suggestions.

Whiteboard tools
Use a Pen from the Pen tray to annotate the pages in the Notebook file.

🖥 Pen tray

🔣 Select tool

🖊 Highlighter pen

The heart and circulatory system

Learning objectives
QCA Unit 5A 'Keeping healthy'
● That the heart and lungs are protected by the ribs.
● That the muscle in the walls of the heart contracts regularly, pumping blood around the body.
● That blood vessels carry blood around the body.

Resources 💿
'Keeping healthy' Notebook file; writing materials.

Links to other subjects
PSHE
PoS (3a) What makes a healthy lifestyle, including the benefits of exercise and healthy eating, and how to make informed choices.
● Use this lesson to inform other work on healthy eating and lifestyles, with regard to heart disease.
ICT
PoS (2b) To monitor events and respond to them.
● Use datalogging equipment to measure pulse rates before and after exercise.

Whiteboard tools
Use the Spotlight tool to focus on the heart diagram.

🖥 Pen tray

🔖 Select tool

📝 Highlighter pen

🔦 Spotlight tool

❎ Delete button

Starter
Display page 8 of the Notebook file. Drag and drop each layer of the diagram to the side of the screen. Ask the children to identify each layer. (Skin, muscle and skeleton.) Explain that the skin is one organ itself – the largest in the body.

Note the position of the heart within the rib cage and discuss why it is located there (for protection) and what other organs are similarly protected (the lungs). Ask the children why these organs are so well protected. Explain that they will be looking in detail at the heart and its function within the body.

Whole-class shared work
● Discuss and highlight facts about the heart on page 9.
● Tell the children that surgeons use a powerful light source in operations. Go to page 10 and use the Spotlight tool 🔦 to examine the cross-section of the heart, looking at its various features (chambers, valves, large blood vessels).
● Explain that the heart consists of four chambers (called atria and ventricles), which contract (squeeze) to pump blood between them and the rest of the body. Tell the children that:
    ● the chambers contract in a set pattern (atria together then ventricles together, which produces the 'du-dum' rhythm of the heart);
    ● the heart performs two main jobs: the right atrium and ventricle pump blood to the lungs to oxygenate the blood, and the left atrium and ventricle pump blood to the rest of the body;
    ● the valves are one-way, which stops the blood from flowing in the wrong direction.
● Using page 11, discuss the different blood vessels and their functions within the circulatory system.
● Go to page 12. Ask: *What lifestyle factors do you think might cause heart disease?* (Smoking, poor diet, lack of exercise, obesity.)

Independent work
● Ask the children to imagine that they work for an organisation like the British Heart Foundation and to write an article entitled 'The heart: the most important organ in the body' for a junior school audience.
● They should clearly explain how the heart and circulatory system work.
● Encourage them to use features of explanation texts, such as the present tense, cause-and-effect connectives and technical vocabulary.
● Provide less confident learners with a list of technical words and their meanings.
● Encourage more confident learners to include features of a persuasive text, to persuade readers why and how the heart should be kept healthy.

Plenary
● Ask some of the children to read out their articles. The rest of the class should judge them on clarity and accuracy.
● Use page 13 to test and consolidate children's knowledge and understanding. Use the Delete button ❎ to delete the green boxes, revealing the answers hidden underneath.

Pulse rate investigation

Learning objectives
QCA Unit 5A 'Keeping healthy'
● To measure pulse rate and relate it to heart beat.
● To identify factors affecting pulse rate and predict the changes.
● To plan what evidence to collect (the number of measurements of pulse rate/ the number of children to use).
● To present results in a bar chart, explaining what these show and whether they support the prediction.

Resources 💿 🅿
'Pulse rate investigation' Notebook file; photocopiable page 129 'How to take your own pulse' for each child; clocks or stopwatches showing seconds. (Microsoft Excel is required to view the embedded spreadsheet in the Notebook file.)

Links to other subjects
PSHE
PoS (3a) What makes a healthy lifestyle, including the benefits of exercise and healthy eating.
● Investigate how exercise and diet affect pulse rate and general fitness.
ICT
PoS (3a) Share and exchange information in a variety of ways, including email.
● Send a copy of the completed spreadsheet to an appropriate recipient, such as the school nurse.

Whiteboard tools
To enter data into the spreadsheet, select the cell and use the On-screen Keyboard, accessed through the Pen tray or the SMART Board tools menu, to type.

🖥 Pen tray

⬚ Select tool

⌨ On-screen Keyboard

Starter
Ask the children to describe the location and function of the heart and make notes on page 2 of the Notebook file.

Discuss their experiences of a doctor listening to their heartbeat (using a stethoscope). Explain that the doctor could measure your pulse (the rate at which your heart is beating) this way, and that pulse is measured in beats per minute (bpm). Ask each child to place a palm on his/her chest to 'feel' the beat. Ask: *Is this an effective way of measuring your pulse?* Explain that your pulse can be measured more clearly elsewhere on the body (for example, on the wrist or neck) without a machine or instrument. Tell the children that they will be measuring their own pulse rates when they are at rest.

Whole-class shared work
● Hand out copies of photocopiable page 129 and stopwatches.
● Demonstrate how to take your pulse at the wrist and neck.
● Ask the children to measure and record their resting pulse rate three times on the sheet. They will need to time each measurement for 15 seconds, and then multiply the result by 4 to get the bpm measurement.
● Go to page 3 and press the box to open the spreadsheet. Use the On-screen Keyboard to enter a set of data, from five children, into the spreadsheet cells under the 'Resting pulse (bpm) 1' column.
● This will automatically create a bar chart on the right-hand side of the sheet. Inform the children that bar charts can be used to present results clearly, so that comparisons can be made more easily. Discuss the bar chart and ask the children to suggest why the pulse rates were not the same each time. Discuss why it was important to make several measurements.

Independent work
● Ask the children to measure and record their resting pulse rates twice more and to choose the result that they think is the most accurate.
● Less confident learners may need support to ensure that their calculations are made and recorded accurately.
● Extend more confident learners by asking them to predict what the most common resting pulse rate will be in the class.

Plenary
● Take the children's most accurate results, and input them under the column heading 'Resting pulse (bpm) 2'.
● Examine and discuss the resultant bar chart. Ask the children to identify the highest and lowest rates, the most common rate and the average rate for the class. Discuss whether in general it is easier to extract this information from the table or chart. Make a note of the children's observations on page 4 of the Notebook file.
● Explain that there is no 'correct' pulse rate, and that the normal resting pulse rate for children varies between 60 and 100 bpm.

Medicines and safety

Starter
Display page 14 of the Notebook file and discuss what the items shown might be. Note down answers, which might include 'medicines' or 'drugs', or that it is not possible to identify them. Tell the children that all these answers are correct. The items shown are all medicines – which are types of drugs – but it is not possible to identify *which* medicines are shown. Question the children's perceptions of the differences between drugs and medicines, drawing out the difference between legal drugs (alcohol, nicotine, medicines) and illegal drugs.

Whole-class shared work
● Go to page 15 and discuss who in the family might require the medicine in the bottle. (Any of them.)
● Discuss who is and who is not responsible for the medicine in the family.
● Ask who might be at risk from the medicine, and why. (Any of them.)
● Ask: *What is missing from the bottle that would help the person responsible?* (Details and instructions.)
● Hand out empty packets and bottles of medicine and their instructions. Ask the children to examine the labels and instructions carefully and discuss them.
● On the blank bottle on screen, write examples of some of the common details found on the labels (name, date of birth, name of medicine, brief instructions including quantities and durations).
● Draw out that the written instructions tend to give much greater detail about the medicine, including side effects and contra-indications.
● Discuss the two red warning signs on page 16 and their meaning (the skull means poisonous, the black cross means irritant) and where these might be found (household cleaning products, not medicines).
● Using page 17, encourage the children to come up with a number of safety rules for medicines in the home, using the imperative form (for example, *Always take the correct dose at the right time*).

Independent work
● Ask the children to design a poster to inform other children of the safe way to look after and take medicines at home. Tell them that their posters will be judged on the effectiveness of the safety message and their visual impact.
● Less confident learners may need support in writing imperative phrases.
● Extend more confident learners by asking them to complement their imperative phrases with slogans and further textual explanation of points of safety (for example, not finishing a course of antibiotics means that the infection might not have been fully eradicated and so might return).

Plenary
● Ask the children to share their posters and discuss their visual impact and the effectiveness of the message.
● Display page 18 and ask the children to highlight the hidden words in the word search. Reinforce the meaning of the vocabulary.

Seed dispersal

Learning objectives
QCA Unit 5B 'Life cycles'
● That seeds can be dispersed in a variety of ways.
● To make careful observations of fruits and seeds, to compare them and use results to draw conclusions.
● That many fruits and seeds provide food for animals, including humans.

Resources 💿
'Life cycle of plants' Notebook file; selection of labelled fleshy fruits that contain seeds or stones (for example, apple, tomato, cherry, strawberry, avocado or mango); selection of labelled seeds or seed cases that don't come from fleshy fruits - for example, wheat, sweet corn, dandelion seeds, sycamore seeds (do not use nuts, especially peanuts, to avoid potential allergic reactions); chopping boards; knives; magnifying glasses.

Links to other subjects
PSHE
PoS (3a) What makes a healthy lifestyle, including the benefits of exercise and healthy eating.
● Link this to work on a healthy, safer lifestyle and the five-a-day fruit and vegetable message.
English
PNS: Creating and shaping texts
● Write a short explanation of how a seed is dispersed by its parent plant.

Whiteboard tools
Use the Delete button to reveal the hidden answers.

🖥️ Pen tray

🔖 Select tool

🖊️ Highlighter pen

❌ Delete button

Starter
Display the selection of different fruits and seeds. Ask: *Why do plants produce seeds?* Explain that plants make new plants like themselves by producing and dispersing (spreading) seeds that grow into new plants.

Display page 2 of the Notebook file and discuss the best position for a seed from the tree to land and for the new plant to grow. Ask a volunteer to drag and drop the new plant into this position. Review the children's knowledge of the conditions required for healthy growth. (Light, water, minerals and space.)

Whole-class shared work
● Go to page 3, about the four main methods to disperse seeds (explosion, animal, water, wind). Tell the children that they will be observing the selection of fruit and seeds to decide which method of dispersal each plant is using.
● Using page 4, discuss and write down some of the probable characteristics each seed might have (for example, seeds spread by wind tend to be small and light with wing-like structures).
● Demonstrate how to dissect a couple of fruits or seeds, using a suitable knife on a chopping board.

Independent work
● Let the children dissect the fruit and seeds and study them with magnifying glasses. Ask: *What role may fleshy fruit play in seed dispersal?*
● Remind the children not to taste the fruit or seeds and to wash their hands when finished.
● Tell them to write down the name of each of fruit or seed and which method of seed dispersal the parent plant uses.
● Less confident learners may need support in linking characteristics of different seeds with the probable method of seed dispersal.
● Extend more confident learners by asking them to differentiate between seeds that are dispersed externally and those that are dispersed internally by humans and other animals.

Plenary
● Share and discuss the children's work. Ask them to justify their answers from their observations. Make notes on page 4.
● On page 5, study the properties of the seed in the picture. Vote and highlight the correct method of dispersal from the list on the tree. Use the Delete button ❌ to delete the blue box to reveal the answer.
● Repeat the activity for pages 6 to 10.
● Discuss the children's answers and any misconceptions that may arise.
● Emphasise that humans and animals play an important part in seed dispersal. Edible fruit and berries provide food for animals. These seeds pass through the animal's digestive system and are excreted far from the parent plant. Externally, seeds such as acorns or hazel nuts are collected and buried by animals and, if forgotten, will germinate. Likewise, so-called 'hitchhiker' seeds have hooks, barbs or sticky surfaces that allow them to attach onto an animal's fur and to be carried away from the parent plant.

Pollination investigation

Learning objective
QCA Unit 5B 'Life cycles'
● That insects pollinate some flowers.

Resources 💿 🅿
'Life cycle of plants' Notebook file; photocopiable page 130 'Pollinator observation sheet' for each child; magnifying glasses; sticky tape; clipboards; access to a garden containing a number of different plants in flower (do this investigation on a sunny day in the summer months).

Links to other subjects
ICT
PoS (2c) To use simulations and explore models to identify patterns and relationships.
Mathematics
PNS: Handling data
● Use the results of the investigation to build a database of pollinators.

Starter
Ask the children how a flowering plant produces a seed. Draw out that this can only be brought about by pollination, and that the term *pollination* is related to the word *pollen*. Make a note of this on page 11 of the Notebook file. Ask the children what they know about pollen and hay fever. Tell them that pollen is like a small packet of information that must be sent from one plant to another, which tells that plant how to grow the seeds for a new plant. Explain that the children will be studying how insects are involved in the process of pollination. Introduce the term *pollinator*.

Whole-class shared work
● Go through pages 12, 13 and 14 to explain how insects are involved in transferring pollen between flowers. Highlight and annotate the pages if required.
● Explain that different insects are attracted to different flowers and that the children will be observing flowering plants in order to study this.
● Provide each child with a copy of photocopiable page 130. Explain how to complete both parts of the sheet.

Independent work
● The independent work needs to be carried out in a garden or flower area.
● Assign the children to a number of different flowering plants and ask them to complete the first part of their photocopiable sheets.
● Next, tell them to record each time an insect visits the flower on their sheets, using a tally. Allow the children ten minutes for this.
● Demonstrate how to 'lift' pollen gently from the anthers of a flower, using a piece of sticky tape.
● Tell the children to do the same, being careful not to damage their plant, and to stick the sample to their sheets.
● For less confident learners, reinforce the process of pollination from flower to insect to another flower, and the associated vocabulary.
● Extend more confident learners by asking them to suggest other ways that pollination occurs (for example, by the wind).

Plenary
● On page 15 of the Notebook file, use the chart to tally the total number of different pollinators that visited the flowering plants.
● Discuss what can be learned from this simple tally chart, drawing out its limitations. (It only shows the main pollinators that visit the garden and not their preferences.)
● Discuss the observations the children recorded of interesting or repeated behaviour of the pollinators. Make a note of the observations on page 16.
● Ask the children to think up questions that may provide a more detailed examination of the results, such as: *Which flowers were most popular with one particular pollinator? Does the height of the flower affect the type of pollinator? Which colour flowers do bees prefer?*
● Examine whether it is possible to answer such questions from the results collected, and what ICT could be used to do this. (Spreadsheets and databases.)
● Draw out that pollen is not only dispersed by pollinators but also by the wind.

Whiteboard tools
Use a Pen from the Pen tray to write on the Notebook page.

▭ Pen tray

🖈 Select tool

✐ Highlighter pen

Parts of a flower

Learning objective
QCA Unit 5B 'Life cycles'
● That plants produce flowers which have male and female organs, seeds are formed when pollen from the male organ fertilises the ovum (female).

Resources 💿
'Parts of a flower' Notebook file; large flowers for dissection, such as tiger lilies or gladioli; plastic knives; chopping boards; heavyweight paper for mounting; glue; magnifying glasses; sticky tape.

Links to other subjects
Design and technology
PoS (4c) How mechanisms can be used to make things move in different ways.
● Design a flower bud that opens, using cam mechanisms to create movement.
History
PoS (11a) To study the impact of significant individuals.
● Link this work to the drawings of flowers made by Charles Darwin.

Starter
Display your bouquet of flowers. Ask the children what purpose flowers have, other than for our enjoyment. Draw out some of the typical characteristics of flowers (scent, colour, different sizes and shapes). Record the children's responses on page 2 of the Notebook file.

Whole-class shared work
● Hand out the flowers for the children to study, with the naked eye as well as with magnifying glasses. Encourage the children to handle and examine the flowers carefully, without damaging them or removing any of their parts.
● Ask them to identify any distinctive parts that the flowers have, and to suggest possible functions for those parts.
● Go to page 3 and tell the children that you are going to dissect a flower and describe each part and its function. (See page 4 for a simple description of these functions.)
● Remove the stem and explain its function. Highlight the appropriate words on the board.
● Repeat the activity for the sepals and petals.
● Repeat the activity for the stamen, separating the anther and filament. Touch the anther and show how the pollen has rubbed off on your finger tip. Show the children how to collect a sample of pollen from the anther using a piece of sticky tape.
● Repeat the activity for the pistil, separating the stigma, style and ovary. Make a careful lengthways cut down the ovary to reveal the ovules (eggs), which should be visible with a magnifying glass.

Independent work
● Tell the children to dissect their flowers in a similar manner. They should stick each part (including a sample of pollen) onto their mounting paper, and label each part accurately using the terms on page 3.
● Less confident learners could identify and name each part orally and then in writing. Reinforce understanding of the different functions of each part.
● Extend more confident learners by asking them to think up ways of remembering the names of the different parts, such as through rhymes or mnemonics.

Plenary
● Invite the children to display their mounted flower parts.
● Using page 5, ask the children to think of ways of remembering the names and functions of the parts of a flower, such as through rhymes and mnemonics. For example, *stamen* contains the word 'men', and *stigma* contains the word 'ma' (as in *mother*), or *sepals keep flower buds safe*.
● Without reference to their work, use the 'Parts of a flower' labelling activity on page 6 to test the children's recall of the names and functions of the parts of a flower.

Whiteboard tools
Use a Pen from the Pen tray to write on the page.

🖳 Pen tray

🖰 Select tool

The life cycle of a flowering plant

Learning objective
QCA Unit 5B 'Life cycles'
● To learn about the life cycle of flowering plants including pollination, fertilisation, seed production, seed dispersal and germination.

Resources 💿 🅟
'Life cycle of plants' Notebook file; photocopiable page 131 'Build the life cycle' for each child; scissors; glue sticks.

Links to other subjects
ICT
PoS (2a) How to develop and refine ideas by bringing together and organising text and images.
● Use graphical modelling software to compose and label an image of the life cycle of a plant or animal.
English
PNS: Creating and shaping texts
● Write an explanation about the life cycle of a plant or animal.

Starter
Spend a few minutes reviewing prior learning about the stages in the life cycle of a flowering plant: ask the children to name and explain each of the stages they have studied. Address any queries and misconceptions, particularly the difference between seed dispersal and pollen dispersal. Use page 17 of the Notebook file to make notes.

Whole-class shared work
● On page 18, list the names of the stages in order: seed dispersal, germination, growth, pollen dispersal, pollination, fertilisation, seed production.
● Choose a starting point and ask the children to use the Lines tool ✎ to draw arrows from one term to another to show the correct order of stages.
● Discuss the limitations of displaying the information in this way. (It looks clumsy, the arrows cross, it is hard to follow.)
● Explain to the children that because these stages are repeated in a cycle, a circular layout would be more suitable.
● Read the instructions on page 19 and go to page 20. This shows labels and pictures to represent the life cycle of a bean plant, but everything is mixed up.
● Tell the children that they will need to solve the problem on paper first, before solving the problem on-screen together at the end of the lesson.

Independent work
● Hand out copies of photocopiable page 131.
● Ask the children to cut out the images and stick them in the correct order on a separate piece of paper or in their books.
● Tell them to label each stage appropriately with the terms discussed and listed.
● Encourage them to label each stage with the same term or with more than one term if necessary. (For example, the image with the visible flowers could be labelled 'flowering, pollen dispersal and pollination'.)
● Less confident learners may need support in recognising, ordering and labelling each stage.
● Extend more confident learners by asking them to write short notes next to each label, to explain what is happening at that particular point of the cycle.

Plenary
● Ask the children to share their work and discuss what they found difficult about the task.
● Using page 20, repeat the task as a class by asking the children to drag and drop the images into their correct position around the cycle. Tell them to use the labels to guide them.
● If required, display the correct cycle on page 21.
● Emphasise the correct order of the cycle and ask the children to explain the difference between the more complicated stages (for example, pollen dispersal and seed dispersal, and pollination and fertilisation).
● Explain that life cycles can be drawn for all living organisms, whether plant or animal (for example, cat to kitten to cat, or frog to frog spawn to tadpole to frog). Challenge the children to think up some similar life cycles.

Whiteboard tools
Select an arrow from the Lines tool to draw arrows on page 18 of the Notebook file.

🖥 Pen tray

🔖 Select tool

✎ Lines tool

The many gases around us

Learning objective
QCA Unit 5C 'Gases around us'
● That there are many gases and many of these are important to us.

Resources ◉
'Gases around us' Notebook file; secondary sources about gases and their uses; quality paper or card suitable for posters.

Links to other subjects
Design and technology
QCA Unit 5B 'Bread'
● This lesson links with the use of yeast in bread making.
PE
PoS (4a) How exercise affects the body in the short term.
● Discuss how the lungs and circulatory system work in transferring gases to and from muscles during exercise.

Starter
Point out of the classroom window and ask the children what the air in the sky is 'made' of. Recap any prior work on the fact that air has weight and is made of gas. Go to page 2 of the Notebook file. Ask the children to name any gases that they think are found in air and note them down.

Whole-class shared work
● Go to page 3. Discuss the names of the gases found in air and ask the children to estimate and record what percentage of air that each gas makes up (children will typically believe that oxygen makes up the largest percentage).
● Vote to predict which gas is the most prevalent in air. Discuss the results and rank the gases in order of highest percentage to lowest.
● Reveal and discuss the percentages on page 4. Ask: *Were your predictions correct? Do you find any of the results surprising?* Draw out the children's knowledge of the effect of rising carbon dioxide levels in global warming.
● Ask the children to circle or highlight the items on page 5 that they think contain gas. (All six contain gas.)
● Use pages 6 and 7 to discuss how the items all contain or use different gases.

Independent work
● Go to page 8 of the Notebook file. Explain the task to the children and leave the page on display to remind them of the focus of their work.
● Allow them to use a variety of secondary sources, such as reference books, internet searches and CDs, to find out about how different gases are used.
● They should then design a small poster to inform other Year 5 children about a gas and its use(s). Tell them that their leaflets or posters will be judged on their visual impact and the clarity of the information.
● Support less confident learners in their research (for example, by helping them to perform effective internet searches).
● Extend more confident learners by asking them to complement their specific information with more general statements about gases.

Plenary
● Ask the children to share their posters. Discuss the posters' visual impact and the clarity of the information. The children's work can be scanned and inserted as link objects on page 8, as a record.
● Go to page 9 and ask the children to highlight the hidden words in the word search. Reinforce the meaning of the vocabulary. After they have completed their search, pull the tab on the left-hand side across the screen to reveal the answers.

Whiteboard tools
Use a Highlighter pen to highlight the hidden words in the word search on page 9.

▭ Pen tray

▱ Highlighter pen

▚ Select tool

Air in soil investigation

Learning objectives
QCA Unit 5C 'Gases around us'
- That soils have air trapped within them.
- To measure volumes of water carefully.
- To recognise whether measurements need to be repeated.
- To use their results to compare the air trapped in different soils.

Resources 🔵 🅿
'Gases around us' Notebook file; photocopiable page 128 'Investigation planning sheet' for each child; photocopiable page 132 'Air in soil results' for each child; good quantities of at least five different soil types (including sand, clay, and a loam soil with more or less equal proportions of sand, silt and clay); plastic containers; sticky labels; weighing scales; measuring cylinders; water.

Links to other subjects
Mathematics
PNS: Measuring
- This investigation develops skills in measuring weights and volumes accurately.
ICT
PoS (1c) To interpret information, to check it is relevant and reasonable.
- Use the results from the lesson to help teach children to evaluate information, checking accuracy and questioning plausibility.

Whiteboard tools
If you do not wish to use the word bank provided on page 12, enable the Screen Shade before you turn to this page.

🖳 Pen tray

🔲 Screen Shade

🔖 Select tool

❎ Delete button

Starter
Discuss page 10 of the Notebook file. Some children may recognise that soil is a solid that contains liquid if it's wet. Read page 11 and pour some water onto a small amount of soil to demonstrate how the water forces air bubbles out of the top of the soil. This proves that air is trapped between the tiny rock particles in the soil.

Ask: *Why are air and water useful in soils?* Reveal the answer by selecting the bottom box and then pressing the Delete button ❎.

Tell the children that there are three main soil types (sand, silt and clay) and that they will be testing a number of different soils to find out how much air is trapped within each.

Whole-class shared work
- Go to page 12. Discuss how the amount of air in different soils could be compared in an investigation. Establish the resources needed and how the children could make the test fair: what will they keep the same (amount of soil), change (soil type) and measure (how much water has been soaked up, when the bubbles cease to appear). Write notes, or drag and drop phrases from the word bank (use the Screen Shade 🔲 to cover this part of the page if you do not wish to use it).
- Using page 13, discuss and record the children's predictions as a comparison (for example, the smaller the particles, the greater the amount of air).
- Demonstrate how to fill a measuring cylinder and read the scale accurately, and how to work out how much water has been soaked up by subtracting the volume left in the measuring cylinder from the original amount.
- Ask the children to complete the 'Investigation planning sheet' (photocopiable page 128).

Independent work
- Provide each child with a copy of photocopiable page 132.
- Invite the children to weigh out the same quantity of each soil into plastic containers and label them. They then pour water carefully onto the first soil, bit by bit, until the air bubbles stop escaping. Having done this, they should calculate and record how much water was soaked up.
- They should do this with three different soil types. Discuss the benefits of repeating the measurements using the same quantity of dry soil.
- Support less confident learners by ensuring that they accurately calculate and record volume measurements.
- Challenge more confident learners to provide reasons for their predictions.

Plenary
- Complete the results table on page 14 of the Notebook file and rank the soils.
- Discuss how repeated measurements help establish a consensus (or highlight inconsistencies). Establish that the amount of air in a soil is affected by the soil type (in general, the larger and more irregular the rock particles are, the more space there is between them, meaning more air is trapped).

Evaporation investigation

Learning objectives
QCA Unit 5D 'Changing state'
● Evaporation is when a liquid turns to a gas.
● Investigating ideas, making predictions, deciding what evidence to collect and constructing a fair test.
● Making careful measurements, recording them in tables and graphs; identifying trends and drawing conclusions; indicating whether the results support the prediction.

Resources ⊙ 🄿
'Evaporation investigation' Notebook file; photocopiable page 128 'Investigation planning sheet' for each child; photocopiable page 133 'Evaporation results' for each child; assorted plastic containers, with same and different-sized or shaped necks or openings, from bottles to ice-cream tubs; measuring cylinders; water. (Microsoft Excel is required to view the embedded spreadsheet in the Notebook file.)

Links to other subjects
Mathematics
PNS: Measuring
● Encourage the children to develop their skills at measuring volumes accurately.

Whiteboard tools
To enter data in the spreadsheet, select the cell and use the On-screen Keyboard to type.

🖳 Pen tray
🄺 Select tool
📖 On-screen Keyboard

Starter
Go to page 2 of the Notebook file to recap prior work on evaporation. Compare rapid, visible evaporation (steam from a kettle) to slow, invisible evaporation (puddles drying up in the playground). Note the link between evaporation and heating. Discuss other variables that might affect how fast a liquid evaporates.

Whole-class shared work
● Hand out copies of the 'Investigation planning sheet' (photocopiable page 128).
● List the possible variables that could be tested (heat, wind, amount of liquid and surface area of liquid) on page 3 of the Notebook file.
● Establish and note down a testable question for each variable and discuss how this could be investigated.
● Go to page 4. Ask: *How will you make the test fair? What will you keep the same? Change? Measure?* (The volume of water.)
● Demonstrate how to fill a measuring cylinder and read the scale accurately.
● Allow the groups to decide which variable they want to investigate (for example, temperature, or surface area) and ask them to complete the 'Investigation planning sheet'.
● Discuss the children's predictions and record them on page 5.

Independent work
● Provide each child with a copy of photocopiable page 133. Give each group three suitable containers.
● The groups should set up their investigations in safe and appropriate locations, recording their starting data on their sheets.
● Over a period of one to two weeks, they should make and record six more measurements.
● Support less confident learners by ensuring that they make and record their volume measurements accurately.
● Challenge more confident learners to provide reasons for their predictions.

Plenary
● Discuss what the children discovered.
● Tell them that line graphs can present a change over a period of time, so that comparisons can be made more easily.
● Open the Microsoft Excel spreadsheet on page 6. Enter a set of data from one of the investigations into the spreadsheet cells.
● Examine and discuss the resultant line graph, using it to explain how the particular variable has affected the rate of evaporation. (The amount of heat is the key variable. Heat from light 'excites' molecules on the surface of the liquid, releasing them as gas into the air. Wind speeds up this process, as the gas molecules are dispersed faster, making way for more molecules to change state. Greater surface area also speeds up evaporation, as there is more area where evaporation is occurring. If surface area and other variables are the same, then the amount of water should not affect the rate of evaporation because it is only occurring at the surface.)
● Compare the results with the children's predictions. The Excel workbook provides eight sheets, for eight groups to record their results.

Condensation

Learning objectives
QCA Unit 5D 'Changing state'
- That condensation is when a gas turns to a liquid.
- That condensation is the reverse of evaporation.
- To make careful observations and draw conclusions, explaining these in terms of scientific knowledge and understanding.
- That air contains water vapour and when this hits a cold surface it may condense.

Resources 💿
'Changing states' Notebook file; ice cubes; mixing bowl and spoon; jelly cubes; cling film; hot water; paper and drawing materials.

Links to other subjects
Geography
PoS (5b) Recognise how and why people may seek to manage environments sustainably, and to identify opportunities for their own involvement.
- Use this investigation to inform children's work on water supply around the world.
Music
PoS (2b) Explore, choose, combine and organise musical ideas within musical structures.
- Compose a repeating pattern of music, using tuned and untuned instruments, to represent changes of state.

Starter
Discuss page 2 of the Notebook file. Some children will recognise that the water is known as 'condensation', but probably won't know why or how it occurs.

Go to page 3 and discuss the red and blue arrows, which are either side of the window pane to represent the meeting of cold and warm air. Draw blue dots to represent the condensation. Explain the term *condensation*: when a gas (in this case, water vapour) cools and so changes state into a liquid.

Go to page 4. Discuss how the same process occurs on a much larger scale when cold and warm air fronts meet in the atmosphere.

Whole-class shared work
- Tell the class that you are going to make some jelly and cool it down as quickly as possible. Dissolve the jelly cubes in hot water, cover the solution with cling film and place several ice cubes in the middle of the cling film.
- Ask the children to observe your jelly experiment carefully. They should see droplets of water dripping down from directly underneath the ice cubes.
- Ask them to explain what is happening. (Children will often believe that the ice is melting and leaking through the cling film.)
- Go to page 5. Annotate it to explain that water is evaporating from the jelly solution and condensing under the ice (the coldest part of the underside of the cling film). Emphasise that the cling film is waterproof and cannot leak, and that the ice is changing state from solid to liquid because of the heat from the solution.

Independent work
- Enable the Screen Shade 🔲 to cover page 5 and ask the children to create a diagram of the apparatus. They should use labels and symbols to explain what happened.
- Emphasise that the children's illustrations should indicate where any changes of state are occurring, especially condensation.
- Support less confident learners by reinforcing their understanding of the processes taking place.
- Extend more confident learners by asking them to make links with other examples of evaporation/condensation (for example, the water cycle).

Plenary
- Invite the children to share their diagrams. Ensure that they understand the process and are able to explain it in their own words.
- Display page 6 and ask the children to highlight the hidden words in the word search. Reinforce the meaning of the vocabulary. If you wish, a timer from the Gallery 🖼 can be used to impose a five-minute time limit to complete the search. Stop the clock whenever a word is found and ask the children to use the word appropriately in a sentence before restarting.

Whiteboard tools
Use the Screen Shade to hide certain areas of the screen.

- 🖳 Pen tray
- 🔲 Screen Shade
- ◤ Select tool
- ▨ Highlighter pen
- 🖼 Gallery

The water cycle

Learning objectives
QCA Unit 5D 'Changing state'
● That water evaporates from oceans, seas and lakes, condenses as clouds and eventually falls as rain.
● That water collects in streams and rivers and eventually finds its way to the sea.
● That evaporation and condensation are processes that can be reversed.
● To interpret the water cycle in terms of the processes involved.

Resources 💿
'Changing states' Notebook file; writing materials.

Links to other subjects
Geography
PoS (4b) Recognise some physical and human processes and explain how these can cause changes in places and environments.
● Use this investigation to inform children's work on water supply around the world.
ICT
PoS (5a) Working with a range of information to consider its characteristics and purposes.
● Conduct an internet search on rainfall patterns around the world.

Starter
Display page 7 of the Notebook file and ask the children to identify the processes at work in the images. Review any prior work on evaporation and condensation, emphasising that the two processes are reversible.

Whole-class shared work
● Look at the water cycle on page 8 and explain that the processes of evaporation and condensation are constantly at work in the atmosphere.
● Demonstrate the passage of a single water droplet around the water cycle, starting in the ocean, by dragging and dropping the image of the droplet (at the top of the page) to appropriate areas on the screen.
● Label and explain each stage (evaporation, condensation, precipitation and accumulation), drawing out the children's understanding of why evaporation and condensation occur.
● Point out how the river and water sink into the earth (infiltration).
● Use page 9 to test the children's ability to identify and correctly label each stage of the water cycle. Emphasise that although water does travel in a cycle, each stage of the cycle occurs simultaneously.

Independent work
● Display the writing frame on page 10 of the Notebook file.
● Ask the children to suggest some key words and write them in the word bank box.
● Tell them to use the writing frame to write a clear explanation of the main stages of the water cycle. Emphasise that their explanations should include relevant vocabulary from the word bank.
● Support less confident learners by reinforcing their understanding of the stages.
● Challenge more confident learners to include an introduction and a concluding paragraph.

Plenary
● Encourage the children to share their explanations.
● Pose the questions on pages 11 to 15. The children should vote on the correct answer. Press on the answer with the majority vote. If it is correct, it will automatically take you to another page revealing more information.

Whiteboard tools
Convert handwritten words to text by selecting them and choosing the Recognise option from the dropdown menu.

🖳 Pen tray

🖰 Select tool

Day and night

Learning objectives
QCA Unit 5E 'Earth, Sun and Moon'
● That it is the Earth that moves, not the Sun, and the Earth spins on its axis once every 24 hours.
● That it is daytime in the part of the Earth facing the Sun and night-time in the part of the Earth away from the Sun.

Resources 💿 🄿
'The Earth, Sun and Moon' Notebook file; photocopiable page 134 'World time zones map' for each child; torches; colouring pencils; modelling clay; toothpicks; glue sticks; globe; a set of world atlases.

Links to other subjects
Geography
QCA Unit 18 'Connecting ourselves to the world'
● Ask the children to consider how they could set up international links with a school in a different country. Discuss why emails would be used for communication and the time differences between their school and the international school.

Whiteboard tools
Convert handwritten words to text by selecting them and choosing the Recognise option from the dropdown menu.

🖳 Pen tray

🔲 Screen Shade

🔺 Select tool

🗙 Delete button

Starter
Display page 2 of the Notebook file. Discuss the 'movement' of the Sun, sinking down beneath the horizon during a sunset, and the next day rising up again over the horizon at sunrise. Ask the children what is really happening and draw out that the Sun is not moving at all; instead it is the movement of the Earth that creates this impression.

Whole-class shared work
● Display page 3 and review prior learning on how the Earth orbits the Sun. Discuss the fact that although the Moon and Sun look the same size in the sky, the Sun is very much bigger. It only looks small because it is so far away.
● Explain that this diagram represents a bird's eye view of the Earth, looking down at the North Pole. Select the 'Earth' and then press and drag the green dot to rotate it anti-clockwise. Explain that the Earth rotates on an axis through its centre, from the North to the South Pole. Demonstrate using a ball of modelling clay with toothpicks placed at the opposite poles.
● Ask the children how this knowledge might help explain the existence of night and day.
● To demonstrate, use the Screen Shade 🔲 to cover half of the Earth and rotate the Earth anti-clockwise. Draw out that at any time, half of the Earth will be in light, while the other half will be in darkness.
● Using page 4, explain that people have divided the world into different time zones. Ask the children to identify some of the countries or continents on the map and label them.

Independent work
● Provide each child with a copy of photocopiable page 134. Ask the children to use an atlas to identify, label and colour countries on their maps.
● Demonstrate how to roll the sheet into a tube with the map on the outside, sticking it together along the International Date Line.
● Tell the children to hold the tube upright, shine a torch at it from one side and rotate the tube to investigate which continents and countries are in darkness when others are in light. Ask them to record their investigations.
● Less confident learners may need support in labelling and colouring the map using an atlas. Ask them to identify continents and look at how many time zones each continent covers.
● Extend more confident learners by asking them to work out the time in different cities.

Plenary
● Discuss the children's discoveries.
● Use pages 5 and 6 to check the children's understanding of night and day in different parts of the world. Use the Delete button 🗙 to delete the blue box to reveal the answer hidden underneath. The globe and torch could be used to either find out the answer before voting, or to check whether the majority answer is correct.

Sunrise and sunset

Starter
Before the lesson, ask the children to record on different days the general direction of the sunrise or sunset, using a magnetic compass. Remind them never to look directly at the Sun.

Review any prior work on day and night, reminding the children that sunrise and sunset are caused by the rotation of the Earth and not by any movement of the Sun. Display page 7 of the Notebook file and discuss the children's discoveries about the general direction of the sunrise (east) and sunset (west). Move the Sun on screen to show the path of the Sun across the sky from east to west during the day.

Whole-class shared work
● Display page 8 and explain what the graph shows. (The time of sunrise in London on the first day of each month in 2007.)
● Discuss the trends and patterns in the graph (that the sunrise gets progressively earlier until June and July, and then gets progressively later).
● Using annotations, encourage the children to read the values on both axes carefully, especially where they fall between increments.
● In the summer it does not actually become light at 4am as the graph indicates. Due to British Summer Time, the clocks are deliberately put forward one hour, so it actually becomes light at 5am. You may wish to discuss this with the children.
● Tell the children that they will be plotting a similar line graph for sunset times in London for 2007.

Independent work
● Hand out copies of photocopiable page 135. Tell the children to plot each time carefully on the graph and to join each point using a ruled line.
● Ensure that they accurately plot points that fall between increments on the time axis.
● Encourage them to discuss their graphs and the trends and patterns produced by the data.
● Support less confident learners in plotting data.
● Challenge more confident learners to consider why sunrise and sunset times change during the year.

Plenary
● Reveal the sunset times for London on page 9 and ask the children to compare their graphs to this one.
● Ask them why sunrise and sunset times change during the year (some children will recognise that these are seasonal changes).
● Display page 10 and, with the aid of a globe, explain how this is caused by the tilt of the Earth in its orbit.

The changing faces of the Moon

Learning objectives
QCA Unit 5E 'Earth, Sun and Moon'
- That the Moon takes approximately 28 days to orbit the Earth.
- That the different appearance of the Moon over 28 days provides evidence for a 28-day cycle.

Resources 💿
'The Earth, Sun and Moon' Notebook file; powerful torches or directional lamps; dark room.

Links to other subjects
RE
PoS (1b) To describe the variety of practices and ways of life in religions.
- Investigate how some religious and secular celebrations are based upon the lunar months, which is why the dates change from year to year. The Chinese, Hebrew and Islamic calendars are all based on lunar months, although they calculate the year in slightly different ways.

Starter
Ask the children about their experience of 'star gazing' and use of binoculars and telescopes. Ask them to describe the appearance of the Moon's surface, either to the naked eye or under magnification. Display page 11 of the Notebook file. Emphasise at this point that the Moon is not a true source of light, as moonlight is sunlight reflected off the surface of the Moon.

Whole-class shared work
- Display page 12 and introduce the task.
- Enable the Spotlight tool 🔦. Resize the spotlight to increase or decrease the difficulty of the activity. Go to page 13 and use the spotlight to examine the shape of the visible Moon.
- On page 14, ask the children to write down and draw some of their observations (the shape changes or the different amounts of the Moon that can be seen).
- Discuss the children's explanations for these changes and tell them that they will be conducting an investigation that will help them explain fully.

Independent work
- Divide the children into groups of six and display page 15. Tell them that the group in the middle represents the Earth, the child circling them represents the Moon and the lamp represents the Sun.
- Ask the children to carry out the instructions in their groups.
- Emphasise that this is an observation exercise and encourage the central group and lamp operator to describe and discuss what happens to the light and shadow on the child's face. As the child circles, a greater or lesser amount of his or her face will be cast in light or shadow.
- Encourage the children to draw parallels with their observations and the changing 'shape' of the Moon.

Plenary
- Invite the children to describe their observations.
- Display page 16 and discuss the basic phases of the lunar cycle: new moon, half moon (waxing), full moon, half moon (waning) and back to new moon.
- Tell the children that it takes 28 days from new moon to new moon (the lunar cycle). Ask: *What is this evidence for?* (It takes 28 days for the Moon to orbit the Earth.)
- Use the interactive activity on page 17 to reinforce the order of the phases of the lunar cycle.

Whiteboard tools
Use the Spotlight tool to highlight different aspects of the Moon on page 13.

🖥 Pen tray

🔖 Select tool

🔦 Spotlight tool

Sound and states of matter

Learning objective
QCA Unit 5F 'Changing sounds'
● That vibrations from sound sources travel through different materials to the ear.

Resources 🔘 P
'Changing sounds' Notebook file; photocopiable page 136 'Sounds survey table' for each child.

Links to other subjects
Geography
PoS (1d) Identify and explain different views that people, including themselves, hold about topical geographical issues.
● Use this lesson to inform work on the environmental effect of traffic noise.
English
PNS: Engaging with and responding to texts
● Link this lesson with work on fairy tales and fables.

Starter
Review prior work on sound being caused by vibration. Ask the children to name ways that they can prove that sound is caused by a vibrating object. Ask the class to sit in silence for one minute and to try to memorise all the sounds they can hear inside and outside the classroom. Without drawing attention to the fact, ensure that any doors and windows are closed beforehand. Ask the children to describe what they could hear. Make a note of their responses on page 2 of the Notebook file.

Whole-class shared work
● Read the text on page 3 and then show the picture on page 4.
● Read page 5. Return to page 4, reminding the children that the characters are in an enclosed space.
● Ask the children for a possible solution to the question on page 5 (for example, sound somehow 'escapes'). Don't comment on whether responses are correct or incorrect, or that sound travels through solids.

Independent work
● Provide each child with a copy of photocopiable page 136.
● Ask the children to visit various areas of the school and listen to the sounds around them. They should record the location, what was heard, the volume of the sounds and whether the sound was from an open or enclosed space.
● Help less confident learners to complete the sheet.
● Ask more confident learners to propose other ways of judging and classifying volume levels (for example, on a scale of 0 to 10) and relate this to other standard scales they may know (for example, the Beaufort wind scale).

Plenary
● Ask the children to share their work and discuss their findings.
● Discuss any difficulties they had in identifying sounds and assigning volume levels. Talk about other possible scales and more accurate methods of measuring volume (for example, a data logger).
● Display page 6. Ask: *How do you hear sound(s) from within enclosed spaces? How does the woodsman?* (Sound must be travelling through solid materials.)
● Go to page 7. Contrast the behaviour of sound to light, which does not travel through opaque solids.
● Go to page 8 and ask the children to draw on the dotted lines to indicate how far they think a sound would travel through each material in one second. (Give them the clue that the maximum distance is 6000 metres.)
● Press the red arrow to reveal the answers. Address the common misconception that the speed of sound through air is the fastest. Emphasise that solids are better conductors of sound vibrations than liquids and that liquids are better conductors than gases. Draw comparisons with electrical conductors.

Whiteboard tools
Use a Pen from the Pen tray to write or draw on the board.

🖵 Pen tray

🖢 Select tool

Muffling materials investigation

Learning objectives
QCA Unit 5F 'Changing sounds'
● That some materials muffle sound.
● To test how well different materials muffle sound.
● To use a prediction to help decide what evidence to collect.
● To devise a fair test.
● To collect reliable evidence.
● To decide whether results support or do not support the prediction.

Resources 🔴 ▣
'Muffling materials' Notebook file; photocopiable page 128 'Investigation planning sheet' for each child; ticking clocks, metronomes or small radios; basic pair of ear protectors; sheets of insulating materials (such as newspaper, felt, cotton wool, bubble wrap, polystyrene and foam); metre rulers. (Microsoft Excel is required to view the embedded spreadsheet.)

Links to other subjects
Mathematics
PNS: Measuring
● This work develops the children's skills in measuring distances accurately.
ICT
PoS (5b) Work with others to explore a range of information sources and ICT tools.
● Use a data logger in the investigation, to measure sound levels accurately.

Whiteboard tools
To enter data in the spreadsheet, select the cell and use the On-screen Keyboard to type.

🖥 Pen tray

🔖 Select tool

⌨ On-screen Keyboard

Starter
Go to page 2 of the Notebook file. Discuss what the children know and make notes. Draw out that some solid materials are better at reducing the volume of a sound than others.

Go to page 3. Tell the children that you need their help in designing a new pair of ear protectors, by testing which would be the best material to line the inside of the ear protectors to muffle sound.

Whole-class shared work
● Hand out copies of photocopiable page 128.
● Provide objects that make a regular and constant sound – such as a ticking clock, metronome or untuned radio making 'white' noise – and a range of possible sound-proofing materials.
● Ask: *How could you use these resources to find out which material would be best for muffling sound? How could you make an investigation?*
● Go to page 4. Ask: *How can you make the test fair? What would you keep the same* (volume of sound) *and change* (materials)?
● Ask: *What will you measure to compare the effectiveness of the materials?* (The distance they need to stand away from the sound before it can no longer be heard.) *Why would this be better than trying to judge the volume of the sound by ear alone?*
● Go to page 5 and record the children's predictions.
● Ask the children to complete the photocopiable sheet.

Independent work
● The children should carry out their investigations, recording their results in a suitable table.
● Remind them to make sure that they are carrying out the comparisons fairly.
● Encourage them to make repeat measurements to ensure results are accurate.
● Less confident learners may need help in designing a suitable results table.
● Extend more confident learners by asking them to provide reasons for their predictions.

Plenary
● Discuss what the children discovered.
● Discuss any drawbacks of the investigation (for example, noise interference, or difference in results being hard to discern). Ask: *Is your evidence good enough to help you decide on the best material to line the ear protectors?*
● Open the Microsoft Excel file on page 6. Inform the children that bar charts can be used to present results clearly so that comparisons can be made more easily.
● Enter a set of data from the investigation into the spreadsheet cells.
● Examine and discuss the resultant bar chart, using it to explain why certain materials may be better than others at muffling sounds. Materials that have loose fibres contain a lot of air, and so make good sound insulators. The sound travelling through them has to move from air to fibre and from fibre back to air. As it progresses, the sound wave loses energy, so that it is muffled or reduced.

Vibrating air investigation

Learning objectives
QCA Unit 5F 'Changing sounds'
● That sounds are made by air vibrating.
● To suggest how to alter pitch and to test the prediction.
● To listen carefully to sounds made, record results in a suitable table and decide whether these support the prediction.
● To describe how pitch can be altered by changing the length of air column in a wind instrument.

Resources ◉ 🅿
'Vibrating air' Notebook file; photocopiable page 128 'Investigation planning sheet' for each child; recorder (or other wind instrument); lots of empty and cleaned glass bottles (33cl beer or milk); water; measuring cylinders or syringes. (Microsoft Excel is required to view the embedded spreadsheet.)

Links to other subjects
Design and technology
PoS (4b) How materials can be combined and mixed to create more useful properties.
● Choose materials to design and make musical instruments.
Music
PoS (4c) How music is produced in different ways and described through relevant established and invented notations.
● Compare the invented notation for the differing pitches (0–100) with established notations.

Whiteboard tools
To enter data in the spreadsheet, select the cell and use the On-screen Keyboard to type.

🖥 Pen tray

🖱 Select tool

⌨ On-screen Keyboard

Starter
Go to page 2 of the Notebook file. Blow into a recorder without covering any of the holes. Discuss what is making the sound and establish that it is the air column inside the recorder – not the recorder itself – that is vibrating to produce a note. Play different notes and ask the children to observe how you can change the pitch of the note by stopping the holes. (Don't reveal at this stage that stopping the holes changes the length of the column of vibrating air.) Tell the children that they will be testing how to alter the pitch of a sound made by vibrating air.

Whole-class shared work
● Hand out copies of photocopiable page 128.
● Demonstrate how to blow over the neck of a small glass bottle to create a sound. Ask: *How could you change its pitch?* (Put water in the bottle.)
● Go to page 3. Ask: *How could you investigate how the amount of water affects the pitch produced? What resources would you need?*
● Go to page 4. Ask: *How could you make the test fair? What would you keep the same* (bottle size and shape) *and change* (volume of water)?
● Discuss measurement: the children will have to judge the pitch of the sound by ear alone, recording the pitch as a value between 0 (very low) and 100 (very high).
● Discuss the children's predictions and record some on page 5.
● Discuss suitable designs for a results table. One example is given on page 6.
● Demonstrate how to fill a bottle accurately using a measuring cylinder or syringe.
● Ask the children to complete the photocopiable sheet.

Independent work
● Invite the children to carry out their investigations, recording their results in a suitable table.
● Encourage them to make repeat measurements to ensure that results are accurate.
● Less confident learners may need help in designing a suitable results table.
● Extend more confident learners by asking them to provide reasons for their predictions.

Plenary
● Discuss what the children discovered.
● Open the Microsoft Excel file on page 7. Inform the children that bar charts can be used to present results clearly so that comparisons can be made more easily.
● Enter a set of data from the investigation into the spreadsheet cells.
● Examine and discuss the resultant bar chart: the greater the amount of water, the higher the pitch of the note. Explain that this is because the vibrating air column is shorter.
● Demonstrate how the same is true with a recorder. Closing more holes consecutively from the top extends the air column because less air is escaping – the longer the air column, the lower the sound.
● Compare the children's results with their predictions.

Musical instruments presentation

Learning objectives
QCA Unit 5F 'Changing sounds'
● To relate their understanding of sound to a range of musical instruments.
● To explain an application of sound using scientific knowledge and understanding.

Resources ● P
'Changing sounds' Notebook file; photocopiable page 137 'Design board' for each child; construction materials (cardboard boxes, tubes, containers, bottles and rubber bands); construction equipment, such as scissors, knives, glue and sticky tape.

Links to other subjects
Design and technology
PoS (1d) Communicate design ideas in different ways as these develop, bearing in mind aesthetic qualities, and the uses and purposes for which the product is intended.
● This lesson links well with this objective.
Music
PoS (1b) Play tuned and untuned instruments with control and rhythmic accuracy.
● Perform a rhythmic/melodic composition in groups with the instruments.

Whiteboard tools
Use the Lines and Shapes tools to draw diagrams on the Notebook page.

⬚ Pen tray

◤ Select tool

☒ Delete button

◣ Lines tool

▣ Shapes tool

Starter
Display page 9 of the Notebook file. Review prior work on how sound is produced (by vibration of an object and/or a column of air). Ask the children to sort the instruments into two groups: those that produce sound through vibration of an object and those that produce sound from a vibrating column of air. Identify instruments that use both (for example, guitar strings vibrate and the sound is amplified by the air vibrating inside the guitar).

Whole-class shared work
● Hand out copies of photocopiable page 137.
● Display page 10 of the Notebook file. Explain that 'The League of Master Instrument Makers' have challenged the children to design and build their own instruments.
● The children will need to think carefully about how their instrument will work: What will vibrate? How will the pitch or volume be changed?
● Demonstrate how to fill in the design board, using a variety of whiteboard tools. Use the Lines tool ◣ and the Shapes tool ▣ to draw a diagram (preferably 3D) of their design, using different colour pens to show different parts, and answering the questions: *What vibrates? What changes?* Show the children how to erase by selecting an object and pressing the Delete button ☒.
● Organise the children into suitable groups and display the construction materials available.

Independent work
● Invite the children to use their photocopiable sheets to design their instruments, leaving the evaluation box blank.
● Once the sheet is completed, each group should complete a design board on screen for use later (pages 11-15 can be used for this purpose).
● The children should then construct their instruments.
● Less confident learners may need help to match the design to how the instrument functions (what vibrates and what changes).
● Challenge more confident learners to propose ways that they could tune their instruments (for example, by adjusting the lengths of a set of rubber bands to correspond to notes from a tuned instrument, such as a recorder or keyboard).
● Ask the children to prepare a short presentation of their instrument, demonstrating it and referring to their design boards on the whiteboard. They should discuss any difficulties they had, and any improvisations they made to ensure that their instruments functioned as designed. They should record these discussions as positive and negative points in the evaluation box on their sheets.

Plenary
● Ask the children to make their presentations. Encourage the rest of the class to ask questions about the information presented.
● Invite the children to suggest possible improvements they could make to their designs.
● If appropriate, give each design a score from 'The Master League of Instrument Makers' and write it in the evaluation box on each design board on the whiteboard.
● Use page 16 to record what the children have learned during this lesson.

Investigation planning sheet

FAIR TESTING

What will you change?
(The variable we are testing.)

What will you keep the same?
(Variables that will be kept constant.)

What will you measure and record?
(Results)

LABELLED DIAGRAM

PLANNING

What are you trying to find out?
(A question that can be tested.)

What do you think will happen?
(Prediction)

What will you use? (Resources)

▪ SCHOLASTIC
www.scholastic.co.uk

How to take your own pulse

◼ Find your pulse on your wrist or neck, as shown in the pictures.

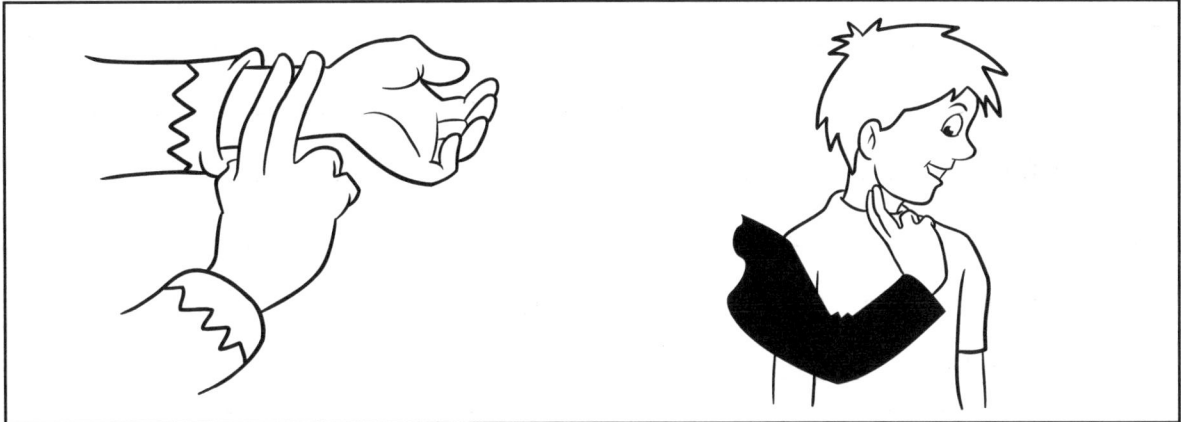

◼ Count the number of beats you feel for 15 seconds and enter it in the table below. Multiply this number by 4 (double it and double it again) to record your resting pulse rate in beats per minute (bpm).

Measurement	Beats in 15 seconds	Beats per minute (bpm)
Measurement 1		
Measurement 2		
Measurement 3		
Measurement 4		
Measurement 5		

Which do you think is your most accurate measurement? _____ bpm

Illustrations © Andy Keylock/Beehive Illustration

Pollinator observation sheet

Part A Find a flower or group of flowers and fill in the following details:

Date: _____   Time: _____

Temperature: _____   Weather conditions: _____

Name of flower: _____

Colour: _____

Arrangement: single flower   group of flowers   (circle one)

Scent: mild   strong   (circle one)

Draw your flower here	**Stick your strip of pollen here**

Part B Tally the pollinators that visit your flower(s) over a ten-minute period.

Time: _____   From: _____   Until: _____

Pollinator	**Tally**	**Total**
Bees		
Flies		
Wasps		
Beetles		
Butterflies		
Ants		
Others		

Write down details of any interesting or repeated behaviour you observed:

_____

_____

Name _____

Build the life cycle

◀ Cut out the pieces and stick them in the correct order on a separate piece of paper. Label each stage appropriately.

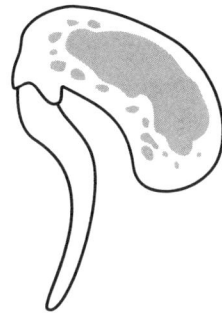

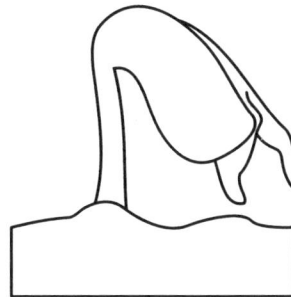

Air in soil results

Soil name: _____

	Starting volume (ml)	Finishing volume (ml)	Amount soaked up (ml)
1			
2			
3			

Soil name: _____

	Starting volume (ml)	Finishing volume (ml)	Amount soaked up (ml)
1			
2			
3			

Soil name: _____

	Starting volume (ml)	Finishing volume (ml)	Amount soaked up (ml)
1			
2			
3			

Evaporation results

Container 1

Variable:

Measurement	Volume (ml)
1	
2	
3	
4	
5	
6	
7	

Container 2

Variable:

Measurement	Volume (ml)
1	
2	
3	
4	
5	
6	
7	

Container 3

Variable:

Measurement	Volume (ml)
1	
2	
3	
4	
5	
6	
7	

World time zones map

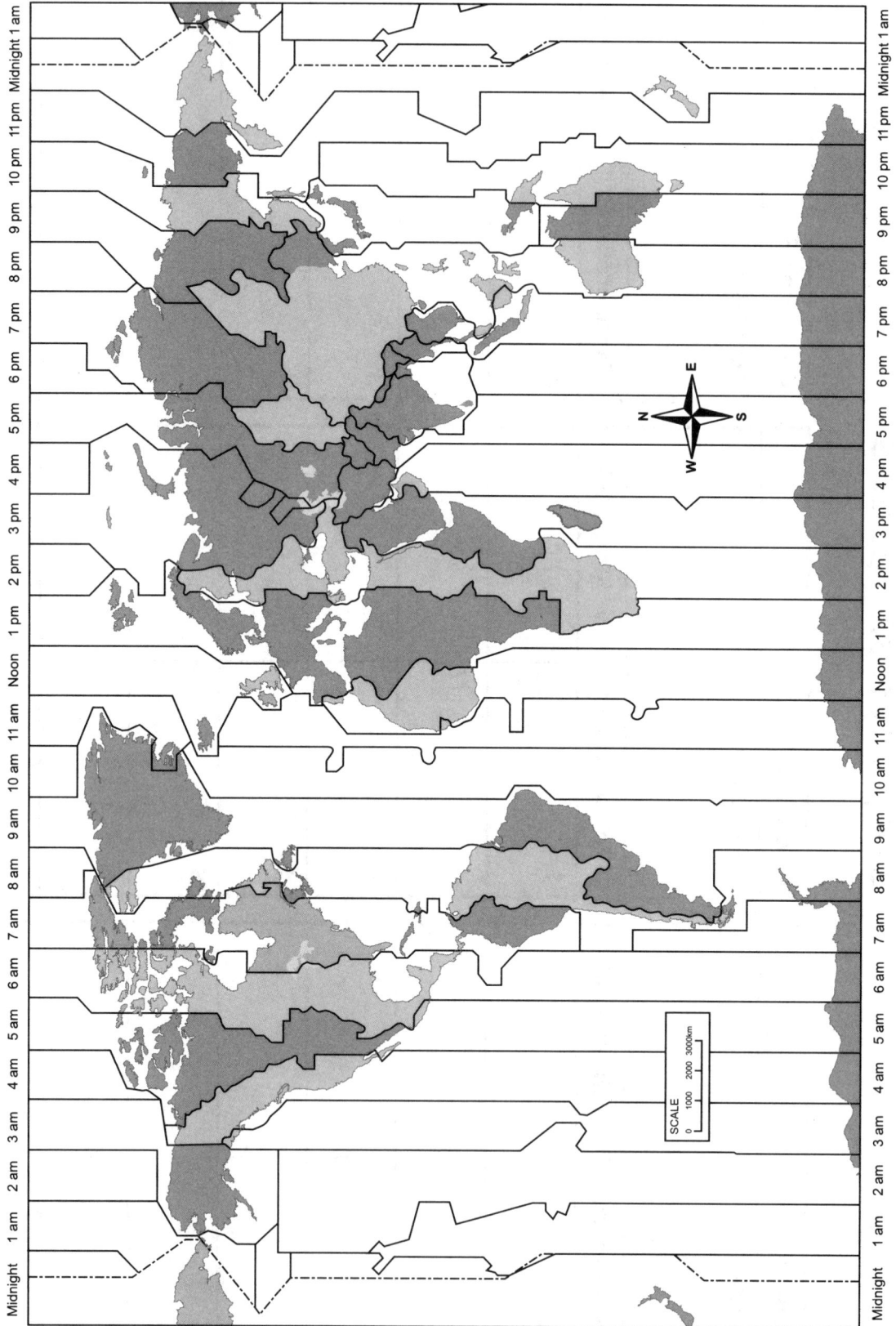

Map © The Drawing Room

➴ S C H O L A S T I C

w w w . s c h o l a s t i c . c o . u k

Sunset times London 2007

■ Plot the times on the line graph below. Remember that there are 60 minutes in one hour.

January	February	March	April	May	June	July	August	September	October	November	December
16:02	16:50	17:41	18:34	19:24	20:08	20:21	19:49	18:47	17:31	16:34	15:55

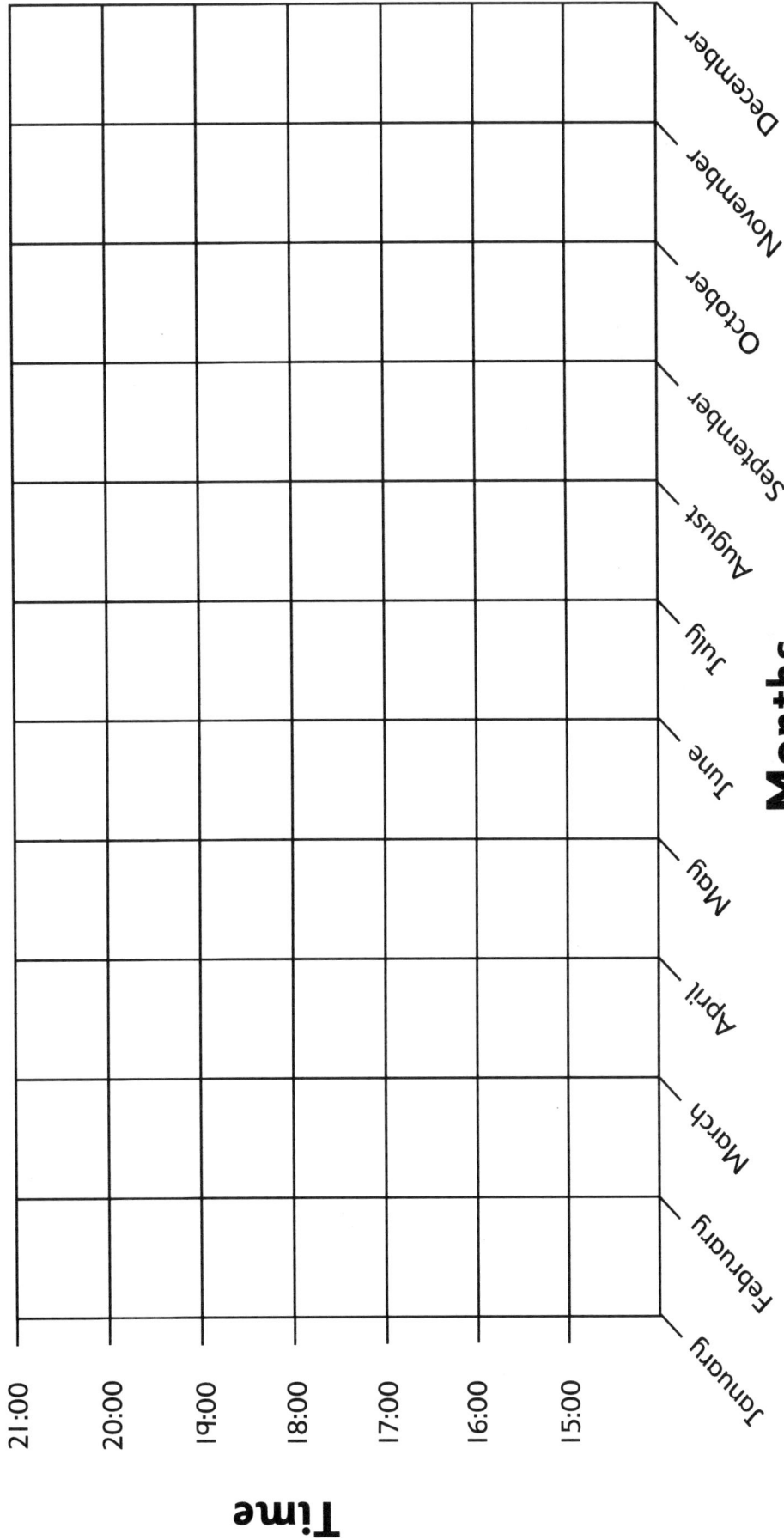

Time

21:00

20:00

19:00

18:00

17:00

16:00

15:00

Months

January February March April May June July August September October November December

Sounds survey table

Location	Description of sound(s)	Volume (as loud as a... whisper/talk/shout)	From an open or enclosed area

Design board

What vibrates?
(material and/or air)

What changes?
(pitch and/or volume)

Materials

Evaluation

Diagram

Foundation subjects

Although foundation subjects cover a multitude of learning experiences, addressing objectives from seemingly disparate curriculum areas, something they all share is their readiness for enhancement with ICT. As educators grow in their experience of, and confidence with, computers, so does their ability to identify opportunities for technology to improve the learning experience.

Modern children are at home with technology and regard it as a natural and exciting part of school life. They are also readily engaged by visual stimuli, and this is where the interactive whiteboard can make a spellbinding contribution. Used simply, it opens up a world of images, photographs and films that can be shared with the whole class. However, the tools and software that accompany the whiteboard can enrich and broaden learners' experiences in art, design, history, geography, RE and indeed the entire curriculum, showing people, places, artefacts, works of art and concepts in an accessible and motivating way.

In response to the changing needs of society, new initiatives have emerged to help children develop as individuals, and to contribute positively to their community. PSHE and citizenship can be powerful tools for improving attitudes, relationships and self-esteem, especially when technology is used creatively to help children find their place in the world.

With the aid of peripherals, interactive whiteboards can motivate the most reluctant children to improve their gymnastic performance while developing self-control and perseverance, at the same time as creating a new audience for performance.

All of the tools, applications and techniques described in the lessons that follow are easily learned and applied. They are also transferable to other curriculum areas, where they can be used to focus attention, model processes, refine ideas, generate interest and generally breathe new life into teaching and learning.

Lesson title	Objectives	Expected prior knowledge	Cross-curricular links
PSHE and citizenship			
Lesson 1: Taking responsibility ⊙	**QCA Unit 2** 'Choices' • To know that our actions (our choices and behaviour) affect others and to care about other people's feelings.	• That our actions have consequences for others and ourselves. • That situations can be seen from a number of perspectives.	**English** PNS Engaging with and responding to texts: Compare the usefulness of techniques such as visualisation, prediction and empathy in exploring the meaning of texts. **Speaking and listening** Objective 54: Working in role helps to explore complex issues.
Lesson 2: Class rules ⊙ ℙ	**QCA Unit 8** 'Class rules' • To understand the need for rules in class, school and society. • To play a purposeful part in creating rules for a good working culture in class.	• How to express an opinion and justify it. • How to challenge an opinion without being disrespectful.	**English** PNS Speaking: Present a spoken argument, sequencing points logically, defending views with evidence and making use of persuasive language. **Citizenship** PoS (2b) Why and how rules and laws are made and enforced.
Lesson 3: Circle time ℙ	**QCA Unit 1** 'Taking part' • To contribute to a discussion and to listen to the views of others. • To develop effective tools for whole-class discussion. • To agree a set of rules for circle time.	• How to take turns in a talk forum. • How to speak and listen respectfully.	**Citizenship** PoS (2a) To research, discuss and debate topical issues, problems and events.
Lesson 4: Daylight robbery ⊙	**QCA Unit 9** 'Respect for property' • To understand that stealing is wrong. • To know some of the ways in which victims of crime can be affected. • To use imagination to develop empathy with victims of crime.	• How to explore situations from more than one point of view.	**English** PNS Drama: Reflect on how working in role helps to explore complex issues. **RE** QCA Unit 5D 'How do the beliefs of Christians influence their actions?'

Lesson title	Objectives	Expected prior knowledge	Cross-curricular links
Lesson 5: Heraldic shields	QCA Unit 5 'Living in a diverse world' • To feel positive about themselves. • To celebrate their worth as individuals by identifying positive things about themselves.	• How to place periods in a chronological framework. • Have a basic understanding of symbolism, perhaps in a religious context.	ICT QCA Unit 5B 'Analysing data and asking questions, using complex searches' Art and design PoS (2b) To apply their experience of materials and processes, including drawing, developing their control of tools and techniques.
History			
Lesson 6: You name it! ◉	QCA Unit 6C 'Why have people invaded and settled in Britain in the past?' • To learn some of the typical Viking place names and their meanings. • To identify the areas where the Vikings settled.	• That settlement is different from invasion. • How to position the main invaders (Romans, Anglo-Saxons and Vikings) on a timeline. • That evidence of settlement comes from archaeology and place names.	Geography PoS (1a) Ask geographical questions; (2c) Use maps at a range of scales; (4a) Recognise and explain patterns made by human features.
Lesson 7: Points of view ◉	QCA Unit 14 'Who were the Ancient Greeks?' • To understand what is meant by *democracy*. • To understand some of the ideas of people living in Athens and Sparta.	• When the Ancient Greek civilisation flourished. • That Greece was made up of city states.	English PNS Drama: Reflect on how working in role helps to explore complex issues.
Lesson 8: What's the point? ◉ ℗	QCA Unit 9 'What was it like for children in World War II?' • To learn that the government disseminated information in different ways and that posters were one way. • To learn that information was provided for different purposes. • To find out about events from different sources (war posters).	• When World War II was and be able to position this on a timeline. • Some of the effects of the war on people's everyday lives, including the threat of invasion.	English PNS Group discussion and interaction: Plan and manage a group task; understand different ways to take the lead and support others in groups. English PNS Drama: Perform a scripted scene, making use of dramatic conventions.
Lesson 9: It's the pits ℗	QCA Unit 11 'What was it like for children living in Victorian Britain?' • To collect information from a range of sources and draw conclusions about the Victorian period. • To understand that ways of life differed greatly across Victorian society. • To write a narrative using historical detail. • To understand that there are many representations of the Victorian period.	• How to use a range of sources. • About the lives of children beyond living memory. • The living conditions of rich children in Victorian times.	English PNS Creating and shaping texts: Adapt non-narrative forms and styles to write factual texts.
Geography			
Lesson 10: Who uses water? ◉	QCA Unit 11 'Water' • To know how water is used in the world. • To investigate similarities and differences in water use. • To be aware of land use patterns.	• That water is essential to life. • That water can be found in the environment.	Science PoS Sc2 (5f) That micro-organisms are living organisms that are often too small to be seen. ICT PoS (1b) To prepare information for development using ICT.
Lesson 11: Local issues ℗	QCA Unit 20 'Local traffic – an environmental issue' • To use maps at a variety of scales. • To identify key physical and human features. • To know how features influence the location of human activities.	• That maps often represent real places. • That issues affect people and the environment.	Science PoS Sc2 (5a) Living things and the environment need protection. English PNS Creating and shaping texts: Adapt non-narrative forms and styles to write factual texts. History PoS (4a) Find out about changes studied from an appropriate range of sources.
Lesson 12: There and here ℗	QCA Unit 13 'A contrasting UK locality' • To use secondary sources. • To use appropriate geographical vocabulary. • To identify the main physical and human features of a locality.	• That not everything we read is necessarily true. • That different people have different views.	Science PoS Sc1 (2l) Decide whether conclusions agree with any prediction made. Design and technology PoS (1d) Communicate design ideas in different ways as these develop.

Lesson title	Objectives	Expected prior knowledge	Cross-curricular links
Lesson 13: Where land meets sea	QCA Unit 23 'Investigating coasts' • To use appropriate geographical vocabulary. • To know about the physical features of coasts and the processes of erosion and deposition that affect them.	• That coasts are the places where land meets sea. • That there is a variety of types of coasts.	History PoS (4a) To find out about the past; (4b) To ask and answer questions about the past.
Art and design			
Lesson 14: Still life	QCA Unit 4A 'Viewpoints' • To collect visual and other information to help them develop their ideas. • To question and make thoughtful observations about starting points.	• Vocabulary: natural and man-made forms, foreground, mid-ground, background.	ICT QCA Unit 5B 'Analysing data and asking questions: using complex searches' RE PoS (3i) Symbols and religious expression: how religious and spiritual ideas are expressed.
Lesson 15: Containers	QCA Unit 5B 'Containers' • To record from first-hand observation. • To explore ideas for container forms.	• How to describe 3D shapes: faces, vertices, shapes of faces and so on.	History PoS (4a) To find out about the events, people and changes studied from an appropriate range of sources of information, including ICT-based resources.
Lesson 16: Telling tales through textiles	QCA Unit 5C 'Talking textiles' • To explore how stories have been represented in textiles in different times and cultures. • To collect visual and other information to help them develop their ideas.	• How to retell main events in a story. • How to produce simple sketches.	English PNS Creating and shaping texts: Adapt non-narrative forms and styles to write fiction or factual texts. History PoS (4a) Find out about the events, people and changes. ICT QCA Unit 5B 'Analysing data and asking questions: using complex searches'
Design and technology			
Lesson 17: Musical instruments	QCA Unit 5A 'Musical instruments' • To investigate, disassemble and evaluate a range of musical instruments. • To relate the way things work to their intended purpose, how materials and components have been used, people's needs, and what users say about them.	• How to classify instruments by type: wind, percussion, stringed. • The names and properties of familiar materials.	Science QCA Unit 5F 'Changing sounds' ICT PoS (1b) To prepare information for development using ICT.
Lesson 18: Investigating breads	QCA Unit 5B 'Bread' • To know there is a wide variety of bread products from a variety of cultural traditions. • To investigate and evaluate bread products according to their qualities and properties.	• How to investigate existing products to inform design ideas. • How to evaluate food products according to appearance, texture and taste.	Science QCA Unit 5A 'Keeping healthy' English PNS Speaking: Present a spoken argument, sequencing points logically, defending views with evidence and making use of persuasive language. ICT QCA Unit 5B 'Analysing data and asking questions: using complex searches'
Lesson 19: Cams in moving toys	QCA Unit 5C 'Moving toys' • To recognise the movement of a mechanism in a toy or model. • To understand that a cam will change rotary motion into linear motion.	• About the working characteristics of some simple mechanisms.	Science PoS Sc4 (2e) To measure forces and identify the direction in which they act. English PNS Speaking: Use and explore different question types and different ways words are used, including in formal and informal contexts.
Physical education			
Lesson 20: Symmetry and asymmetry in routines	QCA Unit 15 'Gymnastic activities' • To perform actions, shapes and balances consistently and fluently in specific activities.	• That you need to practise and refine an action to improve the quality of performance. • How to create a range of different clearly formed body shapes.	Mathematics PNS Understanding shape: Complete patterns with up to two lines of symmetry. ICT PoS (2a) To develop and refine ideas by bringing together, organising and reorganising text, tables, images and sound as appropriate.

Taking responsibility

Learning objective
QCA Unit 2 'Choices'
● To know that our actions (our choices and behaviour) affect others and to care about other people's feelings.

Resources 💿
'Choices' Notebook file; digital camera.

Links to other subjects
English
PNS: Engaging with and responding to texts
● Encourage the children to empathise with different characters in stories and to see events from more than one perspective.
Speaking and listening
Objective 54: Working in role helps to explore complex issues.
● Link the independent work with this objective.

Starter
Open the Notebook file and display page 2. Explain that today's lesson focuses on making choices about the things that we do, and taking responsibility for those choices. Say that for every situation we find ourselves in, we have a choice about how we respond to it. Sometimes it's hard to make a choice about *how* to respond because our emotions get in the way. Ask each child to think about a time recently when they have felt a strong emotion.

Whole-class shared work
● Go to page 3 of the Notebook file. Explain that the class is going to hear about a couple of children who found themselves in a tricky situation and made a choice about how to respond.
● Read the first 'choices' scenario. Ask the children if they've ever been in a similar situation to Jack and Yoshi.
● Ask the children whether they think Jack or Yoshi are responsible and to justify their choices, highlighting the significant words and annotating the text. Make the point that although Jack started the game, Yoshi chose to join in.
● Read the second 'choices' scenario on page 4. Ask the children if they've had similar experiences.
● Again, ask if Pete or Vijaya is responsible (encourage individuals to justify their choices). Make the point that although Pete had been unkind, Vijaya chose to respond in a nasty way.
● Discuss the dilemmas faced by the children in the scenarios. Establish that the children chose to respond to those situations in a negative way. Ask what the consequences of their actions could be and who is really responsible for the outcome.

Independent work
● Split the class into four or five mixed-ability groups. Each group needs to assign the following roles: actors, photographer, director and writer.
● They then devise a series of three 'freeze frames' telling the story of one of the scenarios. (More confident learners could be challenged to create a whole new scenario.) The actors, assisted by the director, must use stance, gesture and facial expression to develop the plot, which should be photographed once the group is happy with it.
● Transfer the pictures to the computer and help the groups to insert them into page 5 of the Notebook file, resizing as necessary. Add more pages if you need them by selecting Clone Page from the dropdown menu in the Page Sorter.
● Show the children how to use the Shapes tool 🖼 to insert speech bubbles beside the characters in the photos and type in purposeful dialogue to develop the story further.

Plenary
● Share the children's completed 'choices' storyboards with the class, and celebrate their success.
● Recap what the children have learned about choices on page 6 of the Notebook file.
● Conclude by reiterating to the children that whatever situation we find ourselves in, we have choices about how we react. It's no good blaming others for our own actions because we must be responsible for ourselves.

Whiteboard tools
Use the Shapes tool to add speech bubbles to the children's work in the independent work.

🖥 Pen tray

🔲 Select tool

✏️ Highlighter pen

🔲 Shapes tool

🖼 On-screen Keyboard

🔳 Page Sorter

Class rules

Learning objectives
QCA Unit 8 'Class rules'
● To understand the need for rules in class, school and society.
● To play a purposeful part in creating rules for a good working culture in class.

Resources ● ▣
'Class rules' Notebook file; photocopiable page 161 'Class rules', one for each pair.

Links to other subjects
English
PNS: Speaking
● Encourage the children to express opinions and debate them in order to reach agreement.
Citizenship
PoS (2b) Why and how rules and laws are made and enforced.
● Compare class rules with laws and evaluate their impact on the lives of those who are subject to them.

Starter

Display page 2 of the Notebook file. Explain to the class that as it's the beginning of the year, it is necessary to think about the kind of class that children (and adults) want to be a part of. Emphasise the importance of everyone contributing, as agreements made today will influence the life of the class for the rest of the year.

Give out copies of photocopiable page 161, and ask the children in pairs to quickly generate three to five statements about the kind of class they would like to belong to.

Discuss the children's responses and draw out any common themes that arise. Ask them to justify their statements, and to explain how these will influence the life of the class.

Whole-class shared work

● Go to page 3 of the Notebook file. Ask individuals to choose the statement that they feel is most important.
● Invite children to come up to the board and write their statement in the circle they feel it belongs, until a good bank of statements is on display.
● If some statements don't fit in one of the categories on the board, discuss this with the class. Use the Shapes tool ▢ to add any other circles that are felt to be necessary.

Independent work

● Ask the children, working collaboratively in pairs or small groups, to mull over the statements on the board, considering how to convert them into a set of rules.
● Encourage groups to discuss exactly how each rule should be worded, making sure that each is concise and unambiguous.

Plenary

● Bring the children back together and ask them to share their rules, explaining and justifying their choices.
● Use majority consensus to decide which rules to accept in the final copy.
● Make a neat copy on page 4 of the Notebook file. Make it personal by using digital pictures of the class at work and play, or ask a talented artist to decorate it with caricatures of the class.
● Save the file, print it out and display the finished result in a prominent position. Refer to it regularly throughout the year, either to applaud positive happenings and attitudes in class, or to remind children who break the rules.

Whiteboard tools
Use the Shapes tool to add circles, if necessary, for the whole-class shared work. Convert handwritten words to text by selecting them and choosing the Recognise option from the dropdown menu.

▢ Pen tray

▢ On-screen Keyboard

▢ Select tool

▢ Shapes tool

Circle time

Starter
Explain to the children that throughout the year, circle time will be used as a forum for discussion. Ask for views on this to gauge their understanding of what circle time is and how it is conducted. Tell the class that an agreed set of rules for circle time is needed. From the SEAL CD (see Resources), open the 'Are We Ready for Circle Time?' poster and ask the children to read it through. Discuss the points it raises and ask the children for any more issues that need to be considered.

Whole-class shared work
● Choose two children to be observers for this circle time, and give them a copy of photocopiable page 162 each. Explain that the observers will make notes, both positive and negative, on what they see during circle time. These notes will be discussed at the end of the lesson and will be used to help refine circle time.
● Start a round, in which everyone makes a statement with a sentence starter. For example: *Something I really like about being in Year 5 is...*, or *Something that worries me about being in Year 5 is...* (Other excellent ideas are given in DfES *Social and Emotional Aspects of Learning* materials.)
● Move on to more personal rounds, commenting on personal goals for the year perhaps, or personal likes and dislikes.
● Ask the observers to feed back to the group, commenting on the quality of contributions, their tone, whether everyone joined in, what they noticed about children's body language and so on. Ask a scribe to note these on the board.
● Discuss the things the observers brought up. Were there any surprises?

Independent work
● Divide the class into mixed-ability groups and explain that each group will work collaboratively to compile a list of rules. These will need to be agreed verbally before a more polished version is written onto large sheets of paper.

Plenary
● Invite each group to share their rules, answering questions and clarifying points. Draw attention to any rules that were common to other groups.
● Tell the class that you are now going to make a class set of rules, using the rules each group has provided as a starting point.
● Explain that the finished set of rules needs to be succinct and kept to a maximum of five (or whatever number you decide).
● Hold a shared writing session to work together to prioritise, agree and record a set of rules.
● Decorate the finished document with images from the Gallery 🖼 and a colourful background. Begin each circle time activity through the year by displaying the rules on the interactive whiteboard and referring to them as necessary.

Daylight robbery

Learning objectives
QCA Unit 9 'Respect for property'
● To understand that stealing is wrong.
● To know some of the ways in which victims of crime can be affected.
● To use imagination to develop empathy with victims of crime.

Resources
'It's only a packet of crisps' Notebook file; writing materials.

Links to other subjects
English
PNS: Drama
● Challenge more confident learners to write a play script telling this story, or one they have created themselves.
RE
QCA Unit 5D 'How do the beliefs of Christians influence their actions?'
● Ask the children to discuss forgiveness. Should Mr Price forgive Bobby?

Starter
Display page 2 of the Notebook file and use it to create a mind map of what the children know about theft. Start them off in small groups, asking them to consider what theft is, who is affected, what things may be stolen and what the consequences of theft are. Give time for the groups to discuss these issues, before bringing the class back together to discuss their responses. Encourage children to talk about personal experiences of theft. Note their responses on the Notebook page.

Whole-class shared work
● Tell the children that you are going to read them a story about a theft. Ask them to consider the points of view of the two main characters, as you read.
● Read the story on pages 3 and 4 aloud to the children, questioning them on their predictions and responses.
● Go to page 5 and discuss Bobby's motivation for the theft. Ask: *Is he so hungry that he has to steal? Or does he do it for excitement?* Note parts of the story that give a clue to Bobby's motivation. Ask: *Could he have been trying to impress his friends with his daring?*
● Next, consider Mr Price's possible reaction to the theft. Ask: *How would Mr Price feel about the theft? What would be the consequences of a theft like this in the long term? What if it kept happening?* Write the children's ideas on page 5.
● Invite individuals to sit in the 'hot-seat'. They can take on the role of either Bobby or Mr Price. Encourage them to dramatise the role, adopting voices and mannerisms to develop the character.
● Invite quality questions from the class that give people in the hot-seat the opportunity to develop their characters beyond their responses to the immediate situation.

Independent work
● Ask the children to rewrite the story in the first person from the point of view of one of the characters: Mr Price, Bobby or one of his friends.
● Encourage children to get into role, reflecting on the points of view explored earlier in the hot-seat.

Plenary
● Choose one or two good stories, perhaps one from each point of view, and scan them onto the whiteboard.
● Read the children's stories. Then ask others to highlight parts of the text that really develop the point of view of the narrator.
● Conclude with a discussion on theft and why it is wrong, both for the thief and for the victim. Try to expose as many negative consequences as possible. Write your conclusions on page 6 of the Notebook file.

Whiteboard tools
Use a Highlighter pen to highlight the main points on the Notebook file.

Pen tray

Highlighter pen

Select tool

Heraldic shields

Learning objectives
QCA Unit 5 'Living in a diverse world'
● To feel positive about themselves.
● To celebrate their worth as individuals by identifying positive things about themselves.

Resources
Picture of heraldic crest (for example of the school, local borough council or football team) inserted into the whiteboard software; paper for sketching; paints or colouring pencils; internet access.

Links to other subjects
ICT
QCA Unit 5B 'Analysing data and asking questions, using complex searches'
● Ask the children to research a local crest, using the internet and other resources.
Art and design
PoS (2b) To apply their experience of materials and processes, including drawing, developing their control of tools and techniques.
● Challenge able artists to make a suit of armour or a banner to add to the display.

Whiteboard tools
Use the Lines tool and the Shapes tool to draw the shields.

🖥 Pen tray

🖈 Select tool

◥ Lines tool

▣ Shapes tool

Starter
In a circle time session, ask the children to comment on things they like about themselves - appearance, attitudes, abilities and so on. Make the contributions more focused by asking them to identify personal attributes that they are proud of: being hard-working, conscientious, having a sense of humour, a caring nature, being a good friend, and so on. Write this list on the whiteboard.

Whole-class shared work
● Ask the children if they know of any organisations, clubs or businesses that have a symbol or sign to represent them. Explain that in modern times, many groups adopt an instantly recognisable symbol.
● Show the children the heraldic crest and explain its local origins. Encourage them to speculate what any individual symbols might mean.
● Explain that heraldic shields like these have their origins in medieval times, when rich landowners would go to war when called upon by the king. In order to recognise which soldiers belonged to which side during chaotic battles, shields and banners would be embellished with the heraldic crest belonging to the landowner. These crests were also used to decorate seals, buildings and armour.
● Find some shields on the internet, and explain that the shield shape, colour and the symbols put on it all had meaning and significance to people in medieval times.
● Use the Lines tool ◥ and Shapes tool ▣ to draw a blank shield shape and divide it into sections. Into each section, draw a symbol for an attribute that makes you proud: a book may represent knowledge, a football could suggest prowess at sport, and so on. Fill each area of the shield, explaining what the symbols represent and what they portray about you. Get the children thinking by asking them to suggest how best to symbolise one of your attributes!

Independent work
● Ask the children to choose a shield shape and sketch it on a sheet of paper, trying hard to make it symmetrical (less confident learners may benefit from using a card template).
● Tell the children to identify the qualities, skills and interests they want to show on their shield, and then divide it up into the appropriate number of sections.
● Help them to create a symbol for each of the attributes they want to portray. The shields can be decorated with paint or colouring pencils in bold colours.

Plenary
● Ask children to share their designs with the class and celebrate their work. Scan a couple of examples onto the whiteboard and invite comments from the rest of the class.
● Let the children help to decide where the shields could be displayed.

You name it!

Learning objectives
QCA Unit 6C 'Why have people invaded and settled in Britain in the past?'
● To learn some of the typical Viking place names and their meanings.
● To identify the areas where the Vikings settled.

Resources 💿
'You name it!' Notebook file; copies of sections of modern maps with evidence of Viking place names (for example, areas around York, Lincolnshire or Keswick), one copy for each child; printouts of page 8 of the Notebook file, one for each child; highlighter pens (or crayons) and pencils.

Links to other subjects
Geography
PoS (1a) Ask geographical questions; (2c) Use maps at a range of scales; (4a) Recognise and explain patterns made by human features.
● Ask the children to consider where human settlements were established after the Viking invasion.

Starter
Open page 2 of the Notebook file. Revise what the children know about the Viking invasion and settlement, noting their responses. They should be aware of the difference between settlement and invasion.

Go to page 3 and study the map. Point out the countries where the Vikings originated and the routes they took. Ask: *Where will most evidence of Viking settlement be found in Britain, and why?* Use the Lines tool ◥ to mark this on the map. Explain that the Norsemen, rather than the Danes, sailed round the north of Scotland and settled many of the islands and west coast areas.

Whole-class shared work
● Explain that place names change only slowly over time, and so provide good evidence of settlement.
● Remind the children of suffixes that suggest Roman settlement (such as -*chester* or -*caster*, both of which mean 'camp' or 'fortified place') and Anglo-Saxon settlement (-*ton* and -*ham*).
● Pages 4, 5 and 6 of the Notebook file look at Viking place names. Invite the children to add other place names ending with -*by*, -*thorpe* and -*thwaite*.
● Go to page 7. Tell the children that the prefix of the place name often related to a personal name, usually a man's. Ask them to work with a partner to make up a name that would be evidence of Viking settlement – for example, Tomthwaite or Janeby. Ask: *What do these place names mean?* (Tom's meadow, Jane's farm.)

Independent work
● Give out the copies of maps, and the printouts of page 8 of the Notebook file.
● Ask the children to locate and highlight Viking settlements on the modern maps. On the printout, they should write the names of the settlements in the first column, and the meanings of those names in the second column.
● Less confident learners could be provided with a simple map.
● Encourage more confident learners to think about what the name tells us about the area.

Plenary
● Go to page 8 and discuss the names of settlements that the children found, and their meanings. Ask volunteers to write examples on the board. Ask: *What do the place names tell us about the area?* (For example, good farming land.)
● Ask: *Is there evidence of earlier Anglo-Saxon or Roman settlement?* Explain that sometimes place names were 'hybridised': Viking personal names and Anglo-Saxon suffixes were joined (for example, Bagley).
● Ask if any children know which part of the country their map represents. Display page 9 of the Notebook file and locate the areas shown on the children's maps.

Whiteboard tools
Use the Lines tool to point to areas of the map, and a Highlighter pen to highlight areas of the map or parts of words.

🖥 Pen tray

◥ Select tool

◥ Lines tool

🖊 Highlighter pen

Points of view

Starter
Display page 2 of the Notebook file and ask for volunteers to drag and drop the labels onto the map. Ask: *When did the Ancient Greek civilisation flourish?* Revise what the children know about Ancient Greece and make notes on page 3.

Remind the children that Ancient Greece consisted of city states and explain that they will be learning more about two of these.

Whole-class shared work
● Display page 4 of the Notebook file. Help the children to label the map.
● Point out the two city states of Athens and Sparta. Remind the children that there were other city states as well as these. Explain to them that these states had their own rulers, laws and currency.
● Ask: *What differences are there between the locations of these two states? How might the locations influence the ways of life of the people?* Note down the children's responses.
● Display page 5 and tell the children that the two states were different in other ways. Encourage them to use the subheadings to help them sort the statements.
● Elaborate on each statement, to give the class a greater understanding of the similarities and differences.
● Display page 6 and ask the children if they have heard of the word *democracy*. Tell them that *demos* is the Greek word for 'people', and that Britain is one example of a democracy. As a class, define democracy and add the definition to the Notebook page.
● Repeat this exercise for *oligarchy*.
● Tell the children that the Spartans didn't write, so our knowledge of their way of life comes from Athenian writings. Ask them to comment on the accuracy or bias that may be portrayed in these writings.

Independent work
● Tell the children to imagine that they are residents of either Athens or Sparta. Ask them to write a speech in praise of the way of life of their chosen city state, compared with the other.
● They should include information about the everyday lives of men, women and children, as well as government.

Plenary
● Divide the class into the two groups of residents. Ask for volunteers from each group to make their speeches. After each speech, and with your support, encourage the rest of the class to question the orator.
● Go to page 7. Ask the children whether they think there are some good features for each society, and discuss these. Write them in the boxes and take a vote on which city the children would like to live in.

What's the point?

Starter
Ask: *What different ways do we get information and advice today?* List responses on page 2 of the Notebook file (for example, television, the internet.) Ask: *Did people receive information the same way during the Second World War? What was the same and what was different?* Highlight examples that were available in wartime Britain. Tell the children that much of the information and advice we receive comes from different government departments.

Whole-class shared work
● Explain that in wartime Britain many posters were printed on behalf of the government to provide information and advice.
● Display the first poster on page 3 of the Notebook file. Ask: *What does this show? What impact does it have?* Make notes of the children's ideas.
● Ask the children to identify the message (security, economy, the war effort) and the intended audience, and make notes.
● Repeat the activity using pages 4, 5 and 6. Ask what the message is each time and how it differs from the other posters.
● Summarise the different categories of information.
● Discuss the humour that is used, and in what way it may be appropriate for wartime Britain.

Independent work
● Ask the children to work in pairs or small groups to create a short radio playlet to perform to the rest of the class. It must convey the same message as one of the posters.
● Remind the children that:
  ● the message has to be conveyed using only sound;
  ● the message should be set in a new context (not the context used in the poster);
  ● humour is important;
  ● the message must be clear and unambiguous.
● Give out copies of photocopiable page 163. These are to plan the playlet (emphasise that the children do not need to write formal scripts).
● Organising children into mixed-ability groups should ensure that more confident learners support those who are less confident. Check that all children are making a contribution to their group's work.

Plenary
● Ask groups of children to perform their broadcasts. The rest of the class must identify which poster provided the inspiration. Display the poster with its annotations, and compare these with the content of the broadcast.
● Encourage the rest of the class to comment on and discuss each broadcast.
● Explain that this sort of information is called *propaganda*. This means spreading information (whether true or false) nationwide.
● Ask: *Which method of conveying information might have reached the widest audience in wartime Britain? Why?*
● Ask: *Which method would be used today? Why?* Write the children's ideas on page 7 of the Notebook file.

It's the pits

Learning objectives
QCA Unit 11 'What was it like for children living in Victorian Britain?'
● To collect information from a range of sources and draw conclusions about the Victorian period.
● To understand that ways of life differed greatly across Victorian society.
● To write a narrative using historical detail.
● To understand that there are many representations of the Victorian period.

Resources 🅿
Photocopiable page 164 'The Lancashire Spectator' for each child; computer with internet access; pictures of children working in the mines and factories; printouts of the simplified text from the Learning Curve reports, one between two; pencils.

Links to other subjects
English
PNS Creating and shaping texts: Adapt non-narrative forms and styles to write factual texts.
● The independent work links well to this objective.

Whiteboard tools
🖥 Pen tray

🖼 On-screen Keyboard

🖱 Select tool

Starter
Write 'Victorian children' as a title on a blank Notebook page. Ask: *What would life have been like for Queen Victoria's children?* Make notes under the subheading 'Rich children', on the left side of the page. Ask: *How was life different for poorer children?* List suggestions on the right side of the page, under the subheading 'Poor children'. Type each sentence as a separate text box. Encourage the children to identify the obvious similarities and differences between the lives of the two social groups. Re-arrange the second list, so that contrasting statements are adjacent.

Whole-class shared work
● Tell the children that you are going to show a movie about the working conditions of poorer Victorian children. Explain that some of the pictures in the movie are contemporary woodcuts and others are modern illustrations, but that the movie is modern.
● Open the web page **www.bbc.co.uk/schools/victorians/flash.shtml** (last accessed 13/6/2007). Select 'Work' then 'Learning' and 'Play the movie.'
● Press the Pause button from time to time, to make short notes on the content on a new Notebook page.
● Listen to David Pyrah's account of working in a mine, by selecting 'Work', 'Learning', then the musical instrument on the right of the screen. Make notes on your Notebook page.
● Ask: *How long had David been off work? What impact might this have had on his family?*
● Go to the web page **www.learningcurve.gov.uk/victorianbritain/ industrial/default.htm** (last accessed 13/6/2007).
● Select Source 4. Work through the tasks on the left and annotate the pictures.
● Ask: *What do these sources tell you about working conditions for children in Victorian mines?*

Independent work
● Give out copies of photocopiable page 164. Ask the children to write a newspaper account for an imaginary 1841 edition of the *Lancashire Spectator*. The account will be about the working conditions of Victorian children.
● Discuss how this work might be structured, and note these comments on a new Notebook page.
● Ask the children to use quotations from the reports where appropriate.
● Provide less confident learners with a more structured writing frame, and appropriate quotations.
● Challenge more confident learners to take on the role of a reformer and write, expressing and justifying a personal view.

Plenary
● Share the newspaper accounts, encouraging the children to question the writers on the source of their information.
● Discuss with the children how the Victorian age has been represented in the resources used in this lesson, in contemporary pictures and text, and using modern technology. Ask them to tell you other representations that they might have come across - for example, the film *Oliver*. Ask them to reflect upon the authenticity of the representations.

Who uses water?

Starter
Display page 2 of the Notebook file and revise the map symbols used to represent water features. Look at a map of the local area on the whiteboard, identify any water shown on the map and annotate it. (**NB** It is not permitted to take screenshots of these annotated maps.) Ask the children to recall what is at the actual location where the water symbols are:
- Is the water still there?
- What is it like?
- Have there been any changes to it?
- Is the water used for anything?

Whole-class shared work
- Go to page 3 of the Notebook file. Ask the children to suggest different uses of water, writing these up on the board. Ask: *Are uses by industry and farming included?*
- The pictures on page 4 show various uses of water. Let the children first study the pictures, then ask them to come up one by one, and decide where to put each picture in the Carroll diagram on page 5. Invite them to explain their choices.
- Once they have done this part of the activity, ask them to complete the second Carroll diagram activity on page 6, about the amount of water used.
- Ask: *How does our water get to our taps?* Visit the website of a local water provider to look at water purification and sewage treatment.
- Use page 7 of the Notebook file to note key points about water processing. Include vocabulary that the children will need for their independent work.

Independent work
- Ask the children to make a diagram showing the processes of cleaning water and disposing of dirty water.
- If possible, complete this work using desktop publishing software. The children will then be able to insert pictures and re-arrange items as the work progresses.
- Provide the basic headings for less confident learners, to help them to organise their research.
- Children who are able to work quickly and independently might like to present their research in a digital multimedia presentation.

Plenary
- Go to page 8. Introduce the idea of keeping a diary of water use at home and at school. Ask: *What categories might be included?* Explain that the children need to collect similar data so that it can be entered into a spreadsheet and analysed (see the Year 5 geography lesson on water conservation on the DfES *Learning and Teaching using ICT* CD).
- Devise headings for the data collection. Suggest that the children keep a tally of the times each type of water use occurs. The quantity of water used can then be built into the spreadsheet, so that it will work out the totals used. Set this work as homework.

Local issues

Learning objectives
QCA Unit 20 'Local traffic – an environmental issue'
● To use maps at a variety of scales.
● To identify key physical and human features.
● To know how features influence the location of human activities.

Resources **P**
Photocopiable page 165 'Development report' for each child; URLs for internet mapping sites, for example OS Get-a-map at **www.ordnancesurvey.co.uk/oswebsite/getamap** (last accessed 13/6/2007) (**NB** Annotating and saving the OS maps is only allowed if your school is part of the LEA OS Map Licensing Scheme); a local development issue to be the focus of the work.

Links to other subjects
Science
PoS Sc2 (5a) Living things and the environment need protection.
● Consider how living things may be affected by the development.
English
PNS: Creating and shaping texts
History
PoS (4a) Find out about changes studied from an appropriate range of sources.
● Use a series of maps to investigate the changes in a settlement over time.

Whiteboard tools
Use a Pen from the Pen tray to annotate the maps. Taking snapshots of the annotated maps means that they can be saved for use at other times.

▭ Pen tray

▣ Select tool

▣ Capture tool

Starter
Display old and new maps of the local area. Ask: *What differences can you spot? Are all the differences linked to human features? Are natural features such as rivers still the same?* Point out that many changes are linked to human activities, but some may be natural (such as coastal erosion). Annotate the old map and use the Capture tool ▣ to take a snapshot of it.

Whole-class shared work
● Introduce the local development and ask: *What have you heard about it? Have you read about it in the local papers?*
● Tell the children that they are going to look at maps to find out where the development is, what is near it and its effect on the area around it.
● Load up a current map of the area. Zoom the map in as close as possible to the development site. Ask: *What is the grid reference of the development?* Explain that this is a large-scale map. Continue to refer to the scale of the map throughout the lesson.
● Ask: *What human features are near the development? What natural features are near? What has been or will be changed?*
● Annotate the map and save it.
● Zoom out one or two units and ask: *What has changed on the map? Will any of the things now on the map be affected?*
● Review the impact of the development.
● Annotate and save the map.
● Zoom out again, until the likely boundaries of the sphere of influence of the development are reached. Annotate and save the map.
● Go through the series of maps again.

Independent work
● Provide each child with a copy of photocopiable page 165. Ask the children to make notes on the sheet, and then write a brief report about the development.
● Revise the key elements of report writing. Suggest a suitable audience (a local councillor, a residents' group or a government minister, for example). Suggest success criteria that will be used to judge the effectiveness of the reports.
● Display the most useful map on the whiteboard and provide printouts of any annotated maps that may assist the report writing.
● Provide less confident learners with a framework for report writing.
● Encourage more confident learners to think about other ways to research the development – for example, by reading newspaper or online reports about it.

Plenary
● Allow the children to read each other's reports. Ask them to use the success criteria to evaluate the reports.
● Discuss other possible research aspects of the analysis of the local development, and make notes of these on the photocopiable sheets. For example:
  ● What fieldwork might be possible?
  ● Who else will be interested in discussing the development?
  ● When will the effects of the development be felt?

There and here

Starter
Start by constructing a mind map of the local area on the whiteboard. Look at the photocopiable sheet for ideas on what to include. Write the name of the locality in the middle. Ask the children to add words and phrases, and then to drag these to suitable locations on the mind map. Move words and phrases about as the links begin to appear – for example, *cinema* and *swimming pool* go together as places for relaxation. The word *leisure* might then be added as a central word for the two activities to branch from.

Save the finished mind map. It may be worth printing out some copies to provide useful headings for the next part of the work.

Whole-class shared work
● Tell the children that they are going to research a contrasting locality. If you are linking this work to a field trip, tell them that they will be able to compare what they find out on the trip with the expectations they form as a result of this research.
● Explain that to record their findings easily and in a sensible order, they are going to construct a mind map similar to the one they worked on in the Starter. They will use a variety of secondary sources, including the internet, books, maps and leaflets.
● Give out copies of photocopiable page 166 and go through the headings together. The children should consider the usefulness of these as they carry out their research.

Independent work
● Provide the children with the resources on the contrasting locality for their field trip. Supply the URLs ready-linked in a word-processing document, or added to Favourites in the web browser.
● Ask the children to work in small groups, taking turns to access the various types of resources. Monitor the presentation of the work.
● Less confident learners could be provided with an adapted photocopiable sheet that includes useful vocabulary.

Plenary
● Bring the children back to the whiteboard. Collect together the findings from their research. Add them to a second mind map, and re-arrange items as the discussion progresses. Complete the task as for the local area in the Starter.
● As the points are collected, ask the children to comment on similarities and differences with the local area.
● Save the mind map and explain that the children will be constructing another mind map of this contrasting locality after they have visited it. They will be able to print out copies of these expectations ready for comparison with the results from the visit.

Where land meets sea

Learning objectives
QCA Unit 23 'Investigating coasts'
● To use appropriate geographical vocabulary.
● To know about the physical features of coasts and the processes of erosion and deposition that affect them.

Resources
'Where land meets sea' Notebook file; digital images of coasts; printouts of page 12, with the location of the school marked on it, one for each child (alternatively, use outline maps of the UK if they are readily available). (Microsoft PowerPoint is required to view the embedded slideshow in the Notebook file.)

Links to other subjects
History
PoS (4a) To find out about the past; (4b) To ask and answer questions about the past.
● Compare photographs of historical sites from the same period. The use of a map to plot known sites of interest for a certain period can also show interesting patterns, particularly in work on Invaders and Settlers.

Whiteboard tools
Use the Spotlight tool and Screen Shade to focus the children's attention on particular parts of the photographs.

▭ Pen tray

▣ Spotlight tool

▭ Screen Shade

▣ Select tool

Starter
Open page 2 of the Notebook file and let the children view the slideshow of coastal photographs. Discuss the photographs with the children.

Whole-class shared work
● Display page 3 of the Notebook file. Allow the children to place the labels correctly on the map.
● Ask: *What is a coast?* Make notes on page 4.
● Read through page 5 and then go to page 6. Move the Screen Shade ▭ to reveal the picture bit by bit. Encourage observations, asking: *What can you see? What might you see next?*
● Look at pages 7 and 8. Use the Spotlight tool ▣ to focus in on different aspects of the photographs, such as the strata in the rock. Find examples where erosion by sea, wind or rain has changed the rocks.
● Compare pages 9 and 10. Ask the children to drag and drop the vocabulary to appropriate places on the photographs, and to justify their choices. Ask: *What are the similarities and differences between these two beaches?* Make notes on page 11.
● Ask: *Which coastal areas have you been to?* Ask for three volunteers to locate and label areas on the map on page 12. List other suggestions of place names at the bottom of the page.

Independent work
● Provide the children with printouts of page 12, with the school location marked on it. You may wish to add two or three locations for them to label which are in more unusual parts of the United Kingdom. (Check that they are in the atlases that the children are going to use.) Give them atlases or access to a mapping website. Ask them to mark the exact locations of the coastal places listed earlier.
● Provide less confident learners with extra clues to locations by giving them maps with some of the main cities and coastal towns already labelled. These can act as points of reference.
● Ask more confident learners to use a scale ruler to work out the distance of each location from the school, as the crow flies.

Plenary
● Ask the children to label the coastal places they have located on page 12 of the Notebook file. Ask them how they would identify the correct location on a map of a different size: *Would you use clues in the shape of the coast? Would you use places as points of reference?*
● Encourage the children to make adjustments to their work as a result of the sharing of information.
● Suggest that the children might start a collection of coastal images. These could be postcards, photographs or cuttings from newspapers and magazines. They should retain the place names to be marked on a map.

Still life

Learning objectives
QCA Unit 4A 'Viewpoints'
● To collect visual and other information to help them develop their ideas.
● To question and make thoughtful observations about starting points.

Resources
Still-life arrangement in the classroom; prepared Notebook file showing a still-life painting from the Art section of the Gallery; on a separate page scan in a digital photograph of the classroom still-life arrangement); a digital camera; objects and artefacts to form the basis for still-life arrangements.

Links to other subjects
ICT
QCA Unit 5B 'Analysing data and asking questions: using complex searches'
● Ask the children to search CD-ROMs and the internet to find examples of still-life images or information on the lives and works of famous painters.
RE
PoS (3i) Symbols and religious expression: how religious and spiritual ideas are expressed.
● Link work to this objective by giving the children religious artefacts to include in their arrangements.

Whiteboard tools
Use the Spotlight tool to focus in on aspects of the Starter painting. Use the Screen Shade to reveal the digital image slowly in the whole-class shared work.

🖼 Pen tray

▨ Select tool

▭ Screen Shade

🔦 Spotlight tool

🖼 Gallery

Starter
Show the image of the still-life painting from the Gallery 🖼 and ask the children for their thoughts and feelings: *Can you tell what medium this image is in? Can you guess when it was painted? Do you know the name for this type of painting?*

Use the Spotlight tool 🔦 to focus on certain aspects of the painting. Discuss the children's responses and explain that still life involves inanimate objects, such as flowers, fruit or objects, in painting, drawing or photography. Help the children to become aware of the arrangement of the piece, by pointing out objects in the foreground, mid-ground and background, and discussing relative sizes.

Whole-class shared work
● Show the children your still-life arrangement in the classroom. Point out individual items in the arrangement, describing their shape, texture and size, and explaining your reasons for including them.
● Now go to the Notebook page showing the digital photograph of your still-life arrangement. Before you show it to the children, enable the Screen Shade ▭, then slowly move the screen across the page to reveal the image underneath. Ask the children for their comments and discuss.
● Look again at the still-life arrangement in the classroom, and ask the children to comment on the relative sizes of the objects, reinforcing the foreground, mid-ground and background vocabulary.
● Go back to the Notebook page. Using a colour that will stand out, ask volunteers to use a Pen from the Pen tray to carefully draw around the outline of an object in the foreground. Repeat for objects in the mid- and background, drawing the children's attention to relative sizes and positions.

Independent work
● Use a safe search engine to find other examples of still life on the internet.
● Arrange the children into small groups and ask them to collect interesting objects for a still-life arrangement - for example, artefacts, fabrics, books, flowers and pottery.
● Challenge the children to organise an interesting arrangement, perhaps with a fabric draped in the background.
● More confident learners could be presented with the additional consideration of how to use natural light to illuminate focal points in their still life, experimenting with light direction and shadows for added effect.
● Allow time for arrangements to be completed and for the children to individually sketch their still-life work.
● While the children are sketching, ask an individual from each group to take a digital photograph of their still life.

Plenary
● Display the digital photographs of the still-life arrangements on a new Notebook page.
● Discuss the choice of objects in the different arrangements, as well as their relative sizes and positions.

Containers

Starter
Describe your day, explaining how, from getting up to beginning this lesson, you have used containers: toothpaste tube; water tumbler; laundry basket; kettle; mug; bowl; washing-up liquid bottle and so on. Give the children one minute with a talk partner to list the containers they have used today. Explain that they will be exploring how containers are made, what they are used for, who uses them and how all of these things are linked together.

Whole-class shared work
● Open the British Museum website at **www.thebritishmuseum.ac.uk**. Follow the links to Explore>Families and children>Online tours. Select 'Containers' to begin a fascinating tour of containers, each from distant parts of the world and different cultures.
● Explore these, enlarging the images and reading the accompanying description.
● Engage the children with questions on the containers: *Where were they made? When? Where are they from? What are they made from? How were they used? How and why are they decorated?*

Independent work
● Provide each child with a copy of photocopiable page 167. Using these, and digital cameras (or sketchbooks if these are unavailable), the children should explore the school, finding examples of different containers.
● The children should examine the vessels they find so that they can comment later on their properties: materials, purposes, decoration, ownership and location. They should photograph or sketch the containers, and write their comments on the photocopiable sheets.

Plenary
● Insert the images onto the prepared Notebook page containing the Venn diagram (see Resources), resizing them to make them smaller.
● Ask individuals to come up and talk about the containers they've found, classifying them as functional or decorative - or both.
● Annotate the pictures with the children's comments. Invite volunteers to drag and drop into the correct area of the Venn diagram, justifying their choices as they do so.

Learning objectives
QCA Unit 5C 'Talking textiles'
- To explore how stories have been represented in textiles in different times and cultures.
- To collect visual and other information to help them develop their ideas.

Resources
A traditional tale, myth or legend that is familiar to the children; internet access to the website **www.bayeuxtapestry.org.uk** (last accessed 13/6/2007); digital cameras or sketching materials; blank templates on paper, and drawing materials, for the children to plan their own sequence of events for a tapestry frieze.

Links to other subjects
English
PNS: Creating and shaping texts
- The content of this lesson could act as a starting point for the children to write their own legend, myth or fable.

History
PoS (4a) Find out about events, people and changes.
- Retell events from historical periods in appropriate mediums (for example, a Roman tale told on a scroll).

ICT
QCA Unit 5B 'Analysing data and asking questions: using complex searches'
- Help the children to search the internet for examples of other tales told through art.

Whiteboard tools
Use the Screen Shade to reveal the scenes from the Bayeaux tapestry bit by bit.

🔲 Pen tray

🔖 Select tool

🖊 Highlighter pen

🔲 Screen Shade

🖼 On-screen Keyboard

Telling tales through textiles

Starter
Display the Bayeaux Tapestry website at **www.bayeuxtapestry.org.uk**; open it at the first tapestry screen, but hide the image with the Screen Shade 🔲.

Ask the children (with a talk partner) to list as many different ways to tell a story as possible. Discuss responses and ask which ways may have been available to storytellers of the past – before film, television or radio. Explain that, long ago, stories were depicted in picture form, because many people could neither read nor write.

Whole-class shared work
- Direct the children's attention to the whiteboard, and explain that you are going to reveal a story told in an unusual way. Ask if they can suggest the medium as you slowly reveal the tapestry.
- Allow time to take in the scene. Ask the children to be history detectives: they should try to deduce what is happening and then explain their observations.
- Tell the class about the Norman invasion of 1066 and describe the battle scenes as they appear on the tapestry.
- Use a Highlighter pen 🖊 to focus on one character. Ask the children to look carefully at this person. With a talk partner, they should describe the person's appearance, actions and feelings. Discuss how the character is represented through stance, expression and dress. Write a list of these points on the whiteboard.
- Tell the children that they are going to make a frieze, showing the main events from a story.
- On a new Notebook page, write up the main events (in note form) from a traditional tale studied previously. Divide the children into groups and give each group one event, making sure that more complex events are given to more confident learners.

Independent work
- Ask the groups to discuss their events, identifying the points that will need to be illustrated for the frieze.
- The children should get into role as characters from the scene and perform a freeze frame, using stance, expression and gesture to communicate the story. The freeze frame can be quickly sketched, or photographed digitally, to be used as reference for the children's drawings.
- Give out the prepared frieze templates (see Resources). Each group should then negotiate the best way to develop the characters pictorially, before recreating them on the template.

Plenary
- Scan the children's work onto the whiteboard. Discuss their images, celebrating achievements and suggesting improvements. Pay particular attention to the ways in which characters and plot have been developed through visual details.
- Explain that the images created today will later be refined and reproduced on fabric, using fabric crayons and dyes, printing techniques or embroidery.

How instruments work

Learning objectives
QCA Unit 5A 'Musical instruments'
● To investigate, disassemble and evaluate a range of musical instruments.
● To relate the way things work to their intended purpose, how materials and components have been used, people's needs, and what users say about them.

Resources
'Musical instruments' Notebook file; a tambourine; a range of musical instruments for the children to handle and play, including string, wind and percussion instruments; recordings of orchestral music featuring a range of instruments; paper and pencils.

Links to other subjects
Science
QCA Unit 5F 'Changing sounds'
● The work in this lesson links well to this unit, which focuses on musical instruments and the scientific workings of sound.
ICT
PoS (1b) To prepare information for development using ICT.
● Challenge the children to create a database for a range of instruments.

Starter
Display page 2 of the Notebook file. As the children enter the room or gather at the front of the class, play a piece of orchestral music. Ask them to listen carefully and try to identify individual instruments and comment on how they contribute to the whole piece. Summarise the children's comments on the Notebook page.

Whole-class shared work
● Display page 3 of the Notebook file and ask the children to name each instrument. Delete the red rectangles to reveal the name of each one as the children identify them.
● Listen again to a short piece of music and ask the children to list on their whiteboards which instruments they can hear.
● Explain that all of the instruments are designed and constructed to make sounds, and that the children are going to investigate each one to understand how it works.
● Go to page 4 of the Notebook file and model how to explore an instrument – in this case, a tambourine. With a real tambourine to hand, describe its shape, construction and materials, the various ways it can make sounds and refer to the kinds of music you've seen or heard it being used in. As you do so, delete the coloured boxes on the labels on the Notebook page. Read the Page notes that accompany the picture, referring to the real instrument as you do so.
● Explain that you want the children to investigate their instruments in the same way, and record their observations.

Independent work
● Divide the children into groups. Give each group an instrument to explore.
● Ask them to complete a sheet showing an accurate picture of the instrument, with annotations to show the instrument's construction, the materials that have been used to make the instrument, and notes on how to produce a sound.

Plenary
● Ask a spokesperson from each group to share the findings with the class, referring to the sheet and the real instrument.
● Explain that instruments can be divided into groups according to how they produce their sounds: wind, percussion and string (point out that there are other musical groups, but these are the ones that you are looking at today).
● Study the diagram on page 5 of the Notebook file, and ask the children to consider which group their instrument belongs to. Invite an individual from each group to come up and drag and drop the image of their instrument into the correct category, justifying their choices.

Whiteboard tools
Use the Delete button to reveal the names of the instruments in the whole-class shared work.

⬚ Pen tray

↖ Select tool

✕ Delete button

Investigating breads

Starter
Discuss the kinds of bread children enjoy at home, making notes of these on page 2 of the Notebook file. Show a range of real breads – for example, a traditional tin loaf, naan bread, ciabatta, tortilla, a baguette, soda bread, pitta and any others you can think of. Help the children to learn their names and in pairs talk about the main differences between them.

Whole-class shared work
● Explain that bread is a staple food around the world – in wealthier areas, it is a cheap and nourishing accompaniment to meals, while in poorer places, it forms a large part of a sustenance diet.
● Discuss how bread can be a part of a balanced diet.
● Explain that although many different cultures produce bread, it can look, taste and be used in different ways.
● Go to page 3 of the Notebook file. Ask the children if they can remember the names of the breads seen so far. Ask them to come out and use the Fill Colour tool 🔳 to reveal the name of each type of bread.
● Invite the children, one at a time, to place each bread on the world map in the approximate area of its origin, using the Lines tool 🖊 to insert arrows if necessary.
● Tell them not to worry about any they can't place, and ask how they could find out where that bread belongs.

Independent work
● Set the majority of the children the task of evaluating the bread products explored earlier. Ask a small group (selected for their ICT ability) to explore the internet to discover more information about each of the breads, focusing on their geographical origin.
● Encourage the children to look at each type of bread in turn, describing its shape, texture and colour.
● They should slice or tear a piece of each and describe how it looks and feels on the inside.
● They can then sample each bread and describe taste, texture and personal preference, thinking of some way to rate each bread.
● The children should record their observations on photocopiable page 168.

Plenary
● Each group should feed back their observations on one type of bread, so that everyone gets to talk in detail. They should begin with the name and origin of the bread, progressing to a description of characteristics and finishing with an account of how the bread is intended to be used (to soak up soup, to scoop up sauce, to wrap foods and so on).
● The ICT team can supplement each mini-presentation with their research findings.
● Ask the children to survey people at home on their bread preferences, and to find out how the availability of foreign breads has changed in recent decades. Let them use the table on page 4 of the Notebook file to summarise their findings.

Cams in moving toys

Learning objectives
QCA Unit 5C 'Moving toys'
● To recognise the movement of a mechanism in a toy or model.
● To understand that a cam will change rotary motion into linear motion.

Resources ◉ 🅿
'Cam mechanisms' Notebook file; photocopiable page 169 'Cam toy' for each child; a range of simple toys with cam mechanisms.

Links to other subjects
Science
PoS Sc4 (2e) To measure forces and identify the direction in which they act.
● This lesson links well to this objective.
English
PNS: Speaking
● Encourage the children to discuss how the mechanisms work in their own words.

Starter
Prior to the lesson, ask the children to collect and bring in a range of simple toys, which may include cams. Examine these with the class, commenting on which parts move, and how.

Whole-class shared work
● Go to page 2 of the Notebook file and press the thumbnail image to open the mechanisms activity and set the toy in motion.
● As it moves, talk through the whole structure, explaining the purpose of each component: the framework provides rigidity and attaches the mechanism; the axle secures a mount for cam; the cam itself, with its elliptical shape, and the follower, which move the swan up and down.
● Now show the children how the cam turns, producing a rotary motion, and how the follower then converts this into a linear motion.
● Ask the children to consider what materials the parts may be made from and what properties the materials would need. Write their ideas on page 3 of the Notebook file.
● Move on to ask how this toy could be made more attractive, with cladding perhaps to conceal the framework.
● Discuss how this might be achieved, what materials might be used and how they could be fastened. Ask: *How could the toy be made more attractive?* Write the children's ideas on page 4 of the Notebook file, for reference during the independent work.

Independent work
● Share out the moving toys between the groups and ask the children to investigate how they work.
● Tell them to focus on who the toy was made for, what materials have been used to make it and how it moves, and in particular, how a cam achieves movement.
● Hand out copies of photocopiable page 169. The children can use this to sketch a picture of their toy and write notes about how it works.
● Tell the children to be prepared to talk about their findings in the Plenary. They will need to share out the roles for the presentation - someone to demonstrate the toy in motion, somebody to describe who it was intended for, another to describe its materials and finally one more to explain how the cam works.

Plenary
● Give each group the space and time they need to demonstrate their toy and their findings to the group.
● Display page 5 of the Notebook file to remind the children of what they need to talk about in their presentations.
● Encourage them to use the correct terminology for each material and part.
● Invite questions from the rest of the class.

Whiteboard tools
Use a Pen from the Pen tray to make a record of the children's ideas in the whole-class shared work.

🖳 Pen tray

🔧 Select tool

Symmetry and asymmetry in routines

Starter

Go to the BBC site at **http://search.bbc.co.uk** and select the option at the top of the page, BBC Audio and Video. Type 'gymnastics' into the search bar and choose a video clip. Play the video and discuss the performance of the professional gymnast. Draw the children's attention to the quality of the movements, and the control of the gymnast. Summarise the main points on a Notebook page.

Whole-class shared work

● In the hall, warm up, describing the effect that exercise is having on the body – increased heart rate, faster breathing and warmer muscles. Ask the children to crouch, still and silent. Then slowly – without wobbles – 'grow' very gradually, extending their body, limbs and head to their full height. Hold the stretch for five seconds.
● Increase heart rate by jogging on the spot, increasing and decreasing pace at your command.

Independent work

● Ask groups to set up apparatus, using the photos as a guide (see Resources).
● Challenge the children to investigate a range of body shapes, both symmetric and asymmetric. Remind them to aim for complete control of every action, like the professional gymnast on the website.
● Working with similar ability partners, the children should create a sequence that includes symmetric and asymmetric movements, shapes and balances.
● They should include a variety of speeds, direction changes and varying levels (with body shapes extended or crouched). More able gymnasts could extend their repertoire by working in tandem with a partner, or producing mirrored actions.
● Ask different pairs to photograph elements of each other's sequences, using a digital camera.
● Invite volunteers to display their sequences, asking others to offer positive but constructive feedback.
● Cool down with some stretches and return the apparatus.

Plenary

● Transfer the digital pictures to a folder on the computer.
● Open your movie-making software (for example, Windows® Movie Maker), and explain to the children that you are going to make a gymnastics presentation. In Movie Tasks, import the pictures taken earlier from their folder into Collections.
● Next, drag suitable pictures from the collection and drop them onto the storyboard at the bottom of the screen. With this complete, select Edit Movie. Here you can add a title screen at the beginning, drag and drop video transition effects between the photos and add a scrolling list of credits at the end of the movie. As you work, make explicit to the children what you are doing so they can become familiar with the package and use it more independently in future.
● Finally, run the storyboard and ask the children to comment on their work, perhaps setting targets for the next lesson. Make a note of the children's comments on a Notebook page.

Our class rules

I want to belong to the kind of class where

I want our class to be

I'd like to be part of a class where

I want to belong to the kind of class where

My idea of a great class is

Circle time observation

Name of observer	Date	Focus for circle time

Focus of observation	Comments for feedback
Did people speak audibly?	
Did everybody contribute?	
Did everyone listen all the time?	
Did people make eye contact when they spoke?	
Did people use a confident tone of voice?	
Did everyone seem to enjoy the circle time?	
Did circle time end on a positive note?	

Name _____

Radio broadcast

Character   Played by:

_____

_____

_____

_____

- Include some information about each character, such as age and occupation.

- We are basing the script on this poster.

- Give a brief description of the poster.

The message in the poster is

_____

_____

The intended audience is:

_____

_____

Special points. For example, humour, sound effects, accents.

_____

_____

- Outline of the broadcast

1. _____

2. _____

3. _____

4. _____

5. _____

The Lancashire Spectator

By our special reporter _____ **March 3rd 1841**

Children at work in our mines – the facts

_____

_____

_____

_____

_____

_____

_____

What the children say

_____   _____

_____   _____

_____   _____

_____   _____

_____   _____

_____   _____

_____   _____

_____   _____

_____   _____

_____   _____

Illustrations © Andy Keylock/Beehive Illustration

Development report

Local development issue: _____

Date of development: _____

Grid reference of the development: _____

Nearby features: _____

Physical features	Possible effect of development

Human features	Possible effect of development

Groups of people affected: _____

_____

_____

Environments affected: _____

_____

_____

Mind map

■ Make a mind map of your locality.

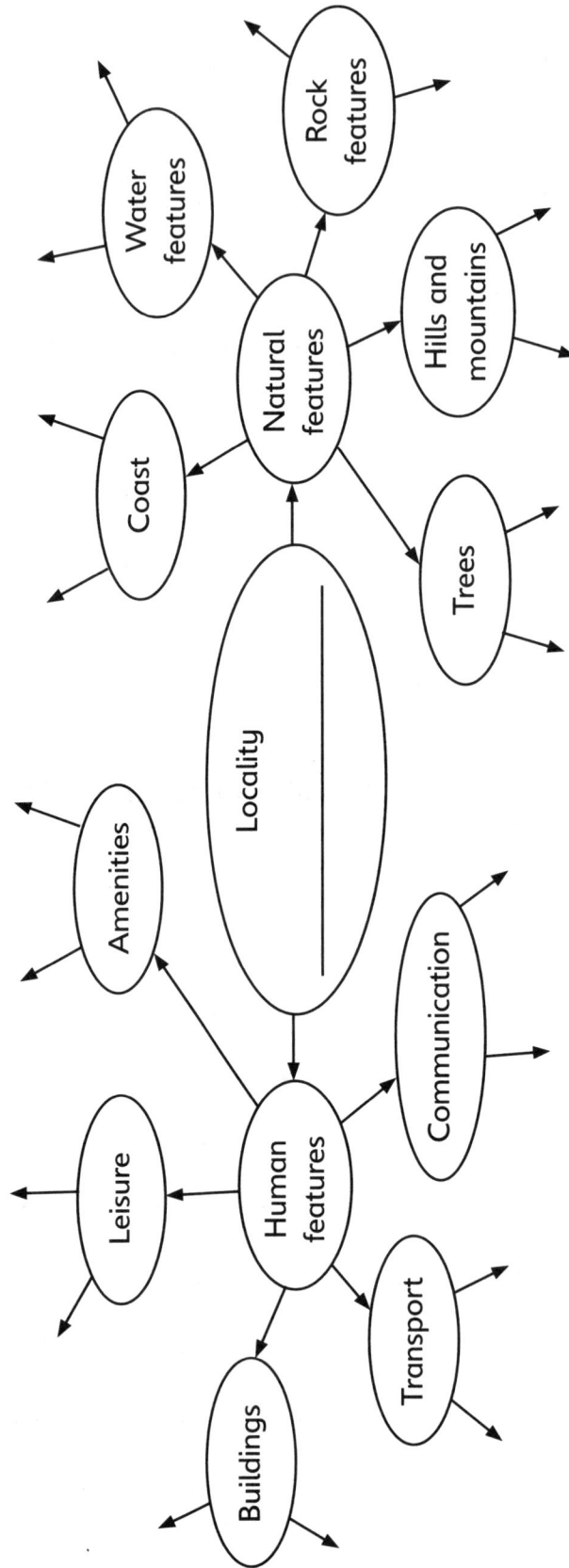

Natural features
- Water features
- Rock features
- Hills and mountains
- Coast
- Trees

Locality

Human features
- Amenities
- Communication
- Leisure
- Transport
- Buildings

Remember! You will not need all of these headings. You may need other headings that are not shown.

Containers

Container	Properties	Materials	Purposes	Decoration	Ownership and location

Investigating bread

Appearance	Taste	Other observations	Rating

Cam toy

◼ Draw an annotated picture of your toy here.

Don't forget to label moving parts and show the different materials used to make it.

Who is the toy intended for? How can you tell? _____

_____

_____

_____

How is your toy decorated? _____

_____

_____

_____

Explain how the cam in your toy works. _____

_____

_____

_____

Whiteboard diary

Teacher's name: _____

Date	Subject/ Objective	How was the whiteboard used?	Evaluation

Whiteboard resources library

Teacher's name: _____

Name of resource and file location	Description of resource	How resource was used	Date resource was used

Using your SMART Board™ interactive whiteboard

This brief guide to using your SMART Board interactive whiteboard and Notebook software is based on the training manual *SMART Board Interactive Whiteboard Masters Learner Workbook* © SMART Technologies Inc.

Your finger is your mouse

You can control applications on your computer from the interactive whiteboard. A press with your finger on a SMART Board interactive whiteboard is the same as a click with your mouse. To open an application on your computer through the interactive whiteboard, double-press the icon with your finger in the same way that you would use a mouse to double-click on your desktop computer.

The SMART Pen tray

The SMART Pen tray consists of four colour-coded slots for Pens (black, red, green and blue) and one slot for the Eraser. Each slot has a sensor to identify when the Pens or the Eraser have been picked up. You can write with the Pens, or with your finger, as long as the pen slot is empty. Likewise, if you remove the Eraser from the slot you can use either it or your hand to erase your digital ink.

    The Pen tray has at least two buttons. One button is used to launch the On-screen Keyboard and the second button is used to make your next touch on the interactive whiteboard a right-click. Some interactive whiteboards have a third button, which is used to access the Help Centre quickly.

The On-screen Keyboard

The On-screen Keyboard allows you to type or edit text in any application without leaving the interactive whiteboard. It can be accessed either by pressing the appropriate button in the Pen tray, or through the SMART Board tools menu (see page 173).

    A dropdown menu allows you to select which keyboard you would like to use. The default Classic setting is a standard 'qwerty' keyboard. Select the Simple setting to arrange the keyboard in alphabetical order, as a useful facility for supporting younger or less confident learners. A Number pad is also available through the On-screen Keyboard.

    The Fonts toolbar appears while you are typing or after you double-press a text object. Use it to format properties such as font size and colour.

On-screen Keyboard

Floating tools toolbar

Aware tools

SlideShow toolbar

The Transparency layer

When you remove a Pen from the Pen tray, a border appears around your desktop and the Floating tools toolbar launches. The border indicates that the 'transparency layer' is in place and you can write on the desktop just as you would write on a transparent sheet, annotating websites, or any images you display. The transparency layer remains in place until all the Pens and the Eraser have been returned to the Pen tray. Your first touch of the board thereafter will remove the border and any notes or drawings you have made.

Ink Aware applications

When software is Ink Aware, you can write and draw directly into the active file. For example, if you write or draw something while using Microsoft Word, you can save your Word file and your notes will be visible the next time you open it. Ink Aware software includes the Microsoft applications Word, Excel, PowerPoint; graphic applications such as Microsoft Paint and Imaging; and other applications such as Adobe Acrobat. Ensure that the SMART Aware toolbar is activated by selecting View, then toolbars, and checking that the SMART Aware toolbar option is ticked.

When you are using Microsoft Word or Excel, you will now notice three new buttons that will be either integrated into your current toolbar (as shown on the left), or separated as a floating toolbar. Press the first button to insert your drawing or writing as an image directly into your document or spreadsheet. The second button converts writing to typed text and insert it directly into your document or spreadsheet. Press the third button to save a screen capture in Notebook software.

When you are using Microsoft PowerPoint on an interactive whiteboard, the SlideShow toolbar appears automatically. Use the left- and right-hand buttons on the SlideShow toolbar to navigate your presentation. Press the centre button to launch the Command menu for additional options, including access to the SMART Floating tools (see page 175), and the facility to save notes directly into your presentation.

SMART Board tools

The SMART Board tools include functions that help you to operate the interactive whiteboard more effectively. Press the SMART Board icon at the bottom right of your screen to access the menu.

- SMART Recorder: Use this facility to make a video file of anything you do on the interactive whiteboard. You can then play the recording on any computer with SMART Video player or Windows® Media Player.
- Floating tools: The features you use most are included in the Floating toolbar. It can also be customised to incorporate any tools. Press the More button at the bottom-right of the toolbar and select Customise Floating Tools from the menu. Select a tool from the Available Tools menu and press Add to include it.
- Start Centre: This convenient toolbar gives you access to the most commonly used SMART Board interactive whiteboard tools.
- Control Panel: Use the Control Panel to configure a variety of software and hardware options for your SMART Board and software.

See page 175 for a visual guide to the SMART Board tools.

Using SMART Notebook™ software

Notebook software is SMART's whiteboard software. It can be used as a paper notebook to capture notes and drawings, and also enables you to insert multimedia elements like images and interactive resources.

Side tabs

There are three tabs on the right-hand side of the Notebook interface:

Page Sorter: The Page Sorter tab allows you to see a thumbnail image of each page in your Notebook file. The active page is indicated by a dropdown menu and a blue border around the thumbnail image. Select the dropdown menu for options including Delete page, Insert blank page, Clone page and Rename page. To change the page order, select a thumbnail and drag it to a new location within the order.

Gallery: The Gallery contains thousands of resources to help you quickly develop and deliver lessons in rich detail. Objects from the Gallery can be useful visual prompts; for example, searching for 'people' in an English lesson will bring up images that could help build pupils' ideas for verbs and so on. Objects you have created yourself can also be saved into the Gallery for future use, by dragging them into the My Content folder.

The Search facility in the Gallery usually recognises words in their singular, rather than plural, form. Type 'interactive' or 'flash' into the Gallery to bring up a bank of interactive resources for use across a variety of subjects including mathematics, science, music and design and technology.

Attachments: The Attachments tab allows you to link to supporting documents and webpages directly from your Notebook file. To insert a file, press the Insert button at the bottom of the tab and browse to the file location, or enter the internet address.

Objects in Notebook software

Anything you select inside the work area of a Notebook page is an object. This includes text, drawing or writing, shapes created with the drawing tools, or content from the Gallery, your computer, or the internet.

(ii)

(i)

Manipulating objects: To resize an object, select it and drag the white handle (i). Use the green handle (ii) to rotate an object. To adjust the properties of a selected object, use the dropdown menu.

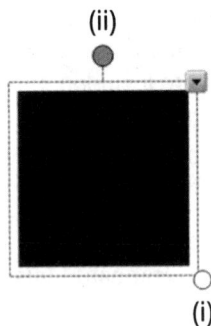

- Locking: This sub-menu includes options to 'Lock in place', which means that the object cannot be moved or altered in any way. Alternatively you can choose to 'Allow Move' or 'Allow Move and Rotate', which mean that your object cannot be resized.
- Grouping: Select two or more objects by pressing and dragging your finger diagonally so that the objects are surrounded by a selection box. Press the dropdown menu and choose Grouping > Group. If you want to separate the objects, choose Grouping > Ungroup.
- Order: Change the order in which objects are layered by selecting 'Bring forward' or 'Send backward' using this option.
- Infinite Cloner: Select 'Infinite Cloner' to reproduce an object an unlimited number of times.
- Properties: Use this option to change the colour, line properties and transparency of an object.
- Handwriting recognition: If you have written something with a Pen tool, you can convert it to text by selecting it and choosing the Recognise option from the dropdown menu.

Tools glossary

Notebook tools
Hints and tips
● Move the toolbar to the bottom of the screen to make it more accessible for children.

● Gradually reveal information to your class with the Screen Shade.

● Press the Full screen button to view everything on an extended Notebook page.

● Use the Capture tool to take a screenshot of work in progress, or completed work, to another page and print this out.

● Type directly into a shape created with the Shapes tool by double-pressing it and using the On-screen Keyboard.

	Pen tray			Lines tool
	Next page			Shapes tool
	Previous page		A	Text tool
	Blank Page button			Fill Colour tool
	Open			Transparency tool
	Save			Line properties
	Paste			Move toolbar to the top
	Undo button			
	Redo button			Capture tool
	Delete button			Area Capture tool
	Screen Shade			Area Capture 2
	Full screen			Area Capture 3
	Select tool			Area Capture (freehand) tool
	Pen tool			
	Highlighter pen			Page Sorter
	Creative pen			Gallery
	Eraser tool			Attachments

SMART Board tools
Hints and tips
● Use the SMART recorder to capture workings and methods, and play them back to the class for discussion in the Plenary.

● Adjust the shape and transparency of the Spotlight tool when focusing on elements of an image.

● Customise the Floating tools to incorporate any tools that you regularly use. Press the More button at the bottom right of the toolbar and select Customise Floating Tools from the menu.

Press the SMART Board icon at the bottom right of your screen to access the **SMART Board tools** menu (shown right).

The **Start Centre** (shown below), is reached through the SMART Board tools menu.

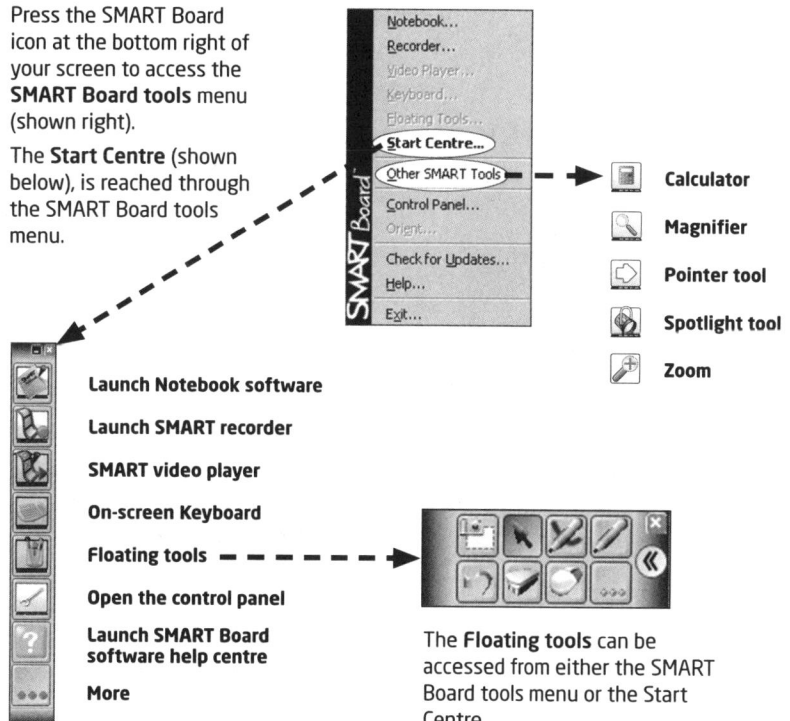

Notebook...
Recorder...
Video Player...
Keyboard...
Floating Tools...
Start Centre...
Other SMART Tools
Control Panel...
Orient...
Check for Updates...
Help...
Exit...

Calculator
Magnifier
Pointer tool
Spotlight tool
Zoom

Launch Notebook software
Launch SMART recorder
SMART video player
On-screen Keyboard
Floating tools
Open the control panel
Launch SMART Board software help centre
More

The **Floating tools** can be accessed from either the SMART Board tools menu or the Start Centre.

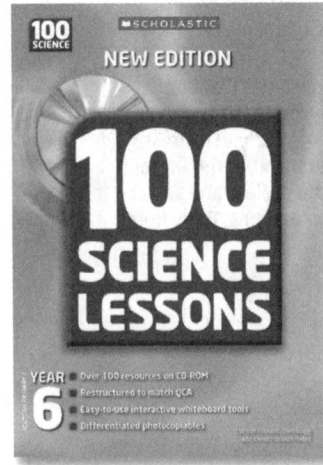